DEAR ALLY,

HOW DO YOU WRITE A BOOK?

ALLY CARTER

DEAR

ALLY,

HOW DO YOU WRITE A BOOK?

Scholastic Inc.

To all the kids who think someone like them can't
do it, from someone who used to think that, too,
but did it anyway.

Copyright © 2019 by Ally Carter

This book was originally published in hardcover by Scholastic Press in 2019.

All rights reserved. Published by Scholastic Inc., *Publishers since 1920*. SCHOLASTIC
and associated logos are trademarks and/or registered trademarks of Scholastic Inc.

The publisher does not have any control over and does not assume any responsibility
for author or third-party websites or their content.

No part of this publication may be reproduced, stored in a retrieval system, or
transmitted in any form or by any means, electronic, mechanical, photocopying,
recording, or otherwise, without written permission of the publisher. For information
regarding permission, write to Scholastic Inc., Attention: Permissions Department,
557 Broadway, New York, NY 10012.

ISBN 978-1-338-21227-3

10 9 8 7 6 5 4 3 2 1   20 21 22 23 24

Printed in the U.S.A.   23
This edition first printing 2020

Book design by Yaffa Jaskoll

TABLE OF CONTENTS

CHAPTER 1
INTRODUCTION

DEAR ALLY,
How do you write a book?

Congratulations! You've asked the question that all writers ask themselves at some point. But do you want to know a secret? It's a question most of us never really *stop* asking.

Every time I sit down to write a new book, I convince myself there must be a way to do it faster, more efficiently, *better*! Surely, after ten years in this business and with a total of fifteen books under my belt, I should know what I'm doing by now.

But I don't, I'm afraid. So I can't really tell you how to write a book. There is no single way to do it, you see.

Every author is different. Heck, every *book* is different. How I wrote my first book is different from the process I'll use to write my next book. Why? Because they're different books. Because I'm at a different place in my life and in my career. Lots of reasons.

Luckily, there are some things that always stay the same, and I'm going to try to cover as many of the basics as I can in this book—things like creating characters, making sure your story has enough conflict, and building a world that feels real to you and your readers.

But just know that what works for me might not work for you.

Really, there's only one thing I can say with absolute certainty: This process will take time.

A few years ago, I did the math and figured out that I spend at least nine hundred hours plotting, researching, writing, and editing every book I write.

STORYBOARDING/BREAKING THE STORY: 4 HRS/DAY FOR 20 DAYS: 80 HOURS
RESEARCHING/THINKING/BRAINSTORMING: 50 HOURS
FIRST DRAFT: 5 HRS/DAY FOR 30 DAYS: 150 HOURS
SECOND DRAFT: 5 HRS/DAY FOR 80 DAYS: 400 HOURS
LINE EDIT: 5 HRS/DAY FOR 25 DAYS: 125 HOURS
COPY EDIT: 6 HRS/DAY FOR 5 DAYS: 30 HOURS
FINAL "PAGE PROOF" EDIT: 8 HRS/DAY FOR 4 DAYS: 32 HOURS
CRYING: 30 HOURS

Nine hundred hours. And that's for just one book. That doesn't include all the hours I spent learning the basics.

A lot of new writers—especially writers in their teens—start out full of ideas and energy, but when they don't immediately write something perfect, they give up. They tell themselves they just can't do it. That's certainly what I did.

I remember when I was in middle school and I got the writing bug. I sat down at our kitchen table one night to write my first novel. My mother (an English teacher) was so proud. I could see her watching me as she cooked dinner. I wrote really hard for a really long time—like ten whole minutes! And then I read what I had written and burst into tears.

"What's wrong?" Mom asked as she stopped cooking.

I could barely catch my breath, I was crying so hard. "It's just . . ." I started. "It's not . . . It isn't as good as the opening paragraph of *To Kill a Mockingbird*!" I exclaimed, and then cried some more.

That's when my mom gave me the best writing advice that anyone has ever given me. She said, "First, that's the greatest novel ever written, so maybe we lower our standards? Second, you should never compare your first draft to someone else's finished draft."

That advice is probably the only reason I was able to write a second paragraph. And a third. And a . . . millionth.

You see, in a lot of ways, writing is like turning on a garden hose that hasn't been used in a really long time. The first water out of the hose is always rusty and dirty and full of gravel and all kinds of gross stuff. But it doesn't stay that way.

Nope. The longer the water runs, the clearer it will be. Writing is the same way.

That first paragraph that I wrote at our kitchen table was dirty water. The story that went with it was dirty water, too. So were the four screenplays I wrote in college and the six short stories I wrote after grad school and the first book I wrote, which to this day has never been published.

Even now, the first draft of every book I do is my "dirty water draft," and that's okay. No one gets to the good stuff right away.

No. To get to the good stuff, *you have to let the water run.*

Writing takes time. It takes work. It takes putting in the hours—sometimes more than a thousand of them—to get the story and the characters and the words just right.

You have to put in the time, is what I'm trying to say.

And that time is up to you. To find it. To use it. To make the most of it because this thing—this writing thing—it's *optional*.

It's something you do because you want to do it. It's something you do because you like to do it. It has to be something that you do for *you*.

Because ultimately, the answer to your question—"How do you write a book?"—is this:

You write a book by putting yourself in a chair and not getting up.

For approximately nine hundred hours.

How did you come up with the idea for this book?

Writing isn't just what I do for a living. It's what I . . . do. Most writers are the same. We've always dabbled or scribbled or played around with stories and words.

When I was in middle school, I started wanting to be a writer, but there weren't a ton of resources available in the small library in my small town. As I got older, I came across some really amazing books about the craft and business of writing—books like *On Writing* by Stephen King, *Bird by Bird* by Anne Lamott, and *Screenplay* by Syd Field (all of which I highly recommend).

I also had the opportunity to join some great organizations and online communities and attend some fantastic conferences.

Most of all, I've been lucky enough to get to know some of the best writers in the world, and whenever two or more of us get together, inevitably we all get to talking about characters and plots and all our favorite tricks. (Not to mention the mistakes we hope we never make again.)

Which is why, whenever I'm at a book festival or tour stop or school visit and someone says, "I'm writing my first book. Do you have any advice?" I want to scream, "Yes! I do! I have so much advice!" but it's hard to answer in a few sentences what, in a way, I've been learning to do my whole life—what I'm *still* learning to do.

When I started looking around for books to recommend to these young aspiring writers, I realized that while there are a lot of great books by adult authors, written for adult writers, there aren't a lot of things written by YA authors for teen audiences.

So that's why I'm doing this: to change that.

Do you have to get good grades in English class to be a great author?

This is an interesting question. And the short answer, I suppose, is: not exactly.

Were most authors pretty good at English in school? My guess is yes. But no publisher is going to ask to see your report card before they offer you a contract. Nope. What they're going to ask to see is your *book*.

Is your book good? Does it have compelling and interesting characters and a well-paced plot and a vivid world? Those are the questions that are going to matter most.

But there will be other questions, too. Like, does this person make silly grammatical mistakes? Is she so obsessed with sounding smart that she uses words she obviously doesn't understand? Is he the kind of person who is going to send out a really important letter without proofreading it first?

Ultimately, publishing is a professional business. You will be expected to write and speak professionally.

And let's not forget, English classes aren't just about writing. A lot of times, they're also about *reading*, and the ability to read carefully and thoughtfully is absolutely essential for anyone who wants a career in this business.

So even though no publisher is going to ask to see your report card, now is the time to develop the skills you're going to need down the line. Just like someone who wants to be a doctor needs to pay attention in science class and someone who wants to be an engineer needs to take good notes in physics, writers pay attention in English class—almost as if our job depends on it (because it kind of does).

I always seem to run out of story before my work approaches book length. How do I craft a story that can go the distance?

First, it's great that you've already started writing! That's the first step.

Second, you should know that not everything has to be a novel. You might not be doing anything wrong at all. Maybe you're simply writing a short story or a novella. There are lots of really great stories that are only a few pages long. And I think, in the beginning, the most important thing is that you actually finish what you start. So if your story is finished after a few pages, that's fine.

But if you think you're ready to try to do something longer, this section might be able to help with that.

First, I'm going to assume that you've read a lot of books. If you haven't, then take my word for it: *Your first job is to read a lot of books!*

Do you have any idea how many people tell me, "So, you're an author? I'm going to write a book someday." And then when I ask them what books they like to read, they almost always reply that they don't have time to read a book. *Then how are you going to have time to write a book?* I want to scream.

So if you take the time to read, you're already way ahead of the game.

Read funny books and serious books. Read long books and short books. Read bestsellers and award winners and dusty books in your school library that only your librarian has ever read. Read everything.

If you're already doing this, awesome.

But your new assignment is to stop reading like a *reader* and start reading like a *writer*.

How do writers read? We pay attention to details, to what is—and isn't—on the page. What happens? When does it happen? Why does it happen?

So how do you do this? It's actually pretty easy (and fun).

STEP 1. Pick up one of your favorite books.

STEP 2. Get ready to take some notes.

STEP 3. Start reading.

STEP 4. As you read, make a list of every big thing that happens. Your job here is to identify all the *scenes*.

For example, if you are reading *Harry Potter and the Sorcerer's Stone*, your list might start like this:

—Dumbledore shows up on Privet Drive.

—Hagrid brings baby Harry to the Dursleys.

—Harry wakes up in the cupboard under the stairs on Dudley's birthday.

—Harry talks to a snake at the zoo.

   etc., etc.

7

STEP 5. After you've finished writing down all the scenes from your favorite book, dig out a fresh piece of paper and do the same thing for the story you're writing.

STEP 6. Put your two lists side by side and compare them.

My guess is that the list for your favorite book is going to be a lot longer than the list for your book . . . but you already knew that, didn't you? The point of this exercise is to illustrate that your problem isn't that your book doesn't have as many *pages*.

Your problem is that your book doesn't have as many *scenes*.

Again, it's possible that your story is just smaller. Instead of taking us all the way to magic school and thwarting a terrible villain while saving unicorns and flying around on brooms, maybe you told the story of a kid who blew up his science lab one day.

If that's the case, you've written a short story. Which is great. Go, you! The only way to turn that into a novel is to have that be the opening scene of a much bigger story. Maybe by blowing up the science lab he turns the class hamster into a dragon that gets loose in the city and he and his friends have to save it? Maybe he opens up a hole in the floor that leads to a secret world beneath the school? Maybe he switches bodies with his twin sister?

You get the idea. *Something else has to happen.* More things have to go wrong. Your characters need more hurdles to jump, more dead ends, more false starts.

You need more conflict.

And you need more scenes to resolve all that conflict.

Look at your lists again. This time, I want you to mark every time the character in your favorite book had something go wrong. Now do the same for your story.

8

That's why your story's so much shorter.

You need more times when things go wrong, and you need more times when things go right.

You need more conflict. You need more scenes.

How do you keep things unique? As soon as I think I come up with a good idea, I read a book that has the same general thing happening in it. It seems like every idea or concept I come up with has already been done.

Okay. True story. Several years ago, I was at my very first writing retreat. There were a lot of amazing authors there, and I was pretty much starstruck, so I tried to keep my mouth shut and stay in the kitchen, cooking and learning from everyone else while they talked shop at the kitchen table.

When Holly Black started talking about her next book, my ears perked up. Then I started freaking out.

You see, the day before I'd left for the retreat, I'd turned in a draft of my book *Heist Society*, about a girl named Kat who grew up in a family of criminals but then cons her way into an elite boarding school in order to try to steal a normal life.

I was really excited about it . . . right up until the point when Holly started talking about her new book, *White Cat*, about a boy who grew up in a family of criminals who cons his way into an elite boarding school in order to steal a normal life.

Holly Black and I had written the same book! Needless to say, I wanted to cry because there wasn't a doubt in my mind that Holly had done it better.

It was all I could do not to burn the cookies. (Oh, who am I kidding? I totally burned the cookies.)

But the more Holly talked, the more differences I saw in what we had each created. *White Cat* has magic and curses and one of the best fantasy worlds that I have ever read. *Heist Society* has art thieves and a crew of geniuses and a teenage billionaire with a private jet.

They are two very different books that are, at first glance, exactly the same.

This is something that new writers often have a hard time grasping. After all, once you get an amazing idea, it's human nature to think you've already done the hard part. We all want to believe that everything else will be easy.

But it's not.

The truth is that, in the long run, ideas are a dime a dozen. It's what you do with the idea that really matters.

A lot of times what people see as similarities are really just staples of the genre or tropes. No one author owns the idea of dystopian futures or vampire romances or boarding schools or kids who have to save the world. The key is to take those tropes and genre staples and turn them into something that is uniquely yours and amazing. You can do it!

How do you avoid taking too much inspiration from other stories you've read?

If writers are supposed to read a lot, then it only stands to reason that they will sometimes be inspired by what they read—they're bound to be! I mean, isn't that kind of the point?

But plagiarism is bad. Very bad. Like don't-joke-around-about-it bad. So where does the line between inspiration and plagiarism lie?

Sometimes that line is fairly clear. While rare, there are instances of people copying whole paragraphs of another author's work and claiming those words as their own. In research papers, you can use quotation marks, cite the original author, and make sure the reader knows they aren't your words, and then that's totally okay. If it's fiction and you want to, for example, use a quote from something in the public domain (like Shakespeare or Austen) then you could cite that as well.

But in cases where someone pulls whole sentences or paragraphs from one novel and plops them down in another and acts as if they're original? Well, those cases are about as close to cut-and-dried as a case of plagiarism can be.

So if a sentence in your book is exactly like a sentence in someone else's book, you've plagiarized them, right? Well . . . maybe. Consider a sentence like *If you don't hurry, you're gonna be late*. That sentence is probably in a thousand novels—a million. Any writer could write that sentence at any time purely by coincidence. But could they write an incredibly similar sentence just before it and an almost verbatim paragraph just below? That's far more questionable.

Words matter. And for writers, our words are our livelihoods, which is why we take charges of plagiarism very, very seriously. And you should, too.

So what about cases where we aren't talking about words—we're talking about *ideas*? That's when things get even more complicated.

First, it's important to understand the concept of tropes. Let's say you love Harry Potter more than anything, and you want to write a book about a kid with magical powers who is the "chosen one" and destined to save the world.

Is that plagiarism? Should you be expecting a call from J. K. Rowling's lawyer? Of course not. If that were the case, then a bunch of other authors would have gotten in trouble long before now. Including J. K. Rowling herself.

Why? Because no one author owns the concept of "the chosen one." No one author could ever own the idea of magic. Those things existed long before J. K. Rowling, and they will exist long after.

But if you were to write about an orphan who finds out he's a wizard and then is taken to wizard school on a big scarlet train and then he learns to play soccer on broomsticks and fights a troll and has a best friend with red hair, etc., etc., then you might be in a totally different situation.

You see, J. K. Rowling doesn't own *wizards*, but she does own *Harry Potter*.

She doesn't own *boarding schools*, but she does own *Hogwarts*.

If that's confusing, you're not alone. I remember several years ago I was working on my fifth Gallagher Girls book, *Out of Sight, Out of Time*, and I really wanted to give my main character amnesia because I love an amnesia story more than anything.

But one of my favorite TV shows of all time, *Alias*, had done a spy-with-amnesia story line not long before. So had *The Bourne Identity*. And a movie called *The Long Kiss Goodnight*. (And probably several others.)

I was talking with my friend Jennifer Lynn Barnes, telling her how I really wanted to give my heroine amnesia but I couldn't because *Alias* had already done it.

"So?" Jen said.

"So I don't want to plagiarize all those other stories," I told her.

Then Jen said something that really made the pieces fall into place for me: "If you can name a half dozen stories that have already done it, then you aren't plagiarizing any of them. You're just writing a trope of the genre."

So, yes, read. Read a lot. Watch movies. Binge TV. Devour comic books. Get inspired. Get exposed to things you never knew existed or things you never knew you loved—that's what reading is for! Then take your new love of boarding schools or magical swords or amnesia and write about them. Most important, make these tropes your own, and put your own spin on them. Because at the end of the day, it doesn't matter where your inspiration comes from. It matters what you do with it.

In your professional opinion, what is the right age to begin a writing career?

Authors hear questions like this a lot. There are so many teens out there who love writing and want to make a career of it—they want to make a career of it RIGHT NOW! And I can't blame them. It is a great career.

But so many teens want to jump right to the getting-published part (which is why I do tackle the "Will publishers take us seriously if we're just teens?" question in the Publishing Your Book section a little later).

I like how this question is worded, though: What is the right age to *begin* a publishing career? The answer is: Whatever age you are right now is the right age to start your career. Why? Because your career starts with *writing*.

You can't query an agent for a book you haven't written. You can't get a publisher for a book you haven't written. You can't promote or market or sell movie rights to a book you haven't written. And writing a book that's worth publishing takes time. Lots and lots of time. And practice. And heartbreak. And probably more than a few missteps and false starts.

You might not get published in your teens, but that's a great time to begin your career. It's a great time to start writing!

DEAR KODY KEPLINGER,

You were really young when you started writing—and publishing! What was that like, and do you have any advice for teens who are looking to do the same?

My first novel, *The DUFF*, sold to a publisher when I was seventeen, right before I left for college. It was, of course, an incredibly exciting time in my life. I'd always dreamed of being a writer, and I was doing it! I was getting started in my career! It wasn't all easy, though. Once I started college, I had both schoolwork and writing work to do. I had deadlines to meet while also trying to keep high grades so I could hold on to my scholarships.

I didn't sleep nearly enough, and I had almost no social life in college. Many times my friends would ask me to go out with them and I had to decline because I had work to get done. I missed out on a lot of college experiences because I already had a career that took up a lot of time and energy.

I don't regret pursuing publication young, but I do wish I'd been more prepared for what that meant. So when teenagers hoping to publish young ask me for advice, I always tell them to really consider what they are pursuing. Getting published isn't just about getting a book on the shelf at your favorite bookstore. It's a job. It takes a lot of time and energy and patience. Once you write a book, the work has only just begun. It's not something to enter into without a lot of thought.

My other piece of advice to teenagers who want to get published young is to just enjoy the work you're doing. If you're only writing to get published, you'll kill your passion for it early. Once you sell a book, there's a lot of pressure. There are edits and deadlines and all sorts of other work to be done. So before you get there, have fun. Enjoy drafting. Remind yourself every day why you love to write. Take risks and make mistakes and learn from them all. Don't put pressure on yourself—the world will put enough on you as it is—and instead let writing be something that makes you happy. When you think you're ready to pursue publication, go for it! But until then, let writing be the outlet that brings you joy, not an obligation.

Maybe you'll be published as a teenager, and maybe you won't. It's okay either way. What's most important is that the first book you publish be one you love and are proud to have written.

CHAPTER 2
GETTING READY

Where do you get your inspiration?

This might be the question that writers get most, which is why it's more than a little embarrassing that I don't have a solid, concrete answer for it. But that's probably because inspiration's not a solid, concrete kind of thing.

Inspiration can come from anything—at any time.

The idea for *I'd Tell You I Love You, But Then I'd Have to Kill You* came to me when I was watching an episode of the TV show *Alias* and I thought I was seeing a boarding school for spies—but it wasn't. It was just a regular orphanage, and I was so upset because, by then, I was super excited about spy schools! So I decided to write one.

Heist Society showed up when I was listening to an audiobook and there was a line about being "a cat burglar in my own house"— which made me want to write a book about a girl named Kat who was a burglar.

My Embassy Row series was born from a librarian telling me that she was worried her son might go into the diplomatic service and then "my grandchildren will have to grow up in embassies all around the world." That, of course, made me wonder what it would be like to grow up on a street where every building is, essentially, a different country— and Grace, my main character, started to take shape.

Not If I Save You First, which is about the daughter of a Secret Service agent in a race to save her former best friend, the president's son, came to me when I was on an Alaskan cruise and I looked out over about a million acres of wilderness without a single light and I thought, *If you got lost here, there's no way you could call 911.*

Ideas can come from things you hear or see, say or do. But most of all, I think they come from asking, "What if . . . ?"

What if you went to a boarding school for spies?

What if your dad was the best art thief in the world and all you wanted to do was steal a normal life?

What if you grew up on a street where every house was, technically, a different country, and ticking off the neighbors could start World War III?

What if you lived in one of the remote parts of Alaska and your best friend was kidnapped during the storm of the year?

Think about the way things are, and ask, What if things were different? What if people were different? What if a rule or law or piece of science were different?

Then see where your imagination takes you.

What's the best writing advice you ever got?	
Shannon Hale	Write for fun! Follow stories that thrill you or interest you or make you excited to sit down and work.

I love writing, but I have so many ideas. How do I know which ideas are the good ones?

You're right. Most writers get ideas all the time—every day! And they aren't all winners. From ideas for new books or series to options for how a plot could unfold, my brain is always swarming with options. And too many options can be paralyzing sometimes.

So this is a big issue—one I'll probably worry about for the rest of my career. After all, writing and publishing a book takes about a year for me. I don't want to pick the wrong idea and regret it in six months. Or a year. Or twenty years! Authors get to write only a small percentage of the ideas that we get. So how do we pick the right ones?

Here are a few of the things that I do to help me (hopefully!) pick well.

1. **SET IT ASIDE FOR A WHILE**. I know those really great ideas grab you and make you want to dig in right now, but that's not always possible. As a rule, any book idea that I'm still thinking about months or years later is probably an idea I should try to do something with.

   For example, I had the idea for *All Fall Down*, the first Embassy Row book, five years before I sold it. So for five years I thought, *What if a girl grew up in an embassy?* When the time came to write something new, I knew that one was probably the one to run with.

2. **TRY WRITING TWO OR THREE CHAPTERS**. If after writing chapter 3 you can't rest until you've written chapter 4, then you've probably got a winner. If, however, you've run out of steam and don't really know where to go, maybe you don't.

3. **TRY TO WRITE THE COVER COPY**. You know, the stuff that's on the back of a paperback or the inside flap of a hard-back? That's the part that's supposed to tell the reader a

little about the book they've picked up and get them excited about reading the whole thing.

Years ago, I had a terrible writing experience—a book I struggled with for over a year. Later, I realized it was because I tried to write the book before I knew what would go on the *back* of the book—what the central conflict would be and what the character would be striving to achieve. I swore right then I'd never again start a book without knowing what would go on the back of the book . . . and that's made all the difference!

	What's the best writing advice you ever got?
Alan Gratz	Keep an idea book! This isn't where you write your stories–it's a notebook where you write down all your crazy ideas for stories and all the writing advice you get from books and teachers.

DEAR CARRIE RYAN,
I know you, like most writers, get a ton of ideas. How do you decide which ones you actually want to write?

Sometimes I feel like the most indecisive author ever! I have an entire file on my computer that's stuffed with ideas. Some of them are one line long, and some are 20,000 words long. In terms of figuring out which ideas I want to stick with, it almost always comes down to the fact that I can't stop thinking about the world and the characters. I itch to get to the computer in the morning, and even if I'm frustrated with the plot, or don't know what happens next, I'm still excited about the story. Unlike a lot of authors, I usually don't know how a story will end when I start drafting it, so if I want to find out what happens, I have to finish writing the book—lol.

Very early in my career, I was trying to figure out what book to work on for NaNoWriMo, and my husband suggested I write what I love. At the time, I was fascinated by zombies but it was 2006 and no one was very interested in zombies. There wasn't really a market for them, and I felt like it would be a waste of time to write a book that obviously wasn't going to sell. Then, while walking home from work one night, the first line of a book popped into my head. When I got home I started writing. I stopped caring about the market, because suddenly I was writing the book *I* wanted to read. This was a book for me, and it was my own desire to see what happened that pushed me to finish it. I'm glad I did because that became *The Forest of Hands and Teeth*—my first published book.

Do you write from personal experience, or do you make it up? Which is easiest?

Personally, I'm not a huge fan of the "write what you know" school of wisdom because I think this advice is easily misunderstood.

When I was a teen, I knew what it was like to go to school and church and family events. I knew what it was like to have friends and worry about my grades. My life was pretty boring and probably wouldn't have been interesting to anyone who wasn't me.

So, good stories can't be about average, everyday things? NO! Not at all. People write amazing stories about super-common things all the time, but . . . (and this is the important part) . . . they always have an *uncommon take* on the common occurrence.

In other words, those stories all have higher-than-usual *stakes*. They have more than an average amount of conflict. They have big issues or questions or challenges that are, by definition, heightened. These stories are always a little bit "more" than what the average person sees in their average life. That's why those stories are more interesting than just reading someone's diary or journal.

In short, at some point every novelist has to make things up.

Where the "write what you know" advice is true, I think, is when we think about feelings and emotions and world. We should all strive to write books that feel real to the reader, and especially when you're starting out, that might be most easily done by writing things that are actually real to you.

So, yes! Pull from your experiences of what it feels like to be betrayed or embarrassed or heartbroken. Take a reader into a house or street or school that maybe they've never seen before.

But don't forget it doesn't do you any good to brilliantly describe your school or a dance competition or summer camp if nothing happens while we're there.

Most of all, make your readers *feel*. Give your characters conflict, and make sure they have something at stake. And don't feel bad if your life story isn't the stuff of great novels—most people's aren't. But that doesn't mean there aren't experiences and emotions and observations around you every day that would make your novel a whole lot better.

Is your favorite genre to read the genre you should write in?

Well, think about it this way: You wouldn't want to spend months or even years of your life writing in a genre you don't enjoy, would you?

But it's also okay to have stuff that you read just for fun. In fact, when I'm writing a YA, I tend to read other things (historical romance being my favorite) because it helps me get out of my own head and not compare what I'm writing to what I'm reading.

In fact, I firmly believe that writers (especially young or beginning writers) should read as much as possible and as widely as possible.

Maybe you love reading YA fantasy novels. That's great, but don't stop there. Read sci-fi and contemporary, too. Read adult romance and nonfiction. Read plays and biographies, mysteries and thrillers. Watch a lot of TV and movies while you're at it.

Then sit down to write the story that uses the stuff you picked up along the way. The more you read, the more tools you're going to have in your tool belt. Don't worry so much about setting out to write an [insert genre here] story. First and foremost, focus on writing a *good* story.

22

How do you decide on an audience? Should I write a book for a specific target age, or is it better to write the book and adjust the content to suit the age targeted?

I didn't set out to be a young adult author. In fact, when I started writing, YA fiction certainly didn't look like it does today. So, in the beginning, I just wanted to write. And I think most published authors are the same way.

Sometimes you might write a whole book thinking you're writing for kids, just to have a publisher decide it would be better off as an adult book. Some books, like *The Curious Incident of the Dog in the Night-Time* or *The Book Thief*, might be published as an adult book in one country and a YA book in another. In many ways, deciding whether a book is adult or YA can be a marketing decision as much as—or even more than—a creative decision.

So I'm not sure it's something you should really worry about yet. For now, just focus on writing the best book you possibly can. The other stuff will work itself out in the long run.

What's the best writing advice you ever got?	
Maggie Stiefvater	Write the book you wish you could find on the shelf but can't.

What is the average word count of your books?

First of all, you're right to ask about *word count* rather than *page count* since the number of pages in a novel can vary widely, depending on font, margins, whether the author uses short or long paragraphs—a bunch of different factors. So when you talk about the length of your work, always talk about word count, and you'll be one step ahead of the game.

Secondly, this is one of those questions where the answer is going to vary. Widely.

Personally, my books probably average about 65,000 words, but that is by no means the "right" length.

A lot of really amazing books come in shorter than that. A ton of really amazing books come in longer.

The only thing you need to remember is that your book should be the number of words it *needs* to be. No more. No less.

In some ways, the genre you're writing in is going to impact that. It's generally accepted that sci-fi and fantasy (or any book with a lot of detailed world building) will be on the longer end of the spectrum (though that isn't necessarily always true).

It's also going to be a function of your voice. Years ago, I was talking with my friend Carrie Ryan. We were comparing physical copies of our books one day, and we realized that they had almost exactly the same number of pages, but her book was tens of thousands of words longer. How could that be? Well, I started looking at the pages themselves. My book had a lot of dialogue and very short paragraphs, which meant there was a lot more white space on each page.

Carrie's voice, however, is much richer and more lyrical, and her book had much longer paragraphs and a lot less white space on the page.

So that's how you get a much longer book that is the same number of pages.

How long your book is will also depend on how big your cast is and how much time your book spans.

Are you writing about a family of six witches, covering a hundred years? Or are you writing about a boy and a girl who get locked in after school one day and are stranded in the huge, abandoned building overnight?

The size of your book will also depend on the size of your characters' goals. After all, in a lot of ways, a plot is like a character's to-do list. The more your character has to do, the more words it will probably take to do it.

Word count will also vary a lot based on the age group you're writing for. A picture book will be shorter than a middle grade novel, which will often be shorter than YA or adult fiction. (Though not always.)

So it really, truly varies. I don't want anyone to get hung up on a certain number, but there are some ranges that generally mean certain things to people in the publishing industry. *Writer's Digest*, for example, gives the following breakdown:

Short story: 1,500–30,000 words
Novella: 30,000–50,000 words
Novels: 50,000 words and up

National Novel Writing Month (NaNoWriMo) gives participants the goal of writing 50,000 words in one month, and that's usually my starting point. If you're having trouble setting your own goal, then 50K might be a good place for you to start, too. Just aim for 50K and keep writing until you reach THE END.

	What's the word count of your shortest book?	What's the word count of your longest book?
Marie Lu	77,000	102,000
Melissa de la Cruz	I think about 48,000 for the Ashleys series, which was middle grade.	I don't tend to write long books, but I think maybe about 100,000 for *Something in Between* and *Someone to Love*. Those books were hard to write.
Daniel José Older	45,000	90,000
Elizabeth Eulberg	38,000	81,000
Julie Murphy	It will likely be the one I'm working on now, which will be about 50,000 words. But of my currently published books: 80,078.	104,078
Stephanie Perkins	74,000	82,000
Marissa Meyer	65,000	240,000
Alex London	740 (it's a picture book!)	120,000
Sarah Rees Brennan	90,000	140,000 My longest unpublished? 300,000 words. I have a problem, okay?

Jesse Andrews	57,000	88,000
Alan Gratz	54,000	72,000
Soman Chainani	97,000	152,000
Holly Black	8,000	110,000
Kiersten White	32,000	117,000
Maggie Stiefvater	77,000	110,000
Zoraida Córdova	77,000	92,000
Gordon Korman	25K for middle grade (10K for chapter book)	65,000
Rachel Caine	80,000	130,000
Dhonielle Clayton	75,000	130,000
Eliot Schrefer	29,000	85,000
Z Brewer	40,000	122,000

DEAR JAY COLES,

What's the best piece of writing advice you've gotten?

The best piece of writing advice I have is to give yourself permission to write badly. Once you get over the hurdle of staring at the blank page, I think one of the best things you can tell yourself is that all you have to do is get the words out and come back to edit later. A second piece would be read, read, read everything in your genre. It's helpful with knowing trends, and in fiction, it helps you learn characterization and strengthens your voice.

GETTING READY!

- Think about some of your favorite book ideas. Now try writing the back cover copy for each one.
- Read five books in genres you don't ordinarily read. In what ways are they like the books you usually read? In what ways are they different?
- Look at your five favorite books. How much white space is on the page? How many pages are the books themselves? Do you see any variation by genre?
- Try writing a short story about an average day in your life. Don't change anything. Just write what happens. Then think about what parts were easy and what parts were hard. What conflict could you add to make your story more interesting?

What's the best writing advice you ever got?	
Kiersten White	Start.

CHAPTER 3
PLANNING YOUR BOOK

Do you find it easier to plan out your entire book before you write it, or do you prefer to just have a basic idea and see where it takes you?

Every writer is different. In fact, every book is different! (Fair warning, I'm going to be saying that a lot because, to be honest, that's kind of the answer to *every* question.)

Some writers wake up one day with a character in their head. Or a line of dialogue. Or a scene or a question or an opening sentence. And then they sit down and they start writing—right then—by the seat of their pants.

That's why these writers are called *pantsers*.

Other writers might start out with a seed of an idea but they don't start writing until they've figured out who the characters are and what their goals might be and every single step that the plot is going to take. They outline, take notes, and often know the ending before they begin writing.

These writers are called *plotters*.

I know writers who start with nothing. And I know writers who start with outlines so detailed they are literally almost as long as the book itself. Neither way is right or wrong, good or bad.

Every writer will have their own individual *process*. Hang out with writers, and you'll hear that word over and over.

"What's your process?"

"I hate my process."

"I'd love to streamline my process."

And inevitably, "I hate it, but it's my process."

Finding your process is a huge part of being a writer (which is probably why we have an entire section in this book called "Finding Your Process"!)

George R. R. Martin (of *Game of Thrones* fame) has a quote on this topic that I absolutely love. Instead of talking about plotters and pantsers, he theorizes that authors are either *architects* or *gardeners*. Either we build and plan and diagram our stories (like an architect), or we plant various seeds, then water and nurture them and see which ones grow (like gardeners). I really like that analogy because I tend to plant a lot of seeds as I write—things that I don't really know what they mean or if they'll grow into anything at all, but it's important for me to have them in there just in case.

I find this especially important when writing series. It's really hard for me to know what will happen two or three books from now, but in the case of my Gallagher Girls series, I knew we would eventually have to answer the question of what happened to the heroine's (missing) father. When I was starting Embassy Row, I knew the royal family of this fictional European country would eventually come into play, so I added a mention of a teenage prince to book one, and sure enough, he was hugely important in book three.

In the end, it doesn't matter if you're a plotter or a pantser, an architect or a gardener. Everyone's writing mind works in its own way, and you will find the process that fits you best. All that really matters is that *you're a writer*.

So write!

DEAR MARISSA MEYER,

Are you a plotter or a pantser? What is your process like?

Definitely a plotter. I get anxious when I don't have a pretty solid idea of where the story is heading at any given point, and I find that it's hard for me to start writing before I have a really structured outline in place. I'll even go so far as to map out the specific beats in each chapter. That said, I've done this enough times to know that things are *always* going to change from the initial outline, so I try to be flexible and let the characters take charge when they need to.

DEAR ALAN GRATZ,

Are you a pantser or a plotter? What is your process like?

I used to suffer from writer's block all the time—I'd be sitting at my computer, ready to write, and have no idea what I was going to write. The clock would tick away, and with it would go the time I had to write that day. Then I'd come out of my office mad that I hadn't gotten words on the page. Then I learned to outline, and that's made all the difference. I now outline every novel I write, chapter by chapter, before I ever write the first word. If I hear a scene in my head, I scribble it down—when the muse speaks, you listen and take notes!—but I never try to push past the inspiration in the outline phase.

Once I know in detail what is going to happen, I sit down at the keyboard and try to figure out how to tell it. Those are two very different processes, but most writers try to tackle them both at the same time. Separating them was a real breakthrough for me. I still get writer's block (of a kind) when I can't figure out what's supposed to happen next during the outline phase, but at least then I don't come out of my office thinking that I've wasted time by not getting words and paragraphs and chapters written. Once I have the outline finished, I never get writer's block—which is important when you're in a mood to knock out first-draft pages. I look at my outline in the morning, read what's going to happen, and then start writing it.

DEAR DAVID LEVITHAN,

Are you a pantser or a plotter? What is your process like?

I am such a pantser. I didn't choose to be that way—it's just the way I am. Which is key. There's no universal right or wrong here—you just have to find out the way your writing mind is wired, and then work with that.

My writing mind is wired to figure out the story as I'm writing it. Part of the joy of the actual writing is, for me, finding out what happens. I always start with a premise—say, "a teen wakes up every day in a different body and a different life"—and then I explore the premise by seeing where it leads me. I will write and rewrite and rewrite my first three chapters to get to know the characters and the voice of the book. Then I'll strike out without a map. Sometimes I'll have some idea of where I want to go. But a lot of the time I won't have any idea of how it's going to end until I get closer to that end. For me, you write a novel in the same way you live a life—time is always moving you forward, and there are certainly things you aim to do . . . but then there will also be detours and unexpected parts that as soon as they happen become part of the story, too. And in order to get my characters' genuine reactions to all the twists and turns, I find I have to be as unaware as they are in regard to what's about to occur.

It's also a great way to keep myself going. Because the only way I'm going to figure out what happens next is to sit down and write what happens next, pulling it from my writing mind and onto the page.

How do you know which point of view to use? If it's first person, how do you pick which character tells the story?

This is one of the things authors worry most about when getting started. Because, trust me, it's not an easy thing to fix if you get it wrong.

The first thing you're going to have to consider is whether you should write in first person, second person, third person limited, or third person omniscient POV. I've written in all but second person (because it is the most rare), and they all have their pros and their cons.

FIRST PERSON, of course, means a character is "telling" the story. Sometimes that means one character. Sometimes an author might choose to have multiple first-person narrators, switching off between sections or chapters. (If you do this, note that the characters should ideally sound really different from each other—have different *voices*—and that's a hard thing to pull off sometimes.)

Choosing first person means that the reader will know only what the first-person narrator knows—and will see only what that person sees. Living in a person's head can be a great way of sucking in readers and making them really care about a character, but it will limit what the reader learns. Which can be a good thing. Or not.

For example, in my Gallagher Girls and Embassy Row books, first person worked really well because I wanted those heroines to be in the dark about what was going on a lot of the time. I wanted them to be confused and worried and maybe a little bit afraid. In fact, I wanted their search for answers to be mostly what the books were about! That's why I wanted to tell those stories through one character's eyes.

So how do you choose your first-person narrator? Well, that should always be the person with the most interesting *view* of the story—not necessarily the most interesting story. Think of it this way: If your book were a movie, your narrator is the camera lens. Most of the time that's going to mean your POV character should be the main character. But sometimes that's not the case. Think, for example, about *The Great Gatsby*. Nick is the first-person narrator of that classic novel, but Gatsby is, in every way, the star of the show.

SECOND PERSON is perhaps the most rarely used POV because, in second person, the narrator is "you" and that's a hard thing to maintain for an entire novel. It's something done more frequently in short fiction or perhaps in segments of a novel.

Third person is another really common POV option. But there are really two versions.

In **THIRD PERSON LIMITED,** you are limited to one person's POV at a time. This means you can only know what's going on inside one person's head at a time. So you might know what your hero is thinking, feeling, hearing, and seeing. If you want to know what your heroine is thinking, you need to have a section break or start a new chapter and switch to her POV.

One of the biggest third-person POV mistakes that new writers make is "head hopping," where you might "hop" from one POV to another in the same scene. For example, your hero might think about how hungry he is and then, in the next sentence, the heroine might think about how mad she is that the hero isn't listening to her. Don't do that. It's confusing for readers and it will make you look like a newbie. (And the goal of this book is to make you look like a pro!)

So, as long as you don't head-hop, you can have as many third-person POV characters as you want, right? Well . . . let's not go crazy.

Any time you give a character a POV—any time you go into a character's head—you are signaling to the reader that that character is important, so the reader needs to perk up and pay attention because this is one of the main characters of the story.

Sometimes writers might break this rule intentionally to fake the reader out or set the story up in something like a prologue, but for your first few books, I'd recommend you pick one or two (or, at most, three or four) POV characters and stick with them. It's often tempting to write in a (minor) character's POV because then we can *tell* what they're thinking, and we don't have to *show* what they're thinking. But that's kind of cheating. And confusing. And you can do better, I promise.

When I was writing *Not If I Save You First*, I had a gut instinct pretty early on that third person limited was the only way to go. Why? Because I wanted the book to have dual leads—as much his story as her story and vice versa. I saw this as the story of two people overcoming external *and* internal struggles to get to know each other in a new way. I wanted readers to be able to see and feel and experience the story through both of the main characters' perspectives.

I could have done it in alternating first person POV—that technically would have worked. But I was worried about making my hero and heroine sound different (about having different voices), and I'd been reading a lot of old-school romance novels, which are almost always told in alternating third person, so it just felt right.

(That's something else to remember: If you're writing in a genre where one POV is dominant, you might want to ask yourself if there's a reason for that and let that factor into your decision.)

THIRD PERSON OMNISCIENT POV is sometimes confused with third person limited because both use *he/she/they* instead of, for example, *I/we*, but there are some really important differences. In third person limited, you're tied to what your POV character(s) know and see and smell, etc. In omniscient, the story is basically being told by some all-knowing, all-seeing narrator who can see inside the characters, and also into the past and the future.

An omniscient narrator knows not just how the characters are feeling but also how the story will end.

The story is being told by *you—the author*—in other words, so everything you know, you can put on the page. Which is very appealing! But it's also where it's easy to get into trouble.

After all, just because you *can* put everything you know onto the page doesn't mean you *should*. In general, new writers often like to "tell" readers everything—all at once. This is often called an *info dump*.

> *Molly was having a very bad day, which was about to get worse with a knock on the door. She opened it to see John outside, and Molly was mad. John was, too. He and Molly used to be friends, but then she ate all the regular M&M's and left only the peanut M&M's even though she knew John was allergic to peanuts, which his parents found out when he had a reaction when he was four and almost died. John also had red hair and green eyes and was taller than Molly now. He liked dogs more than cats and really needed a haircut.*

See? With omniscient POV you could, theoretically, dump every bit of information about every single character and thing right on the page—boom! All in one go. Needless to say, that's not usually a good idea.

Part of being a writer isn't just learning what to write; it's learning what *not* to write—what you should show instead of tell (more on that later) and when you should sprinkle information into the story rather than dumping it all down onto the page.

But that doesn't mean that omniscient POV doesn't have its uses!

When I was writing *Heist Society*, I knew that, most of the time, I'd be in the head of my heroine, Kat, but there would be times I'd have to show the reader stuff that my heroine wasn't present for—like guards

FIRST PERSON:

WHEN I WOKE UP THIS MORNING, I HAD NO IDEA HOW BAD MY DAY WOULD BE.

SECOND PERSON:

WHEN YOU WOKE UP THIS MORNING, YOU HAD NO IDEA HOW BAD YOUR DAY WOULD BE.

THIRD PERSON:

WHEN SHE WOKE UP THIS MORNING, SHE HAD NO IDEA HOW BAD HER DAY WOULD BE.

checking a video surveillance feed or a bank manager checking the locks on a door.

Heist stories are, by definition, pretty complicated. It was important for the reader to see the whole picture—not just what was going on with Kat but also what was going on elsewhere in the world/story. In this case, having an omniscient point of view helped build suspense—the reader could see things that Kat might not know, which would ratchet up the tension and keep readers on the edges of their seats. It also helped the reader to understand all the different pieces that were in play.

Think of it like this: Sometimes your book is like a chess game. Omniscient POV is the best way to allow a reader to see the entire board. Sometimes that's best. And sometimes it's better to see the game only through the eyes of the queen or a knight or whoever your POV character happens to be.

Omniscient POV also allowed the Heist Society books to have a very different voice and scale and feel from my (first person) Gallagher Girls series. We weren't limited to one lens, in other words. The reader could see big, sweeping scenery shots or close-ups and everything in between. And I can't imagine writing that series in any other way.

38

When it comes to picking a POV for your stories, keep all of this in mind. Also, be sure you read a bunch of books done in each. Then sit down and try your story each way. One POV might feel a lot easier than the others once you start writing, and then you'll know exactly what to do.

DEAR JENNIFER LYNN BARNES,
Second person POV is really, really rare, but you've used it! When? Why? How?

I almost always write in first person. That's the point of view that feels natural to me, and I love giving readers the opportunity to live in the protagonist's head and experience things as she experiences them. But when I sat down to write my Naturals series, I knew that I needed a second point of view to really tell the story. The series follows a secret FBI program that trains gifted teenagers to profile serial killers. My protagonist is a "natural" profiler—meaning that she has an innate understanding of how to take little details about a person and their behavior and figure out their big-picture personality, which she can then use to predict how that person will act in the future. I knew that I wanted to write first person from this character's point of view, but I also wanted to give the reader the opportunity to do what the teens in the books are learning to do.

Get inside the heads of killers.

So, in addition to my protagonist's point of view, I also wanted to write some sections in the killer's point of view.

That way, readers could try their hands at profiling the killer and figuring out who they were before the characters did. To start, I tried third person for the killer's sections, but that felt awkward, because I didn't want readers to know who the killer was or to explicitly give away anything about the killer's identity—not their age, not their appearance, not their gender. I briefly considered writing the killer sections in first person, but that felt *too* intimate.

Ultimately, I decided to try writing the killer's point of view in second person. So instead of saying "he picks up the knife" or "I pick up the knife," the killer's perspective would be written as "you pick up the knife." From the moment I first tried the second-person perspective, I knew it was the right one! It allowed readers to be close to the killer, but since second person is such an unusual point of view to write in, it didn't feel like I was normalizing what the killer was thinking. And as a bonus, I soon discovered that most things sound a lot creepier in second person.

Looking back, I think the second-person perspective worked in the Naturals books in a way that it wouldn't have worked in any of my others for two reasons. The first is that the killer's chapters are very short and occur infrequently throughout the book, so I'm not asking readers to spend *too* much time in a perspective that might sound very odd to them at first. The second reason that particular POV works is that I was able to explain my POV choice to the readers in the book itself. As my protagonist is being taught to profile, her FBI mentor instructs her to always profile using either the words *I* or *you*, rather than *he* or *she*, because the former bring you much closer to the killer. So when my protagonist thinks about a killer, she always mentally addresses that person as *you*, and then when readers get to actually see inside the killer's head, the narrative refers to the killer in the same way.

Outside of this series, I've never used second person, but having used it once made me realize just how many options I have when it comes to point of view.

DEAR ELIOT SCHREFER,
How do you pick a POV?

I start with the plot, and then figure out which character is best for that story. Not which character will get through the narrative the easiest—but I'm not out to torture characters either. I come up with a character for whom the story line will be most resonant. In *Endangered*, for example, which is the story of a girl surviving wartime in the Democratic Republic of Congo with an orphan bonobo at her side, I chose a fourteen-year-old mixed-race girl because (a) the bonobos are matriarchal, so a female protagonist would be an interesting way to explore themes of female survival strategies among humans and apes, and (b) I wanted Sophie to feel like an insider at times, and other times like an outsider, and

(c) because she's old enough to be able to take care of a baby ape, whose needs are closer to a human child's than a pet's.

Should my book be written in past or present tense, and what's the difference?

This is a really good—and really important—question! In fact, this is one of the first questions an author will ask themselves about any project. It's one that I worry about a lot because no one—and I mean *no one*—wants to get halfway through a book and realize they've been using the wrong tense and they're going to have to rewrite the whole thing!

So past versus present—what's the difference and when do you use them?

For me, it's about perspective. If a book is written in present tense, then the hero or heroine isn't looking back on things after the fact. No, we—the reader—are seeing things happen *as they happen*, right through the main character's eyes (if it's written in first person or third person limited). We feel the slap of the rain on her face. We hear the thunder. We see the lightning. We are *in the storm*, and that can be incredibly powerful. Just like the characters, the narrator has no idea what comes next, and that adds an extra level of tension and conflict to a story.

But present tense can also be a little disorienting. Sometimes that's what you're going for. My Embassy Row series, for example, was present tense, and I can't imagine it any other way because Grace was a heroine who didn't know who to trust or how she was going to make it. The reader had to be with her—right in her head as things were happening—to really get what she was going through.

In contrast, my Gallagher Girls series was first person past tense. It was about a girl going to spy school, and each book was a "report" about what had happened that semester. By the time Cammie sat down to "write" her report, she'd already lived through the events of the book, and she'd had some time to think about things. To reflect. To consider.

To tease.

For example:

When the person telling the story already knows how the story turns out, you can drop hints about what's to come. Which can be a powerful thing as well.

> *If I'd known how the day would end, I never would have gotten out of bed.*

So how do you decide which to use? Well, when I'm starting a new book, I will often sit down and write the opening chapter a bunch of different ways. Present tense. Past tense. First person, third person, omniscient. I'll write chapter 1 all the ways, and inevitably, there will be one way that just feels right for chapter 2, and that is usually the winner.

What's the best writing advice you ever got?	
Julie Murphy	I've gotten three pieces of advice that have stuck with me: 1. Read as much as you can. It's a free writing education. 2. The sooner you treat yourself like a professional, the sooner other people will, too. You've got to put in the work. 3. Writing advice isn't one size fits all, and it's perfectly okay to ignore advice that doesn't work for you, even when it's from your favorite authors.

How much research goes into writing a book?

That depends on the book!

If you're writing a story about people and places and things you already know really well, then you may not have to do much research at all. Your life has been your research. Start writing!

But if you're working on something taking place in a different time or place or featuring characters really different from you or information you don't know super well, then there should be some research in your future.

SOMETIMES THAT RESEARCH WILL BE ABOUT PLACES: For example, if you have a scene in London, you need to make sure the cars are driving on the left side of the road and taxis are black, not yellow!

SOMETIMES THAT RESEARCH WILL BE ABOUT HISTORY: If you want to write about something that happened during World War II, then you might want to write about food rations and how telephone numbers had letters and numbers in them, and include the fact that a lot of cars didn't have seat belts.

SOMETIMES THAT RESEARCH WILL BE ABOUT PEOPLE: If you're attempting to write characters with different ethnic backgrounds, religions, sexual orientations, and/or abilities than you, then you should do as much research as possible.

Speak to people with those backgrounds. Read books written by people in those communities, both fiction and nonfiction. Watch documentaries and read interviews, and, most of all, remember that people are people. No group on earth is completely homogeneous. Within every culture there's going to be a huge range of interests and hobbies and beliefs. It's your job to create characters that embrace and fit into a group without simply employing stereotypes or making vast generalizations.

SOMETIMES THAT RESEARCH WILL BE ABOUT GENRES: Even if you're working on a fantasy novel—on something in a totally made-up land and featuring things that could never exist in this world—then you would be smart to research the canon of science fiction and fantasy stories that came before you.

Knowing the "rules" of the genre can be a big help in figuring out what you should (and shouldn't) do. For example, if you want to write about unicorns, that's great! But it will probably help to have a good idea of what other unicorn stories have looked like through the ages.

(And for the record, I'm a big believer that a person should never try to write in a genre until they've read at least twenty books from that genre.)

SOMETIMES THAT RESEARCH WILL BE ABOUT SKILLS OR TECHNICAL KNOW-HOW: People ask me all the time how I research my books. I think they're envisioning clandestine meetings in deserted parking garages where people in trench coats tell me all about being a spy. Which . . . um . . . would be amazing! But the truth is I do a lot of research—right up until the point when the research starts getting in my way.

When I was writing the Gallagher Girls, I read a lot of declassified training manuals written for spies in World War II, and I watched a lot of documentaries featuring former government operatives. I gleaned a ton of useful information from the reference books produced by the International Spy Museum.

But at the end of the day, I was writing a story. I was never going to get things exactly right because, to my knowledge, there is no top secret boarding school for teenage girl spies. At some point, I just had to make stuff up.

And at some point, you will, too.

> ## DEAR ALAN GRATZ,
> Do you research before you write or as you go? Do you have any research advice that teens should know?
>
> I research before I write. I write historical thrillers, and it usually takes me about a month of research before I'm ready to build my story. After I build a chapter-by-chapter outline, there are usually a couple of things I need to go back and do more research on. But once that's done, I'm ready to write—and any more research I have to do along the way is usually pretty light!

How do you find good research sources?

This will, obviously, depend a lot on what you're researching.

Nothing compares with visiting real places or talking to real people. If you're working on a book set during World War II or the civil rights movement, then you should try to talk to some of the older people in your family or community. They might be able to tell you what the air smells like after a battle or how windy it was during the march from Selma to Montgomery—the kinds of details you won't read in a book!

But while interviewing people and visiting places are great, they're not always possible. Which is why, these days, most people's first stop will be the internet. You want to know something, you google it, right? Well, that's a great start! But there's a lot of misinformation on the web, and if you're going to spend months (or years) of your life working on a book, you want to make sure you're working with the right information.

When I was working on *Not If I Save You First*, I knew that, in some ways, I was writing my most realistic book yet, and I wanted to make sure that real Alaskans could read my novel without wanting to scream about all the things I'd gotten wrong. That's why I went to the best possible source: Alaskan librarians. They recommended some great books that helped me learn things like what berries are found in the Tongass National Forest, when they're in season, and, most importantly, which ones are yummy and which ones are deadly.

I also trust research-based information from colleges, universities, or government agencies like the USDA and the National Park Service. In fact, when I was working on *Not If I Save You First*, I was really worried that if I set the book during a blizzard, then the bears would all be hibernating (and I really wanted the threat of a bear attack hanging over my characters' heads!). So for a long time, I worried that I was going to have to choose between bears and snow. (What's an author to do?)

But then I found the Alaska Department of Fish and Game's website, and I learned that bears hibernate when they run out of food. So if it's an early snowstorm that follows an unusually warm fall, then it's very possible there will still be berries and other food for bears, so the bears could very much be out and about when the storm hits. I was in luck.

Through the years, I've also gotten some great information by watching documentaries. For example, I remember one documentary about what it's like to work in embassies all around the world. When it showed a horse-drawn carriage taking the new US ambassador to Japan to the palace to present his papers to the emperor, I knew I wanted a scene like that in my first Embassy Row novel, *All Fall Down*.

When I realized that a lot of spy movies employ former spies as consultants and they're often interviewed on the "bonus content" on the DVDs of those movies, I hit the mother lode of great spy info. A ton of that made it into the Gallagher Girls books—including a full scene in *Cross My Heart and Hope to Spy* that is an exact replica of a training exercise that they run at the CIA's covert training facility "The Farm."

In short, the world is full of information. Read books and articles, listen to podcasts, and watch interviews and videos. It has never been easier to learn about things—quickly! Just be sure that you're learning the right things from the right people and always consider the source. (They're definitely not all created equal.)

You'll want to weave that information into your stories, worlds, and characters as seamlessly as possible. Your novel shouldn't read like a textbook, and you should never just cut and paste information into your book. For starters, that's plagiarism. Plus, it's not good writing.

Finally, I've read a lot of books where the author clearly did a ton of research on a subject and didn't want to "waste" any of it, so it was all in there—whether it mattered or not. Whether it was boring or not.

So do as much research as you can; use it. Absorb it. But if it doesn't blend seamlessly and efficiently onto the page, then it probably doesn't belong on the page. And that's okay. It still shaped your understanding of a subject, and that's the most important thing.

DEAR ELIOT SCHREFER,
Do you research before you write or as you go? What are your favorite research tips/tricks?

I try to get all my research out of the way before I start. That always fails, of course—plenty will come up that I hadn't predicted. The biggest enemy in writing a research-heavy book is the feeling of being snowed under by the material. The thing I have to avoid is having a teetering stack of books, Post-it notes sticking out, beside my computer. To prevent that, I note important passages in my research books, then type those quotes into their own document. I print that out and use it as my research bible. A forty-page printout is much easier to manage than a few dozen books.

While I'm writing, I try not to pause to research. I keep a legal pad around and jot down things I'll eventually have to look up. Then, on a day when I'm uninspired to draft anything new, I might go back and do that additional research, then go back and edit in the changes. I'm always looking for tasks I can do even when I'm not in the mood to be writing.

How do I know when I've planned a story enough to start writing?

I don't know that any author ever feels 100 percent prepared to start a book. It's always a little bit scary, like getting up on a really high diving board and looking down, except that if you jump off a high dive, you're at least guaranteed of getting to the end. Gravity will take care of that much.

Maybe you'll feel ready to start writing when you no longer have any big questions that are floating around in the back of your mind. Or maybe, like me, there are some questions that you can't answer until you start writing, and no amount of plotting or planning or research can get you there, so you might as well get the "wrong" version of the story on paper because that's the only way to find the right version.

Maybe you'll want to get started as soon as you find a piece of research that makes everything click together in your head. Or maybe you'll want to keep on researching and outlining and talking about your book with friends because that's a whole lot easier and more fun than actually sitting down day after day and laboring over something that might never be any good.

I spend a lot of time on airplanes, and I've gotten to where, when someone sits down beside me and asks what I do for a living, I never, ever tell them I'm a writer. Why? Because everyone—and I do mean *everyone*—has a book they've been wanting to write. And they will usually spend the duration of that flight telling me how amazing their idea is and that they'd do what I do if they just had the time.

These people all *want* to be writers. They all say that someday they're going to *be* writers. But the act of starting a book is scary. And the actual process is long and painful and sometimes not even a little bit fun.

So these people keep *talking* about the book they'll write someday.

My hope for you is that you'll be someone who stops talking and starts writing.

So how do you do that?

—**SET YOURSELF A DEADLINE.** Maybe it's that you want to start writing during National Novel Writing Month. Maybe you want to be finished by spring break or your birthday. Whatever you choose, even artificial structure can be helpful. The key is picking some kind of deadline and writing it down. And once you do that you can . . .

—**HOLD YOURSELF ACCOUNTABLE.** Maybe that means telling your BFF or librarian. Maybe it means getting a writing buddy and keeping each other honest. Maybe it just means telling your little sister you'll give her twenty dollars if you're still researching in two months. It doesn't matter how you do it, it just matters that there's something keeping you on track so that you . . .

—**DON'T SPEND SO MUCH TIME RESEARCHING YOUR IDEA THAT YOU BECOME SICK OF YOUR IDEA.** Research is a form of procrastination for a lot of people—a way of "working" without having to go out on a limb and start actually writing. But if you're still researching after months, you run the risk of losing your love for the project before you write a single word.

So plan, research, and strategize until you get comfortable with what you need to do, but don't forget, the most important part is that eventually you *do it*!

What's the best writing advice you ever got?	
Kody Keplinger	Don't be afraid to deviate from your plans. Outlines can be incredibly useful, but sometimes your story is going to take you in unexpected directions, and it's okay to change course.

DEAR STEPHANIE PERKINS,
How much of the story do you know when you start, and how do you figure it out?

It takes me about two years to write a novel, which gives me a long time to think about future projects. I always know what my next two or three books are, and I keep huge files of notes about each project. Whenever I think of an idea that would be good for a certain project, I add the note. This means that when it's time for me to actually write the next book, I already know a lot about it! However, I still take a little more time to shape the story before I begin writing.

First, I want to know where the story begins and where it ends. I like there to be some sort of parallel. A similar moment or situation, but something important has changed. After that, I figure out the key plot points that will get me from beginning to end—the turning points and significant realizations. Then I'll start figuring out the most important moments between those key plot points. And so on, working my way down to smaller and smaller moments.

It's not a perfect metaphor, but I think of it as building a spine. I start with the top and bottom, then add big vertebrae in between, then smaller vertebrae in between the big vertebrae, and then even smaller vertebrae between those. I keep adding until my structure is steady and even.

Also, because I write a bit slower than most authors, figuring out the plot before I begin is crucial. I don't have time to be searching for it as I go along.

So is that it? Is your novel totally planned now? Uh . . . probably not. If you don't feel entirely prepared to start writing at this point, don't worry. You want to know a secret? I'm getting ready to start writing what will be my sixteenth published book and I don't feel prepared . . . at all!

I'm not sure anyone ever feels entirely ready to start an undertaking like this, but there are some things you can do to put yourself on slightly more solid ground.

1. Experiment with tense and POV. Trust me, it's a lot less painful to write your opening chapter a few different ways than to get to the middle of the book and realize you've picked the wrong POV character and the whole thing should be in past tense instead of present.

2. Try writing a scene from one of your favorite books from a different character's POV or in a different tense and see the impact that it has.

3. Give yourself a set amount of time to research, and remember, nothing says you have to know everything when you begin. In fact, I'd wager that you don't even know exactly what you need to know yet. You won't know everything until you write it!

4. Be kind to yourself. If you're nervous, that's normal. If you're scared, me too! If you're afraid you're going to waste your time by making the wrong call, just remember that the first draft of anything is a dirty water draft

and, as every writer eventually learns, you can't edit a blank page!

CHAPTER 4
BUILDING YOUR WORLD

How do you go about creating a world that's both realistic and captivating to the reader?

My world-building advice for new authors is pretty simple: Don't go crazy.

When I hear about people trying to get an agent for a thousand-page debut fantasy novel, I start to wonder if maybe they went a little overboard with the world building.

Now, don't get me wrong; I understand the temptation. After all, making up stuff is fun. What if purple were yellow? What if swords were made out of fire instead of steel? What if spaceships looked like old-timey cars and ran on French fries?

And world building probably feels like the key to success. After all, everyone loves Harry Potter and *Star Wars*—big stories set in big worlds! But it's very easy to make your story more confusing than complex, more boring than nuanced.

So how do you know which world-building details matter and which should be cut? Well, I think it really boils down to the type of detail you're talking about.

THROWAWAY LINES are small, inconsequential lines that color the world or characters but aren't really essential. They're like the decorative buttons on a coat. They make the coat look nice and cool and finished, but they don't really serve a function.

Without them, the coat might look too plain, though, so you want some. But if you had nine hundred of them on one coat, that would look ridiculous. So definitely throw in some details that add texture, nuance, and interest, but add them in moderation.

But what about **THROWAWAY LINES THAT AREN'T AS "THROWAWAY" AS THEY SEEMED AT THE TIME**? To be honest, I've often thought that one of the main reasons to have throwaway lines is to camouflage the details that you want to plant now but surprise the reader with later.

My favorite throwaway line ever is in *Harry Potter and the Sorcerer's Stone* when Hagrid says he borrowed the flying motorcycle from Sirius Black. That line doesn't matter at all until you read *Harry Potter and the Prisoner of Azkaban* and realize that Sirius Black is one of the most important characters in the whole series. That moment was the moment I fell in love with Harry Potter and knew I'd follow it to the end because I had no idea where we were going.

But most world building is bigger than mere throwaway lines. Let's call those things . . .

WORLD-BUILDING PILLARS. These are the things that matter so much that if you took them away, a part of the story or world would crumble.

So how do you build those? Well, I think that boils down to your initial question: How do you create a world that feels *realistic*?

That means that every action has an equal and opposite reaction. That means your world-building decisions have to have consequences. They matter. They influence the plot and/or the characters. If you changed your world, you would somehow change your story.

In that sense, every world has to be realistic. It doesn't matter if you're writing a story about a boy who joins a band in Cleveland or a band of warlocks who go to war with an ancient elven race—you have to commit! You have to act and write in every way as if everything you're writing is real.

When I think of examples of realistic world building, I always remember a very small detail in Holly Black's amazing Curse Workers series. In that world, magic is real and people perform magic by touching other people with their hands. So, in Holly's world, everyone wears gloves.

Gloves are essential, and bare hands are edgy and dangerous. I remember a line where the characters go to sanitize their gloves when, in any other book, the characters would be washing their hands.

That's it. Just that one little, simple thing, but I still remember it years later and think about it a lot. Because right then I got it. The fact that the characters wear gloves wasn't just a fun character trait or quirk. It was a part of that world, and it mattered. It mattered so much that it had changed everything about the society—right down to the fact that there weren't sinks in the bathrooms; there were glove-sanitizing stations. In that moment, that world was real to me.

So don't just think about the facts or the quirks or the details of your world. Think about the ripple effect those facts and quirks and details would have.

And remember, in the long run, people may be fascinated or entertained by worlds, but it's the characters we root for. It's the plot that we follow. World building exists to shape and support great characters and great plots. It's never, ever a substitute for them.

DEAR MARIE LU,

What are the steps that you go through when you're building a world?

I usually build a world by first building a character. With *Warcross*, for example, I knew early on that I wanted to write a story about a girl hacker and bounty hunter. Emika's personality, problems, and passions came first to me, and I spent a long time developing her profile before I started thinking about what kind of world would need to exist in order for her to be this person that I created. So, around Emika, I built the world of Warcross—a game that she would hack, technology that she would use in her bounty hunting, and so on. When I decided that I wanted to set this in our world in the very near future, I did a lot of research about real-world tech that is on the cusp of becoming mainstream. I tried to flesh out how those elements would be incorporated into our everyday lives. And within that, I placed Emika. I tend to build a world out about halfway before I start writing my first draft, and as I'm writing that draft, the rest of the world building will fall into place. It's all a very organic, shifting process for me, and I will constantly add to the world as the series goes on.

When you're working with so many different novels and ideas, how can you separate the worlds? Does it all just blend together, or is everything its own universe?

This is something that will, again, vary a lot author to author. Whenever I do events, I'm always asked if the characters in my series could ever meet—do they live in the same world? (Which is why I wrote the novella *Double Crossed* a few years ago, featuring characters from both the Gallagher Girls and Heist Society.)

So the answer is yes, they do live in the same world. But that fact isn't really essential to the stories—it's just something fun I've done for myself and my readers. A lot of authors will call these things "Easter eggs"—little lines you might insert into one series, giving a nod at another.

For example, in *Not If I Save You First*, the hero remembers that someone once told him he would have made a good candidate for the Blackthorne Institute—the boys' school in my Gallagher Girls series. Some readers will catch that and get a kick out of it, but some readers won't, and that's okay.

If you decide to write multiple books or multiple series, you have a few options:

1. You can set everything in what is obviously the same world—where the fact that the worlds overlap *is* essential to the stories. This might be a great idea, especially if you've got a large world or a complicated magical system. Maybe some of the characters from one series might cross over or appear in the other, but the two properties will be linked more by world than by characters.

   Leigh Bardugo is a master of this. So is Cassandra Clare. But it isn't limited to the sci-fi and fantasy genres. All of Sarah Dessen's books are contemporary stand-alones, but Sarah has also built a world in which her characters all exist together (and which her readers love returning to every time there's a new Sarah Dessen book).

2. Another option is to create an elaborate world, and when it's time to write a new series, you decide to create another one! The good news is that, with this model, you get to start with a clean slate and build everything from scratch! But the bad news is . . . you have to start with a clean slate and build everything from scratch.

   There are pros and cons to each. Obviously, if your first series is selling really well and you have a ton of rabid readers, it would probably be smart to keep your next work as tightly linked as possible to the thing that people already love. But maybe your first series didn't sell at all and you're still trying to find an agent? Or maybe it got published but never really found its readership? Or maybe you're just ready for a new world, and getting a fresh start with a fresh slate is what gets you excited to write again.

3. You can also do what I've done, where, yes, I make nods to my other series and characters, but each of my worlds can (and do) stand entirely on their own.

People ask me all the time if I ever get confused while I'm writing. If, for example, when I was working on *Not If I Save You First*, things blurred together and it suddenly turned into a Gallagher Girls or Embassy Row novel. The answer is no, I've never had that problem. Maybe if your worlds are incredibly detailed and complex (and confusing), that could happen.

But if you have a feel for your characters . . .

If you've fully developed your world . . .

If you're really invested in that story and know why all of those back-story and world-building details matter (and they aren't just thrown in for the heck of it), then I don't think you'll have a problem in the long run.

The key to all of these things is that you don't have to decide right now. Right now, you just have to think about the world you want to build for your next novel and try to make that world as amazing as possible. What you do three or four or fourteen books from now? That's a problem for Future You. And that's okay.

DEAR SARAH REES BRENNAN,
What comes first for you: plot, character, or something else?

First for me comes a premise—the premise usually becomes the selling point of a book, what you say when people ask you what it's about. ("Girl falls through hole into magic world" is the premise of *Alice's Adventures in Wonderland*, and "children go through wardrobe to magic land" is the premise of *The Lion, the Witch and the Wardrobe*.) It's the thing you have before plot, where there are some people, and they have a problem to solve, or an adventure to set out on, and for me there's also the mood, a feeling of what might be in store, whether that's wonder, or love, or despair. Then I work out characters—the specific people I want this situation to happen to, who will be brave enough or weak enough or love enough. Only then comes the plot—what happens to the characters, after the premise.

DEAR HOLLY BLACK,

How do you create a magical system that makes sense and enriches your story and world?

There's a temptation when thinking about writing fantasy to believe that because anything can happen, there aren't any rules. Not true! It's on you, the writer, to create rules for your fantasy world—and your magic systems—that are consistent, interesting, and thematically resonant.

Herewith, I am going to ask you a few questions that I hope will help you on your path. Firstly, what can your magic do? It's possible to make a system where there's only one type of magic—like, say, flying—or a magic system where magic does lots of stuff, so much stuff that it would be impossible to list it all. But figuring out what the magic does, insofar as you can, is still a good place to start.

Secondly, what are the limitations of your magic, and what's the cost of using it? Without limitations, there's no story, because magic is going to solve every problem and overwhelm the narrative. And without a cost, magic doesn't have any value.

There are lots of possible limitations to magic, and many of them are also costs—it tires the user out, it drains their life force, it requires years of training, it requires a bunch of rare components, it takes a long time to cast a spell, some of what the spell does affects the caster, there are ways to be immune to magic, spells fade over time, magic users are shunned, magic is illegal, etc. Keep calibrating until the magic isn't overpowering the story you want to tell.

Thirdly, is there a model for how your magic users are organized? Vampires who function like solitary hermits are going to be very different from vampires who are organized like a board of directors.

Fourthly, what is the metaphorical value of your magic? Magic is always metaphorical, whether we want it to be or not. For example, a magic system that has men and women using different kinds of magic is saying that men and women are profoundly different. And what about nonbinary users of magic? You want to be sure that while you're building something cool, you're also building something that says what you want to say about the world.

And lastly, ask yourself how magic will be used by real people to get the things that real people want—power, love, sex, money, etc.

After you're done, recruit friends—especially friends who love gaming—to try to break your story by using the magic you've built to disrupt the world of your story.

And keep calibrating! Good luck!

I want to write fantasy and sci-fi. How is your world building different since your stories take place in the "real world"?

Thanks for asking this! In truth, it's one of my pet peeves when people talk about world building and only include speculative fiction (fantasy, sci-fi, dystopian, etc.). The truth is that every type of author writing every type of book should pay a lot of attention to world building.

I grew up in rural Oklahoma. We had cows and baled hay. I graduated in a class of seventy-six, and I had the grand champion steer at my county fair three times. That's the real world. In fact, that was *my* real world.

But people who live in big cities and ride the subway and go to school with thousands of other students, they're living in the real world, too! It's just a very different world from the one that I knew as a kid.

So if I were to write my story, I'd have to make sure my world felt real to people who have never even seen a steer—much less showed one at the county fair. I'd have to keep in mind that going to school with seventy-five other kids is different from going to school with four thousand.

Those experiences are all going to be very different, and those worlds should feel incredibly unique.

In many ways, writing in the "real" world is far easier than creating an entire world from scratch like people have to do with speculative fiction. After all, I've never had to describe how cars work in any of my books. Cars are just cars. Gravity is just gravity. Europe is just Europe. But I also have the option of building my own little sandbox inside the real world and playing in whatever parts of it I want.

You see, on the surface, my worlds look exactly like the real world, but it's what goes on beneath the surface that allows me to have a lot of fun.

Holly Black was the person who first taught me about **OPEN WORLD FANTASY** versus **CLOSED WORLD FANTASY**, and I think, even if you're writing realistic fiction, you need to keep these concepts in mind.

In an open world fantasy, the fantasy elements are pretty much out in the open. A lot of comic books and superhero stories fall into this category. After all, everyone in the Marvel universe knows that Tony

Stark is Iron Man and that there's a government organization called SHIELD.

Closed world fantasies, on the other hand, exist behind a kind of curtain. Harry Potter might be the best example of this. In Harry's world, there's a whole parallel universe, complete with governments and banks and hospitals—everything we have in this world—but with magic. It exists right beneath our noses and no one has a clue.

In a way, all contemporary authors are writing closed world fantasies. We're all writing the ordinary, regular world, but we're taking our readers behind a curtain into a part of it they've never experienced for themselves.

After all, nobody knows that the Gallagher Academy for Exceptional Young Women is really a school for spies. Nobody knows that a network of amazing art thieves and con artists is being run by a teenage girl out of a brownstone in Brooklyn. Nobody knows that the ruling family of a (fictional) European country is actually embroiled with a powerful secret society and one teenage girl has the power to bring them both down.

This is what I write. And this is how I write it—by asking these questions:

What are the things that are true for everyone in the world?

What are the things that are true for just my characters?

And what are the things that are secret—that only my characters know?

So no matter whether you're writing witches or mean girls, remember that writing realistic fiction doesn't mean that everything has to be 100 percent realistic. It's still a story. It's still fiction. And it's your job to think about what's going to make it feel vibrant. What's going to make it feel real—not just in the sense of "this is a place I know" but also in the sense of "this is a place I *want* to know"?

What's a world that is going to result in the most interesting characters?

Because if you change the world, you will change the characters . . .

And we're going to talk about that next.

For a lot of writers, world building is the fun part. And by all means, have fun! Create your world. Figure out your magic. Name your dragons. But remember . . .

1. World building isn't just for fantasy and sci-fi writers—it's for everyone.
2. Nothing happens in a vacuum. Whatever the elements of your world might be, make sure that those elements impact the characters and plot.
3. World building lives to support interesting characters and plots—it's never a substitute for them.

CHAPTER 5
CREATING YOUR CHARACTERS

How do you make characters (good or bad) that your readers will care about?

The key to great characters is writing characters who we care about. Who we root for (or against). Who make us laugh or cry or just . . . feel. Because it doesn't matter how great your plot is if we don't care about the people involved. It doesn't matter how rich your world is; if we don't care about the people who live there, then we have nothing at stake.

Characters are our portals into those rich worlds. They're how we see ourselves battling dragons or saving the day or falling in love. Characters are how we—the reader—feel like we, personally, have something at stake in this story. They're why we cry when a beloved character dies or why our hearts race when our characters are in danger.

So what makes a good character?

Well, you're going to get a lot of different opinions on this, but I always go back to the age-old question of nature versus nurture.

Are we products of our environments? If you take the same person and plop them down in a different sort of neighborhood or with a different kind of family, would that person grow up to be vastly different?

Or are we products of our DNA? Are some characteristics or traits just naturally ingrained in us, and it doesn't matter if we're raised by the richest people in town or if we grow up struggling to get by? Will we still like a certain kind of peanut butter and have the same favorite song either way?

When thinking about characters, I think it's important for authors to consider both nature *and* nurture. What kind of person is that character just wired to be? And what kind of person has their world turned them into?

And then you have to show how all of that manifests itself—both the good and the bad. Is she someone who gets cranky when she hasn't eaten? Is he someone who always remembers to buy a birthday card? Do group situations make them nervous? Or are they more comfortable when they're lost in a crowd?

These little touches are how you make your characters feel real. And making your characters feel real is how you're going to make people care about them.

Always.

DEAR STEPHANIE PERKINS,
How do you write a compelling hero or heroine?

I write about people who I'd like to know in real life. I give them compelling passions and interests—things that interest me, personally—and I balance them out with genuine flaws and mistakes that make me feel less alone in the world. Perfect people are boring. And irritating. I like characters who have room for growth.

How do you make a character's backstory more interesting?

The first thing I want to say about backstory is simple: Everybody has one.

Unless you're going to start your book with your hero's birth and follow their entire life (which I do *not* recommend), then there's going to be stuff that happened before we showed up to watch. And that's good. That's *essential*. (Even for supporting characters. Especially for villains.)

Something had to make your characters the way they are when the book begins.

The stuff that goes on during the book? That's going to make them another way.

I think a lot of new writers think about backstories and world building as a kind of checklist they can go down, giving characters dead parents or bad childhoods, terrible accidents or tragic health scares. (With maybe a few debilitating romantic encounters thrown in for good measure.)

But not all backstories are tragic or sad. Frodo Baggins had a pretty easy life until the day he had to leave home to go destroy the most powerful and dangerous ring in the world. Nothing in his backstory had turned him into the obvious person for that job. Which, by the way, is what made him the most *interesting* person for that job!

Still, most of us naturally gravitate toward that checklist:

What kind of stuff has your character had to endure?

But that checklist is only part of the picture, and it's almost worthless without the second part:

What kind of coping mechanism did they develop to endure it?

Sometimes those mechanisms translate to the dark sides of a character's personality. Think about Bruce Wayne, who saw his parents murdered and, as a result, focused all his energy on finding their killer. He grew up so intent on vengeance that he became Batman.

Sometimes those mechanisms come through in the good aspects of your character's personality. Steve Rogers was bullied so badly as a kid that, after he became Captain America, he became obsessed with fighting for the little guy.

Whatever the case, backstory isn't the stuff that happened to your characters. Backstory is the stuff that turned your characters into who they are right now.

So don't tell us what the character's backstory is right from the start. Don't go down that checklist. Instead, show us interesting, flawed, and compelling characters and then give them a heck of a good reason for being that way.

DEAR DAVID LEVITHAN,
Do you have any tips or tricks for getting to know your characters?

I am definitely a fan of asking the questions *What does your character have?* and *What does your character want?* in tandem. It can also be helpful if you don't feel you know the character yet to open a blank document and freewrite in that character's voice. Ask the questions—*What's your darkest secret? Who's the most important person in your life and why? Do you like where you live? What have you been listening to*

What is some advice for how a writer can shape their characters and develop unique, interesting personalities for each one?

In a way, I think all characters start out as archetypes. Or stereotypes. Or maybe just types.

You have the hero or heroine. The best friend. The rival. You have the queen bee and the wannabe, the musician and the Goth, the slob and the snob. But whether you're writing a bookworm or a jock, truly great characters happen when we go *beyond* the type.

When the jock writes poetry. When the homecoming queen secretly writes fanfiction. When the macho guy from the wrong side of the tracks is a piano prodigy and the music buff is tone-deaf.

Great characters—and personalities—happen when our characters are *more* than what we have come to expect.

When I first started writing *Not If I Save You First*, there was a stretch of time where I was really worried about the book. I couldn't quite figure out what tone I wanted it to have, and I didn't quite know who these characters were (because I *did* know at that point that the book would have only two or three characters through most of it . . . and that's a lot of book for just a couple of people to carry).

I knew I wanted to write a girl who had survived almost all alone in

71

the Alaskan wilderness for years. I knew she was going to be tough and strong and really, really smart. But I also knew I wanted her to be funny and not the most obvious person to save the day. In short, I needed her to be someone the world might underestimate.

I thought about it for a long time. Maybe she should be a beauty queen? A pop star? A reality TV celebrity?

And then it hit me: yes. I needed her to be underestimated by the world, and to do that all she had to be was . . . *a girl*.

So I decided to make her the girliest girl to ever cut wood and gut fish and use a hunting rifle. I needed her to be the kind of girl who has her own hatchet. And I needed that hatchet to be *bedazzled*.

That was when I knew not just the type of character my heroine was going to be, but the ways she was going to go against type as well. That was when I knew her backstory (girl raised in rural Alaska, fighting for survival) and her personality (girl who refuses to let her circumstances beat the sparkle and life out of her).

How about supporting characters? Well, I always start by asking, Who is my main character and what are her weaknesses? What are his strengths? And then I go about the business of making sure they're surrounded by people who will challenge and help them. I build a cast of personalities that will make my heroines and heroes—and my books—stronger.

As you start your book, you might want to also think about types of characters that you, the author, are going to *need*.

Are you going to need a computer genius or someone who's good in a fight? Will the plot require someone who is fluent in a bunch of languages . . . or just the language of talking to the opposite sex?

And don't forget when you're thinking about your character's strengths to think about their weaknesses as well. Superman is only interesting in a world in which kryptonite exists. Otherwise, he'd win every fight every time and that would never be in question—there would never be any conflict.

So it's not enough to give us characters who are amazing. Give us characters who have room to grow and improve and change as well.

What's the best writing advice you ever got?	
Jesse Andrews	Don't stop yourself from making mistakes before you make them. Because some aren't mistakes at all.

How do you decide when or how to introduce a character (protagonist, antagonist, etc.)?

When and how characters are introduced is one of those things that no one will notice if you get it right—but people *will* notice if you get it wrong. And you might very well get it wrong on the first draft. But, hey—isn't that what second drafts are for? Or third? Or tenth?

So many of the rules about introducing characters aren't even really rules for writers. They're rules for readers. And they're rules that we don't even know we know—we've just encoded them after reading books and watching movies and being told stories all of our lives. They're the things that we've been trained to expect.

For example, I read a historical romance novel a while back that opened with a handsome young man sneaking out of a house in the middle of the night. The next scene showed a young woman. A lifetime of reading told me that those two people were our hero and our heroine. Except . . . no. Actually, the guy was the heroine's brother. We didn't meet the real hero for twenty more pages, and I didn't even know he was the hero at the time because he was just one of a whole bunch of people we were meeting—and one of a whole bunch of points of view we were in.

When I was approximately fifty pages into the book, I had to go read the book's description to figure out who the hero and the heroine were. There were just so many POV characters—and we were meeting characters in such a random order—that I couldn't even start to get my bearings.

Authors have an unwritten contract with readers—things that readers will expect just because they've seen them done that way so often. Especially when meeting characters for the first time.

For example, readers have been conditioned to believe that any character with a point of view (especially early in the book) is an important character. Probably a main character! But what if they aren't? Well, then you might want to kill them off as soon as we meet them (à la Leigh Bardugo's *Six of Crows*) or show in some other way that this is a person who won't be sticking around.

Most of us have also come to expect that the boy we meet first is probably the hero and/or love interest. (I have a theory that a lot of YA love-triangles-that-aren't-really-love-triangles came about because readers were introduced to the not-love-interest first and so they encoded him as a "love interest" even when he wasn't. Example: Gale and Katniss.)

Can you break these rules? Absolutely! Amazing authors do it all the time to great effect. But you need to have a good reason.

Setting aside the unwritten contract that authors and readers have, there are some practical tips that I find make introducing characters a little bit easier.

First, the easiest way to introduce people, places, and things is to have them all be new to your POV character as well.

It's just about a billion times easier to explain stuff to the reader when someone also has to explain it to the hero or heroine. Can you imagine how confusing Harry Potter would have been if Harry had been brought up within the wizarding world? But he wasn't. So we got to hear Hagrid explain about Diagon Alley and Gringotts and exactly what that letter from Hogwarts really meant.

If your POV character(s) aren't new to the world, then you'll need to carefully introduce people in a way that tells the reader something about who they are and the role they'll fill in the story (best friend, love interest, enemy, frenemy) without rehashing old information.

Now, be careful! You're going to be tempted to include a lot of information in dialogue where the characters tell each other things they both already know. Resist this temptation! Why? Because if your characters have a history, then they need to act like it. And they need to talk like it. They should have inside jokes and old grudges. They need to make your heroine gasp and hug them or maybe jump behind a potted plant and hide. You need to write as if they were alive long before the story started. You need to make your reader believe that's true.

Another really easy rule of thumb is that, if you have a large cast, it's probably going to be easier to have the characters trickle in.

Have you ever gone someplace and suddenly been introduced to a big group of people all at the same time? Did you find it hard to remember everyone's names and which of the people were siblings and who was married to whom and which person was the computer genius and which one was going to college on a soccer scholarship?

It's just hard to take in a lot of new people at once in real life. Meeting fictional people is like that, too.

So when I'm writing a big cast, I try to make sure everyone gets their own moment of introduction when possible. It doesn't have to be long or complicated. It doesn't even need its own scene. But I'd avoid mass introductions, if possible. I think your reader will thank you.

Another tip is to give everyone in the group different physical characteristics (or markers). This can make it a lot easier for your reader to differentiate between the guy with the dark hair and the guy with the tattoos and the girl with the braids, etc.

Finally, I should point out that, in some cases, some characters can (and should) be introduced long before they walk into the room. Villains, especially, are often referenced long before we meet them. So you don't always have to meet the important characters early on in your novel, but if you want to "hold" that character's place in your reader's mind, you would do well to hint or reference them early on just to plant that seed.

Is it better to describe a character's physical features like hair and eye color when you first introduce them or incorporate it throughout the book?

As I said in the section before this, I think it's important to work a few key physical characteristics in early on, largely because once a reader mentally "casts" a character, then it's hard to change that impression. For example, if your character is a very tall, very thin brunette, then you don't want your reader mentally casting her as a petite blond. You may never break that first mental picture. Especially if a character has physical characteristics that matter (like Harry Potter's scar).

It's doubly important that you let your reader know what your characters' ethnicities are or if they have any physical features that really shape their personalities. For example, in my Gallagher Girls series, one of the characters is very petite and incredibly clumsy—two things that can pose a challenge at spy school! Another of the girls is black and is the first British student the school has ever had. So I made sure to work those facts in when we first met each of them.

As a rule, it's a lot easier to describe supporting characters because very few people ever think about their own hair or eye color, so it's not a natural thing for a POV character to do. The one thing you *don't* want to do is have your narrator looking at themselves in the mirror, describing their reflections. Editors and agents see this so often from first-time writers that it's frowned upon.

So try other approaches. Maybe another character should comment on the hero's eyes. Maybe the heroine can think about changing her hair.

You don't need a lot. As a rule, a little bit of description goes a long way. But do try to work in a little bit up front. Then make sure your characters are far more than just their eye colors. Because in the long run, that might be the least important thing about them.

Unfortunately, when I talk to new writers and ask them about their characters, I find that a lot of times they will have given a lot of thought to the physical but not much thought to anything else.

"Tell me about your heroine . . ."

"Well, she has red hair, and one blue eye and one brown eye. And she's left-handed. And she's about my height but never wears heels."

Those are all character descriptors. They're not character traits. And that is a really big, really important distinction.

Now, I'm not going to argue that a person's physical appearance can't affect their personality and background—it totally, 100 percent does. And, obviously, ethnicity can and will play a big role in shaping not only a character's cultural background but also some of the ways that they might interact with the world.

But a person's physical description is not all a person is. It shouldn't be all your character is, either.

Finally, I think a mistake a lot of writers make early in their careers is they pick a section of the book to try to *do a thing* and then they set out to accomplish that thing right then. Right there. They put everything they know down on the page like it's mashed potatoes on a cafeteria tray. *Dump.* And then, mission accomplished, they move on to the next thing.

There are times for that—make no mistake. But when it comes to creating characters and making them seem real, then that isn't accomplished by dumping a lot of facts onto the page at one time.

Most characters—like real people—will become more fully formed the more time you spend with them. So don't worry about making sure your readers get everything you know about your characters in one shot. You've got a whole book to flesh them out.

DEAR GORDON KORMAN,
Do you have any words of wisdom for making good characters?

I have to resist the tendency to paint with too broad a brush, so my favorite editorial advice is to find nuance. Villains can still have admirable traits. Scoundrels can be lovable. And it's always intriguing when our favorite characters have to wrestle with their dark sides and make hard choices.

When creating characters, do you already know all of their secrets and details right from the beginning, or do you figure those things out along the way?

This is yet another thing that will no doubt vary case by case and writer by writer, but one thing I find myself saying a lot—especially as I work on my first and second drafts—is that "the characters haven't shown up yet."

Now, that's not to say that I'm missing characters. It's not even to say that I'm writing the wrong characters. It just means that they don't feel real yet. They're pencil sketches, still needing paint and color and texture. I haven't fleshed them out, brought them from archetypes (the nerd, the jock, the femme fatale, etc.) to characters that go beyond type and become something more.

I can't really know someone after one meeting, and I can't really nail a character in one draft.

Even if you know all their secrets and their details, there will be some stuff that's in your head but not on the page. Yet. That's what future drafts are for. It always takes a few drafts for all the colors and details I have in my head to actually make it into my books.

So if your characters don't show up in your first drafts either? That's okay. Just keep writing and rewriting until everyone is there!

DEAR CHRISTINA DIAZ GONZALEZ,
Do you have any tips/tricks for getting to know your characters?

I like to discover a secret (hidden wish, fear, or past event) that the character reveals to no one except me. This gives me insight into their personality and can help shape some of their decisions. It also makes them feel more "real" in my mind.

How do you make your characters three-dimensional? How do you balance writing characters in fantastical situations (super-cool secret agents and smooth-talking cat burglars) while keeping the emotion/experience real and personable?

Real people have pros. And real people have cons. I think a lot of new writers struggle with the cons part. In fact, I think one of the hardest things about starting to write is figuring out that bad stuff has to happen. A lot of writers love their characters. They don't want to see them make mistakes. They certainly don't want to see them suffer.

But mistakes and suffering are conflict. And conflict is gas in the tank (more on that a little later). Sometimes your characters have to make mistakes and/or be a Not Good Version of themselves. That's what will make them feel human.

Real people also have quirks and hang-ups, annoying habits and pet peeves. Giving your fictional people some of these little mannerisms or tendencies can really go a long way toward making them feel more real to your readers.

Maybe your heroine never leaves home without a ponytail holder on her wrist. Maybe your hero doesn't like his foods to touch. Maybe two of your supporting characters finish each other's sentences or always coordinate their outfits.

Any writer can create a character who is "the chosen one" or a girl who has a problem at school or a boy who falls into some kind of supernatural conundrum. But only a truly great writer can make readers believe that these people are real (or wish they were).

And the key—the distinction—is in the details. Because the tropes and the overarching character stuff isn't always that unique or special. But the small beats or moments when a character lets their guard down and shows their soft side to a friend . . . the little habits or quirks that let the reader pick up on the fact that the character is nervous or scared and trying not to let the world know . . . that's where the greatness lies, atop a mountain made out of a million small decisions and precious words. Choose them wisely.

What's the best writing advice you ever got?
Marissa Meyer	Never forget that you're doing this because it's FUN.

What is the best way to pick names for the people and places in your books? Do you name them after people you know, pick a random name, or something else?

I'm always surprised by how many times authors are asked where we get the names of our characters. Maybe because, for me, a character's name isn't that important. In fact, sometimes I don't even come up with names until the last minute, using placeholder names for months and then, right before I turn a book in, doing a Find and Replace for something different.

For some authors, though, names are incredibly important, and they'll spend hours—or days—looking for the perfect names before they write a single word.

A lot of authors rely heavily on online baby name directories when we go name shopping. There are also cool sites that chronicle names through history and in various countries if you're looking for either an old-fashioned name or a name for a historical character. Sometimes you'll hear a cool name at a signing or get fascinated with the name of an actress—really, anything goes. When you're a writer, you're always on the lookout for stuff you might pick up and use someday. Maybe not *that* day. But we're always filing things away for future reference.

I don't often name characters after real people, but it does happen. Rosie in Embassy Row is named for one of my best friends. Maddie in *Not If I Save You First* is named for her daughter, largely because I think "Mad Dog" is the greatest nickname ever and I was dying to use it—especially for that book because . . .

The perfect name is always going to depend on the character.

When I was starting *I'd Tell You I Love You, But Then I'd Have to Kill You*, it seemed really important that the main character's name: (1) Start with a *C* and (2) be a first name that could also be a last name.

Why a *C*? Because I love alliteration, and I knew she was going to be known as "The Chameleon." Why a first name that could also be a last name? Because I wanted her first name to be her mother's maiden name. So "Cameron the Chameleon" was born.

Perhaps my most famous name is W. W. Hale the Fifth from Heist Society. This name came about because, first of all, I needed a name that sounded like Old Money. But I also wanted a guy who was always called by his last name. I didn't know that my heroine, Kat, would have no idea what the *W*'s stood for when I set out to write his character. But that's a detail that came out the first time I wrote them together and it stuck. To this day "What's Hale's first name?" is in the top five questions I get asked. People are obsessed with it! (And, yes, I do know what it is. And, no, I'm not going to tell you.)

Coming up with the names of towns/places/things is much the same.

I worried a lot about the name of Adria (in Embassy Row) because for the first time I was inventing an entire country and I wanted something that was evocative of a region of the world, without already being a place in that region. My editor and I spent a lot of time looking at maps, and ultimately, we decided that a country named after the Adriatic Sea would fit the bill.

So there's no one way to come up with a name. Just keep your eyes and your ears open, and if it doesn't fit once you start writing, that's what Find and Replace is for.

I already have my main character and my world figured out, but I'm having some trouble trying to come up with my antagonist (I don't even know who it is or what they're after) and really just my whole plotline. So how do you create a believable, full-of-depth villain?

Villains are hard. Great villains are (almost) impossible.

I think the key to writing a villain is to spend some time in their skin, thinking about things from their perspective. Spend some time thinking about how you would tell their story from their point of view. Because *all characters—even the "bad" ones—are the heroes of their own stories*.

Perhaps the best villain in recent memory is the character of Killmonger in *Black Panther*. He isn't some one-dimensional bad guy making vague threats or blindly grasping at power. No. He has a legitimate claim to the throne of Wakanda. He was wronged in a very serious and personal way. And he has a very specific goal that is exactly what the hero doesn't want to happen. Killmonger is a character who has gone down a very dark path that he didn't entirely choose for himself, and as a result, his character is sympathetic and dynamic, and it's not hard to imagine what the story would look like with him as the POV character.

As for your villain's goal—well, that depends on what you want your hero to be doing. Are you writing a very personal story about a girl who overcomes bullying at her school? Or are you writing a big, epic tale with battles and quests?

The villain needs to fit the goal, in other words. And in fact, your villain needs to have their own goal, and that goal should probably somehow relate to their personality and backstory. (And needless to say, it needs to run counter to the hero's objective.)

Voldemort is the obvious example. He was a half wizard, half Muggle orphan who so hated his Muggle father that he pretty much dedicated his life to destroying anyone who wasn't a pure-blood wizard.

Even if he'd never attacked Harry Potter's parents, he and Harry would have been on opposite sides of that fight. But he *did* attack Harry's parents, and in doing so, *it became personal.*

In my opinion, conflict is *always* better when it's personal.

It's also important to point out that you don't necessarily need a villain to have conflict. One of the first things my mom (the English teacher) ever taught me is that conflict comes in a few forms.

Man vs. Man—so, a villain or antagonist of some kind is going to try to keep me from my goal.

Man vs. Nature—so, a storm is moving in and there's no shelter and we're going to die if we don't figure something out.

Man vs. Himself—so, a man who hasn't left his apartment in five years is the only person who can stop a murder. But first he has to leave his house. Which he really, really doesn't want to do.

Man vs. A Ticking Clock—this one is my own, but I think it's important to mention. This one works well in conjunction with the other types of conflict because most great stories have a sense of urgency about them. Why this is important. Why it's important *now*. Sometimes, if the stakes are feeling a little low, I'll add some kind of ticking clock. An auction that's going to take place on Christmas Eve. A big dance at school. A storm that's moving in—something to up the stakes and give things a sense of urgency.

DEAR MARIE LU,
One of the things that I struggle with the most—and that you do the best—is creating villains. So . . . how do you do it?

It's both realistic and unsettling to remember that villains are also human, as capable of weaknesses and unique traits as our heroes. I try to go into building a villain remembering that, at one point, they were probably children, too, or had loved or lost someone, or had been somehow molded into who they now are. They likely think that they're the hero of their own story, that what they're doing is fundamentally right and that they can't believe why other people don't see the world as they do. Put that into your villain—however disturbing, get into their headspace and try to understand what makes them tick. Because villains are not monsters; they are humans, because humans are capable of terrible things. Remembering that will not only make your villains fully fleshed out but even more terrifying figures.

What makes a hero a hero?

I suppose the short, technical answer to this question is point of view. As I said in the previous question, if you turn the camera around and look at things through the villain's lens, then that person might very well be the hero of the story. At the very least, they should be the hero of *their* story.

In fiction, we often talk about protagonists. And we talk about heroes (and heroines). More often than not, we use the terms *protagonist* and *hero* interchangeably.

But sometimes protagonists aren't heroes at all. Sometimes they're antiheroes—people who aren't exactly good and aren't exactly right, but they're our gateway into that story and so we find ourselves rooting for them just the same.

One of my favorite movies is *Ocean's Eleven*. It's about eleven criminals who band together to rob a Las Vegas casino. So they're the bad guys, right? Well . . . see . . . they should be. But the casino owner is so mean and the thieves are so utterly charming that the audience never even thinks about rooting against them.

Regardless of how good (or maybe not-so-good) your hero is, the hero of your story should always be a person with a goal. Sometimes that goal is physical (throw the One Ring into Mount Doom); sometimes that goal is emotional (survive your sister's wedding). But whatever the case, we need to be rooting for the heroes to win. To survive. To achieve their goal and be okay afterward. In fact, we want the events of this book to teach our heroes some kind of lesson and make them stronger and better than they ever were before.

The hero is the person we want to have a happy ending.

(Whether or not you give it to them is entirely up to you!)

It's important that, over the course of a novel, a character experiences some kind of personal growth. How do you create that kind of character growth while still maintaining who they are as a person?

You're right—no one wants to read a story about a character who starts out one way and then goes through a huge ordeal that leaves them . . . exactly the same. I, for one, feel cheated when that happens. Like I just watched an hour-long home makeover show where designers and contractors worked tirelessly to turn a house . . . into the exact same house.

No. Your character should always have a *before*. And they should always have an *after*. And the two pictures should always be different in some meaningful way.

So how do you keep your character arc from changing who they are as a person? Well, it might help to think of it like this: In the beginning, your character is clay. You're not changing what they're made of. You're shaping it and honing it and putting it through fire to make it tougher (or softer). Your character is still your character. They're just a more evolved version of themselves.

If you're worried about them changing too much, you might want to think about it like this: The parts of the character that are affected by the plot will change. The parts that aren't affected by the plot won't change.

So if you're writing a book about a boy who is allergic to nuts and loves heavy metal music and has panic attacks around girls . . . and then his mom becomes the headmistress of an all-girls school and he has to live on that campus . . . well, by the end of that book, he will probably have gotten over the nervous-around-girls thing, right? But I bet he'll still be allergic to nuts and love heavy metal music.

So what kind of story are you writing? Is it a story about a person who learns to love or trust or believe in themselves? A loner who finds a family? A member of a family who breaks away to stand on their own? Maybe you're writing a friends-to-lovers romance where a relationship changes forever? Maybe it's a redemption story where someone makes up for a huge mistake in their past.

Just remember, your character is clay. Your plot is fire. Your plot is the thing that will change them.

How do you handle writing characters that come from different cultural/racial/ethnic backgrounds than yours?

This is an incredibly timely and important topic. Diversity and representation are key, not only to writing well-rounded and realistic worlds but to also allowing all types of readers to find themselves in books and for our society to be more empathetic on the whole.

It's definitely not something to do just because it's a "hot" topic or it seems like a way of getting a lot of attention or pats on the back. Representation isn't a gimmick or a shortcut. And it's not something to be done without a great deal of thought, research, and respect.

If you're writing about characters who are really different from you, then you'll want to be especially mindful. You should definitely do a lot of research when writing characters from different ethnic backgrounds or with different abilities or sexual orientations. It's important that your characters represent how people are—not just the (sometimes stereotypical) way that people have been portrayed in the past.

Read books by authors who come from the background you're trying to write, and be open to criticism and advice. In some cases, you may want to have your book read and critiqued by a friend who comes from that background or a "sensitivity reader" who offers these kinds of critiques professionally. Whether you use a friend or a pro, be sure to be respectful of people's time and know that if you're asking someone to perform a professional service, you should be prepared to pay for their work.

Finally, remember that no two people are the same, and no one person is representative of an entire group. There is no way that this group talks or that group thinks or acts or dresses. Characters should always be people, and people are always unique.

DEAR SOMAN CHAINANI,
How do you write a character who's not like you?

You really have to know a character in your bones to make them live on the page, so if I'm going to write a character who's not like me, I have to really have someone in my life or someone in the culture I'm thinking of as I write them. Otherwise, it'll come off too much as a stock character or a series of gimmicks. But the more I write, the more I realize that every character in the world is somewhat like me. As an author, I'm responsible for empathizing and understanding the entire range of human emotion, motivation, and behavior.

DEAR DAVID LEVITHAN,
How do you write a character who's not like you?

As a gay writer and a gay reader, I love to read stories about gay characters. Some of my favorites are by authors who are writing from their own gay experiences and other favorites are by authors who are not gay themselves but have a deep empathy for and connection to what a gay teen might be going through. When writing outside your own identity, I think it's important to ask yourself many questions. I'm going to use a non-gay author writing a gay main character as my example here, though I believe these questions hold no matter what the identity is.

1. *Why is this character gay?* In other words, why do you want to write from this point of view? If the answer is "Well, they could be straight or gay, so I decided to make them gay"—that's not a good answer. It can't be arbitrary. Or done because you think it will draw more readers. It has to be that being gay is important to the character's story, and to the story as a whole.

2. *What is your connection to the character?* Pinpoint the parts of yourself that you're putting into the character and/or the parts of other people you know that you're putting into the character. What is making them feel real to you? What are the parts of this character's life that this connection will not allow you to see? If there are gaps in your knowledge, you'll have to do the research to fill them in. Read other books to fill in the gaps. Talk to people with firsthand experience to fill in the gaps. Try to know as much as you can about the

intersectionality of the identities you're writing about, getting as specific to your character as you can get in your research.

3. *Are you defining this character solely by their gay identity?* If the answer here is yes, then alarms should be going off. The moment you define any character by a sole aspect of their identity, then you are not creating a well-rounded character . . . you're creating a stereotype. Nothing infuriates me more than reading a gay character whose sole purpose in the story is to be gay. That robs them of their humanity— which is the opposite of what fiction should do to a character. So make sure when you're writing that you know more about the character than the fact that they're gay . . . and then make sure that the multifaceted portrait ends up on the page.

4. *Who can tell you if you're getting it wrong?* If you're not gay and your book with a gay main character goes out into the world without a single gay person reading it first, that's a problem. Because you don't know what you might not know . . . and the only way to correct this is to get other opinions. You still have final say over your work, but a book is always stronger after feedback from other readers, especially if you are writing outside your own experience and/or identity. When I wrote my novel *Two Boys Kissing* and had it narrated by a chorus of gay men a generation older than me, my first reader was my uncle, who was of that generation and had lived with AIDS for over three decades. I would not have published the book if he hadn't said I got it right, because I needed a reader who was able from his own experience to tell me if I'd gotten it wrong.

What advice do you have for writing a character of a different gender than yours? I'm worried that when writing male characters in my own stories, the only thing that sets them apart from my female characters is their appearance, name, and pronouns. How do you make them feel more tangible?

I don't know that this is a gender-specific question. Because when you think about it, we're always writing characters who are different from us. (Or we should be!)

I've never been a student at spy school. I've never robbed the greatest museum in the world or broken into the Iranian embassy. I've never been kidnapped in Alaska.

Writing is the ultimate exercise in empathy, so the best advice I have is to try to put yourself in all of your characters' shoes as much as possible. What are they thinking, feeling, wanting? Also, look around. Pay attention to how some of the guys in your class talk. Sit. Move. Make note of some of the mannerisms or quirks that you might see, then go ahead and incorporate those into your writing.

But most of all, remember that not all guys move the same, think the same, crave the same things, or have the same fears. You don't have to write guys well. You just have to write *That Guy* well. And you can do it.

Which do you come up with first: characters or plots?

You might as well ask me which came first, the chicken or the egg!

Some authors—and some books—will clearly start with a character (a girl who goes to a boarding school for spies!). Some will obviously start with a plot (what if you were kidnapped in Alaska?). Some will even start with a world (what would it be like to live on a street where every house is, technically, a different country?).

But no matter which question lands in your brain first, the other aspects of that story shouldn't be far behind.

If you give a plot a different character, you get a different plot.

If you give a character a different world, you get a different character.

For me, worlds, plots, and characters are so intertwined with each other that it's almost impossible to separate them from each other.

I mean, what would Harry Potter have been like if Neville Longbottom had been the chosen one—or if Harry had been raised by a magical family instead of by Muggles? Can you imagine *The Hunger Games* if Katniss's father hadn't died? Would *Lord of the Rings* have looked the same if Aragorn had been tasked with taking the ring to Mordor?

These stories may very well have had the same villains, and these very different characters might have had the same goals, but with different characters at the center of the stories, those stories are bound to have played out quite differently.

All I know for sure is that none of these things exist in a vacuum, and as you write, you're going to be almost braiding those three things together to make your story as strong as possible.

DEAR ZORAIDA CÓRDOVA,
What comes first for you: character, plot, or something else?

My characters have always made themselves known first. They sort of just show up, sometimes unannounced, sometimes a little late, but they always seem to be very loud. Loud enough that they demand attention and say, "This is my story, please write it."

Characters are hard. Sure, people talk about plot twists and they get obsessed with world building, but at the end of the day, none of that matters if your reader doesn't have characters to root for and worry about and love.

There's a reason fans talk about "the feels." People read to feel, and characters are how you make them do it. So give your characters quirks and pet peeves and friends who support them—rivals who test them. Give your characters ups and downs, highs and lows, and make sure they're different at the end than they were at the beginning.

And finally, don't worry if your characters don't feel real to you when you're starting. The more time you spend with them, the better you'll be able to write them. Even if they start out as pencil sketches or archetypes, know that you have as many drafts as you need to make them the kinds of characters that will give your readers all the feels.

CHAPTER 6
DEVELOPING YOUR PLOT

How do you plan a book? Do you plot the entire story before you begin writing, or do you simply have a basic idea and let the story develop as you write?

People frequently ask me if I outline and the answer is no, not really. I know authors who write massive, detailed outlines. They know before they ever write a word how chapter 20 will open and what characters will be in the scene that ends chapter 32.

That is *their* process. That might even be *your* process. And honestly, you won't know until you try.

But I've learned that that isn't *my* process.

I'm just not capable of outlining in that way. To me, everything sounds good in theory, and I won't know if an idea is a dud or a winner until I actually put it on paper.

So I don't really do outlines.

What I *do* do is **STORYBOARD**.

You know that big list of scenes that you wrote down in the introduction? Well, imagine if you wrote every single one of them on a notecard or a Post-it note and then hung them on your wall or laid them out on your bed. If you did that, you'd have the storyboard for that book.

This is an old screenwriting technique (more about that in a moment), and I've used it for every single book that I've ever written. I love it because you can move those cards around, take some out, put some in—really play with all your options while visually "seeing" the entire story.

It's like turning your plot into a giant jigsaw puzzle, and you can experiment with all the different ways that the pieces might fit together.

This is especially helpful for me, because when I start a book, I usually know a few really big things, like my book is a road trip and I know I'm going to drive from New York to Los Angeles. I know along the way I'd like to see the St. Louis Arch and go to the Grand Canyon and drive down the Strip in Las Vegas.

So I know where I'm starting. And I know where I'm going. And I know a few stops that I'd like to make along the way. But I don't know where I might find a diner that serves awesome pie. I don't know where I might get a flat tire and have to go part of the way on bicycle. I don't know all the little things that might happen—both the good and the bad. The storyboard allows me the freedom to mark out the big things but also leave room for surprises.

Another advantage of storyboarding is that it really helps me see what I do—and do not—know. Specifically, it helps me figure out not just what's going to happen but *how* it's going to happen. You see, a lot of times when I start a book, I'll know most of the story, but I won't know the scenes, and—let me tell you—that is a huge distinction.

For example, I knew my book *I'd Tell You I Love You, But Then I'd Have to Kill You* was going to be about a spy in training who meets a "normal" boy—that she'd fall for the boy, and that the pressure of living a double life would put a lot of strain on her grades and her relationships until, finally, she would have to make a choice about whether she really wanted to follow in her parents' footsteps or lead a normal life.

That's the whole *story*, but it took a lot of time and bad drafts to find the *scenes* in which all of those things would become evident.

Where would Cammie be? Who would be with her? What would she want? How would it go wrong?

I have so many Post-it notes on my whiteboards with *heroine realizes it's been a lie* . . . which is great. That's conflict. But *how* does she realize that? Does she overhear people talking? Does she hack into a computer? Is she tipped off by a person in a hooded cloak?

The hardest part of writing, for me, isn't figuring out what's going to happen—it's figuring out *how* it's going to happen because, for me, getting the scenes right is the same thing as getting the book right.

Storyboarding helps me figure out some of it before I ever write a word, but honestly, a lot of it I just have to figure out as I go—take a look around when I get there and try to figure out the best way.

Maybe you're the kind of writer who is going to figure out all of those things before you write a word. Maybe you're the kind of writer who is going to figure it out as you go along. You know what? It doesn't really matter which type you are, just so long as you do it.

Every time I start a book, I tell myself that this is going to be the time when I figure out all the perfect scenes before I start—that this is going to be the time I make it all the way through a first draft without making any big mistakes.

But here's the thing I've come to realize: *The mistakes matter.* The pitfalls sometimes show me the way.

When asked about his thousand failed attempts at creating a light

97

bulb, Thomas Edison famously said that he didn't fail a thousand times. He just found a thousand ways *not* to build a light bulb.

Maybe your first draft . . . or second draft . . . or tenth draft might just be ten ways *not* to write your book.

Even by taking steps in the wrong direction, you learn which way the right direction may be.

How do you know what should happen in your novel? I have a good idea for a story, but I don't even know where to start, and when I think about coming up with a whole novel from scratch, I get overwhelmed and give up.

When I was in high school, I decided I wanted to become a screenwriter. I'm not sure why—probably because I'd always been a reluctant reader, but I loved stories—which meant I loved movies. And the idea of writing movies for a living seemed way too good to be true.

So my mom, being awesome and supportive, bought me my very first writing craft book, *Screenplay* by Syd Field. I don't think it's an exaggeration to say that that book changed my life.

That's where I first learned about storyboards (see above).

That's where I first learned about acts and plot points and that all stories have beginnings, middles, and ends.

When I read about story structure for the first time, it was like being shown a magic formula that could turn all the stories in my head into real live books and movies. That's when stories started making sense to me—when I could actually look under the hood and see all the moving parts and understand exactly how they were working. And why. And it's a lesson I use pretty much every single day.

Because here's the thing: No story is ever really written from scratch. There is, to some extent, a formula that's as old as time, and even though people toss around the word *formulaic* like it's a bad thing, it doesn't have to be. In fact, it could be your best friend.

Because knowing the secret of story structure—knowing the formula—means you never truly have to start from scratch ever again.

So let's start with the basics.

Every story is composed of three parts: Beginning. Middle. End.

I know, I know. That's not exactly mind-blowing stuff, but it's important to keep in mind. Because those are the building blocks upon which all stories are built.

For most modern, commercial stories (think books and movies), the beginning is about one-quarter of the story. The middle is about half. And the end is the final quarter.

BEGINNING　　　　　　　　**MIDDLE**　　　　　　　　**END**

Obviously, there's wiggle room and none of this is set in stone, but that's a starting point you might want to consider. Your three parts may go something like this:

Beginning: Get your characters up a tree.

Middle: Throw rocks at them.

End: Get them out of the tree.

You'll often hear the parts of a story referred to as **ACTS**.

When most people think of acts, they probably think of plays, but in truth, almost all books and movies are comprised of acts, too. An act is simply a segment of the action where the character (and story) is moving in a particular direction.

Then something happens to change that direction.

That's called a **PLOT POINT**.

Maybe that means telling the hero he's been chosen to save a magical world and sending him off on a quest. Maybe it means turning Fluffy the Hamster into a flying, fire-breathing killing machine that your heroine has to track down and turn back into the class pet.

Your first major plot point is the point where the story really starts going—where we know that, from this point on, your character's life is never going to be the same again. The beginning is officially over, and the middle has begun.

So how many acts should a book have? Well, it depends. And forgive me, but this is where it gets a little confusing because, for a lot of people, Beginning, Middle, and End translate into act 1, act 2, and act 3.

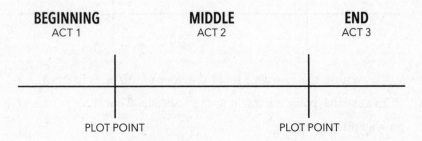

But I think that's a little misleading because that can leave people with the impression that you need only two plot points—two major turns in the story—and that's not true at all.

Stuff is going to have to go right—and wrong—throughout the story. You're going to have to give your characters lots of ups and downs.

This is where storyboarding really helps me.

I never know how many acts (or segments . . . or set pieces . . . or whatever term you want to use) my books will have when I start out, but it generally ends up being eight or so.

When I storyboard, I consider every line of Post-its to be an act.

The very first Post-it on the top line will usually be where we meet the main character or we get introduced to the world—maybe both! Maybe you have a few scenes like that. Then something happens. I call this the "inciting incident," but it's really just a small plot point and it usually comes within the first chapter or two.

For example, my book *Not If I Save You First* starts with our hero and heroine, Logan and Maddie, living in Washington, DC, where Logan is the president's son and Maddie is the daughter of a Secret Service agent. The first line of the storyboard is about Logan and Maddie in DC, living their regular lives. But then Logan's mother is attacked and Maddie's father is injured and neither of them will ever be the same again. (Inciting incident!)

And we go to the next line.

Line two shows us Maddie and Logan six years later. Maddie's living in a cabin in Alaska and Logan isn't the sweet boy he used to be. When he gets in trouble and is sent to Alaska to live with Maddie and her father, we really see how much they've each changed, but they're going to have to find a way to live with each other—or so we think, right up until a gunman appears out of nowhere, knocking Maddie down a cliff and dragging Logan off to some unknown fate.

When Maddie wakes up, she knows she has two choices: She can turn back and get help, or she can follow them. Maddie follows them. (Plot point! Break into act 2!) And the book truly begins.

In terms of the three-act structure, it would look kind of like this:

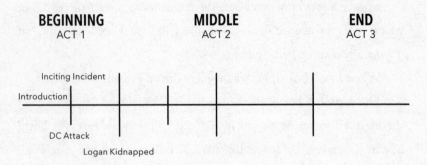

The next line on my storyboard is going to be Maddie trying to track Logan and the kidnapper down, trying to get ahead of them, out-smart them, save Logan. But it's not that easy, is it? Nope. Eventually, Maddie is going to hit a roadblock or make a mistake. Or two. Or seven. And then that is another plot point. And we go down to the next line on my storyboard.

And so on.

And so on.

Until we reach the **MIDPOINT**.

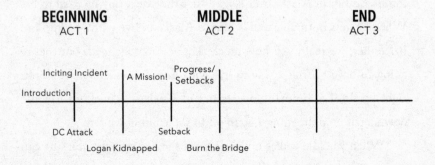

There's a story consultant named Michael Hauge who talks a lot about story structure, and I love his way of looking at the midpoint of a story. Think about it like this: Imagine you're on a plane flying from Hawaii to Los Angeles, and you're out over the ocean when the plane begins to have mechanical problems. If you're closer to Hawaii, you'll probably turn back. But if you've crossed the midpoint of the trip—if you're closer to LA than Hawaii—then you have no choice but to keep going forward.

It's not just the midpoint, you see. It's also *the point of no return*, and for your story, that really, really matters.

Because maybe up until that point, all your character has wanted is to go home, turn back, return to the way life was. But eventually your characters have to cross that point of no return and know that the only way out is through.

I love this construct so much that at the midpoint of *Not If I Save You First* they literally burn a bridge.

From this point forward, stakes will be higher. Things will feel more personal. The bad guys are going to be closing in, and the tension will start to boil. There will be more ups and downs after the midpoint, oftentimes with your characters putting some kind of plan in action. (Which, by the way, is my next row of Post-its or line on the chart.)

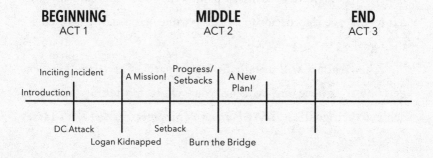

And then something terrible happens. Because let's face it, something terrible always needs to be happening. But *this* something needs to be *especially* terrible.

Toward the end of act 2 (or the middle section), your characters need to experience a setback so major that people often refer to it as the **ALL IS LOST**. Or the **DARK NIGHT OF THE SOUL**. But it doesn't matter what you call it, the key is that your characters have been brought to their lowest point and it doesn't seem like there's a way in the world they can crawl their way out of it.

(Spoiler alert: The last act is them crawling their way out of it.)

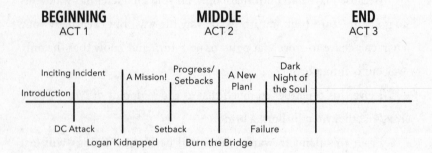

The break into the last act may be your characters rallying the troops for one last fight. Or it might be your heroine finally asking her former best friend for help. Whatever the case, your characters have been brought to their lowest point—they no longer have anything left to lose—so they decide to risk everything on one last try to achieve their goal.

The final act will usually have two parts. The first—and longest/most significant—will be your character taking action to achieve their goal. In *Harry Potter and the Sorcerer's Stone*, it's Harry battling all alone, trying to keep the stone away from Voldemort/ Quirrell.

This is the climax of your story—the big finish. And in a way, your whole book has been building toward this moment.

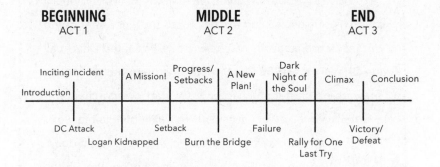

After the big finish, you'll usually want to have a quieter scene or two to show the reader what your characters' "after" picture looks like. Exactly how much have the people and the world changed via this story? This could take place in an epilogue or not, but whatever the case, make sure you give your reader that sense of exactly how everything turned out.

Maybe your story will fit this model exactly. Or maybe not at all. By no means do all stories have to fit this formula, but that doesn't mean that *formula* is a dirty word. Stories in every genre imaginable have followed a structure much like this since the dawn of time.

The bad news is that you still have to decide exactly how your characters and your plot and your world will all come together to fill out this framework. But the good news is you don't actually have to start from scratch.

DEAR JENNIFER LYNN BARNES,
Are there any plotting rules that you live (and write) by?

When I first started writing, I sometimes tended to forget about plot. I wanted to frolic in character and world, and I'd get so distracted by how much fun that was that I occasionally found myself just waiting for the plot to show up. After doing this for far too many first drafts in a row, I adopted what I call the **CHAPTER THREE RULE**. In my first draft, the plot has to show up no later than chapter 3. If I start writing chapter 4 and realize that I don't have anything resembling a plot yet, I backtrack and rewrite the first three chapters so that it does.

Another rule that I live by when I'm coming up with the plots for my book is to **MAKE IT PERSONAL**. I write mysteries, thrillers, and paranormal, so my plots often revolve around finding a killer, solving a mystery, or preventing the apocalypse (you know, normal teen stuff). But regardless of what genre I'm writing, I want the overall plot to be really personal to my character(s). Having to catch a serial killer works well as a plot, but having to catch the serial killer who killed your mother? That's better.

My final plotting tip is to think of a book as a series of **BIG TWISTS** and **REVEALS**. You don't need a ton of them. Over the course of an entire book, I aim to shake things up eight times. For each of my **BIG MOMENTS**, my character realizes something or something big happens that completely changes the direction of the plot. Everything that follows one of these big moments is *because* of this moment, as my characters grapple with the consequences, right up until the next big twist or moment happens. When I start writing, I usually know three to five of the big moments, and the others I figure out along the way. It's intimidating to plot a whole book. But thinking of a few big twists? That's fun!

How integral is setting to plot?

VERY.

Set a story in a different time or place (or world) and you will likely get a very different story. Can you imagine Harry Potter without Hogwarts, or Black Panther without Wakanda? Can you even begin to picture Katniss Everdeen growing up anywhere other than District Twelve?

Most fantasy/sci-fi/dystopian novels are firmly rooted in their otherworldly settings. But what about contemporary fiction?

I'd argue the same is true there as well. In fact, *Not If I Save You First* came about because I asked the question "What would happen if two kids were kidnapped in the Alaskan wilderness and a storm was moving in?" If you took away the setting, that book literally wouldn't exist.

There might not be much difference between a suburban high school in Indianapolis and a suburban high school in Minneapolis— but in those instances it's the suburban-high-school part that matters. If you take that story and move it to a tiny town in rural Oklahoma where there are ten people in your entire grade, then that story is going to change significantly, right? Likewise if you moved it to an army base or an international school in Rome or a gigantic high school in the middle of New York City.

So the setting of your novel is going to have a tremendous impact on your story, particularly as it ties to world building. But I've learned settings can also make a huge difference to individual *scenes*.

Several years ago, I was watching the director's commentary of the movie *Mr. & Mrs. Smith*. (Hint: You can sometimes learn incredibly cool things by watching directors' commentaries!) Near the end of the movie, there's a scene where the hero and heroine are arguing about whether to fight or run—but they're doing it while lying in a storm drain. You can see and hear the bad guys overhead—just a few feet away—all while Mr. and Mrs. Smith whisper and bicker and try to decide what to do.

It's a great scene.

In the commentary, the director talks about how the scene didn't work for a really long time. The dialogue was good. The scene was necessary. But there's something inherently boring about watching two people stand in a room, talking. So he changed the location of that scene to a storm drain with the bad guys lurking just inches away. He didn't change a single word of dialogue. And yet it was a totally different (and vastly improved) scene.

So pay careful attention to where your stories—and your scenes—are set. Settings can provide humor or suspense or conflict. They can practically be another character, driving your plot forward or providing obstacles that stand in your characters' way.

In a lot of ways, *Not If I Save You First* was the easiest book I've ever written, and I think the setting was a huge reason why. My characters faced constant conflict, from the man who kidnapped them, from each other, from snow and ice, steep mountains and hungry bears. There was absolutely no shortage of things that could go wrong at any minute, and as a result, I never once came close to running out of conflict.

So if you find yourself running out of steam, look at the setting of your story (or of some individual scenes). Maybe the part where the heroine's boyfriend breaks up with her would be more dramatic if it happened at halftime of a basketball game—and they were on the court. Maybe the part where your hero finds out he has superpowers would be better if he was actually taking the ACT when his powers kicked in.

It's up to you to use your characters' environment to make the story as interesting as possible.

DEAR GORDON KORMAN,
What are your favorite plotting tips and tricks?

I'm a sucker for unintended consequences. I love it when characters start something in motion with the best of intentions and everything snowballs out of control.

DEAR KIERSTEN WHITE,
Are you a plotter or a pantser? What's your process like? (In other words, how do you write so freaking fast?)

I subscribe to the simmer-and-spurt method: I simmer an idea for months (sometimes years!), and then when it's ready, it sort of spurts out of me in a mad rush. I do some plotting, but my favorite writing experiences are the ones where I can discover the story as I'm writing it.

I'm an aspiring author, and one of my weaknesses is stakes. When I had my first query letter critiqued, everyone asked, "What's at stake? Your stakes aren't high enough." So, how do you know you made the stakes high enough for your characters?

First, congratulations! It sounds like you've already finished some projects, which is a really big deal, and you should be proud of that if nothing else.

Next, know that this is a very common—and incredibly important—question.

In many ways, a novel is only as good as its stakes.

A PERSON WANTS A THING FOR A REASON, AND SOMETHING (OR SOMEONE) STANDS IN THEIR WAY. Boom. That's it! That's pretty much every book ever written in a nutshell.

What's the best writing advice you ever got?	
Holly Black	Characters need to want things. And the force of their wanting is what propels a story.

When we talk about "stakes," we're talking about the *reason*. Put simply, the stakes are what will happen if the main character fails.

A book about a girl who starts her own business because she wants to . . . have a business . . . is less compelling than a book about a girl who starts her own business because her mom just got fired and the bank is going to foreclose on their house if they can't come up with some cash.

A story about a boy who can't find his favorite hat is less interesting than a story about a boy who can't find the hat that gives him super-powers and can start a war if it falls into the wrong hands.

So, in your story, what will happen if the main character fails to achieve their goals?

Is it that she'll be unhappy? Is it that his day will be ruined? Is it something that the character probably won't care about after a good night's sleep? Or is it something that is going to affect their life for years to come—maybe forever?

The really obvious examples of high stakes come from big epic fantasy stories like *Lord of the Rings* or Percy Jackson: Fail and the world as you know it ends.

But the truth is, having stakes simply means that if you fail, the world *as you know it* will end.

What if the love letters you wrote with no intention of sending were actually mailed to the boys you used to crush on? (Like in Jenny Han's *To All the Boys I've Loved Before*?) What if your covert relationship with a boy from town might get you kicked out of spy school? (Like in my novel *I'd Tell You I Love You, But Then I'd Have to Kill You*?)

Stakes don't always have to be life or death. What matters is that they feel that way to your character (and to your reader).

Just remember to always make sure something big is riding on your characters achieving their goals. And when possible, make sure that *something* is as personal as possible. After all "an FBI agent has twenty-four hours to stop a serial killer from striking again" is a high-stakes story. But "an FBI agent has twenty-four hours to stop the serial killer *who murdered her son* from killing again" takes the stakes to a whole new level.

What are your favorite plotting tips/tricks?

The single best trick I have ever discovered is a really simple one. At the end of every writing session, I go to the next blank page and leave instructions for myself. Sometimes it's only a line or two, sometimes a paragraph or two, but always very bare-bones, "here is what needs to happen in this next section." That way, the next time I sit down to write, I'm not faced with an intimidating blank page. I've already given myself a to-do list, and I can dive right in! It's one of the best ways to combine plotting and pantsing. Live in the moment, but have your eye on the next section or two so you know where you're going.

How do you avoid cliché plotlines and tropes?

You can't. Not always. And sometimes you might not want to.

A cliché is a saying or phrase or action that is so commonly used that it's not original anymore (and people kind of make fun of it).

There are some clichés that every new author is probably going to use. For example, most new authors will have their characters describe themselves while looking in a mirror at least once. Most people will use the phrase *deer in the headlights* or *butterflies in my stomach* at some point in their early work.

You can't avoid all clichés—especially when you're just starting out! So if you make them, edit them out and keep writing and try to do better next time.

Tropes, however, are a much more complex subject.

A trope is a plotline or story element that is so common it actually becomes a staple of certain genres. (The hero who is a "chosen one." The heroine on a quest. Enemies who are stuck together for some reason, then fall in love.)

Tropes and clichés became tropes and clichés because they're so common. Which means they can't always be avoided. And do you want to know a secret? Sometimes they shouldn't be.

In the right hands, tropes can be powerful tools.

Avid readers often know what they love, and certain tropes can become "auto buys" for them. For example, I'll read anything where the heroine has amnesia, and I'll watch any movie where there's a prince in disguise.

Neither of those concepts is super original. (Tropes never are.) But the tropes themselves offer a kind of contract with a reader that they can expect certain things to happen. They're buying a particular reading experience.

Think about it like having a story-in-a-box kit that contains all the elements that are common for whatever trope you're writing.

If you're writing a story about a secret prince, then you're going to have a scene where he and the heroine meet. You'll probably have a scene or two where he tries to hide he's a prince. I'm betting there will be a scene where he doesn't know how to do something that servants usually take care of (like work a coffeepot). You can bet there'll be a scene where she learns the truth.

Those are all staples of that genre. Don't worry that every secret prince story has them. That's okay. Readers expect them. Readers *want* them. What matters is how you approach the scenes and the rest of the story.

Perhaps the most important thing when using tropes is learning to walk the tightrope between delivering readers the story they signed up for and giving readers a fresh, new take on a story they've read a million times.

For example, maybe instead of a down-on-her-luck girl getting to the end of the movie and marrying the prince, we learn instead that she's a long-lost princess? That would certainly be a twist on a trope that might please a lot of people.

But what if you got to the end and instead of the prince choosing the down-on-her-luck waitress, he goes ahead and marries the nasty duchess that his mother likes? Well, that's a terrible twist on the genre!

Why? Because it doesn't deliver on the contract you had with your reader. It doesn't deliver the things that fans of that trope love.

The more you read, the more you'll be able to identify the good from the bad, and the more you'll know which ones to use and when. Just know that tropes are not intrinsically bad. They're just common. And as writers, we have to accept that there are no wholly original stories. Everything has been done before (and will be done again). It's up to us to write our own versions of it and make it as strong as we possibly can.

As a reader, what are your "auto-buy" tropes?	
Marie Lu	Characters who are extremely good at what they do. In that same vein, a character with notoriety.
Daniel José Older	Monsters and complex political wrangling.
Elizabeth Eulberg	Anything music-related, boy and girl best friends.

Julie Murphy	Childhood friends turned lovers, enemies to lovers, antihero/villain turned hero, exiled royals/a royal who doesn't know they're royal, boarding school . . . I could go on forever!
Marissa Meyer	Love/hate romances and secret identities.
Sarah Rees Brennan	Fake dating, magic bonding, revenge spree, wicked lady and innocent gentleman, anything with dragons.
Holly Black	Enemies to lovers, con artists, the badass who comes out of retirement, monster girls, fancy boys.
Zoraida Córdova	Revenge, enemies to lovers, road trips or big trips, chosen ones.
Gordon Korman	Underdog comes out on top.
Rachel Caine	Historical murder mysteries! Especially with a twist, gender swap, etc.
Dhonielle Clayton	Magical games, hate-to-love romance, love triangles.

How do you avoid plot holes when writing?

I understand this worry and question, but the truth of the matter is you're not going to avoid every potential plot hole. Especially while writing a first draft. My advice would be to set this worry aside in the beginning. Do your best to answer all the questions your book poses and cover all your bases, but know that it probably won't all get in there the first time through. Which is totally okay.

That's what rewriting is for.

When you're able to stand at the end of the book and look back over the whole thing—that's when you'll see the places where you need to seed in the little hints or tie up loose ends.

I do this with every book, but it was especially important when writing my Heist Society series. In the second book, *Uncommon Criminals*, I just couldn't figure out how I was going to get my characters out of the place they were going to rob (with the priceless emerald, of course). I went through several drafts before I realized that if I just made two of the characters identical twins I could pull off one of my favorite plot twists of all time—and save the emerald, too.

That was it—just one little change that changed everything. I like to call these "linchpin" pieces, and they're essential to making most of my stories turn. And they almost never turn up until draft two or three!

The good news is, you have as many drafts as you need to get this right. No one is expecting it to be perfect right off the bat, so my advice is to stop expecting it of yourself.

What's the best writing advice you ever got?	
Marie Lu	Don't be afraid to write something bad. It's more important to finish that first draft, because you can't make a blank page better.

If you write a character into a corner, how do you write the character out of it?

Well, I suppose that depends on the corner, so I'm afraid I can't offer any specifics, but I can say that this is the goal.

This is always the goal!

With every story, the reader should reach a point where they can't possibly see how the character is going to make it out of that corner. And then it's up to you to get them out of it. I'm sorry to break it to you, but that's the job.

Sometimes you'll figure it out early on—before you even start writing. Sometimes you'll write the entire first draft and still not know what the fix is. Sometimes you'll still be working on the perfect solution on draft ten.

Just know that it's never easy—not for anyone. But do you know what's worse than not knowing how to get your character out of their problem? Not giving your characters any problems to begin with.

So don't shy away from conflict and problems and corners. In the long run, corners are your friend.

How do you write really good plot twists? Do you need to plan ahead? How do you keep it from being too obvious while also not being too ridiculous?

The best plot twists that I have ever written came to me after I'd already started the book—sometimes right at the very moment that the twist itself happened, and I was just as surprised as the readers. Sometimes I knew *some* twisty thing was going to happen, but I didn't have it figured out just yet.

Sometimes I had a really cool, really awesome plot twist all planned out in my mind and then, when it came time to put it on paper, it just didn't work at all.

So if you have a plot twist in mind when you start out, great! Start laying the groundwork for it and planting the seeds (because it's just cheating to have the murderer be someone the reader never met and could never have suspected!).

But keep in mind that your twist might change. Your plot may evolve. And something even better might occur to you at some point along the way.

Also, remember that not every book needs a plot twist. They're great when they happen, but if they don't happen, just focus on making the plot points that you do have as interesting and compelling as possible.

What do you do when your plot just sort of stalls?

If your plot stalls . . . if your story lags . . . if your characters have a goal and yet they don't have anything to *do*, then it's possible that what your story needs is a MacGuffin.

But what is a MacGuffin? Well, in the immortal words of the great director Alfred Hitchcock, a MacGuffin is nothing. And yet, it's also *everything*.

Simply put, MacGuffin is the name of the item that everyone wants and the plot hinges on. The One Ring. The Sorcerer's Stone. The Holy Grail. These are just some of the famous MacGuffins that have been driving stories since the dawn of time.

Sometimes the MacGuffin will be a lost love letter or a microchip with the name of the traitorous spy. Sometimes it will be an item of vast magical power, and sometimes it will be something incredibly sentimental and important only to your characters.

But the only thing that matters is that your MacGuffin has to be the thing that your characters want. And need. And will do almost anything to get/keep/recover/protect. You get the idea.

In my Heist Society series, the MacGuffins were the things that the crew needed to steal. In *Not If I Save You First*, the MacGuffin is actually Logan, the president's son who has been kidnapped by the villain and has to be saved by the heroine.

MacGuffins drive conflict by putting the good guys and the bad guys at odds, battling to control one physical item of great importance. They are the reason we set out on a quest or break into the CIA or befriend the meanest girl in school just so we can get something out of her locker.

Now, it's important to note that not every story can—or should—have a MacGuffin. But if you find your plot is stalled and your characters don't have much to do, try coming up with a literal, physical item that both sides need.

Remember, conflict is gas in the tank. And a good MacGuffin can go a long way toward getting you to The End.

I probably spend more time on plot than any other part of the process because, for me, plot is where characters and world come together. Whether you write by the seat of your pants or plot the whole thing out in advance, just don't forget that conflict is what keeps your story moving forward. And stakes are the reason it all matters.

So think about all the reasons your characters have to succeed. Then think about all the ways they can fail. Whether you're a pantser or a plotter, if you put those two things together, you've got the makings of a plot!

Are you a plotter or a pantser?	
Shannon Hale	Depends on the book! I've discovered that I'm not rigid in my work habits. I don't need to work in a particular place or time of day or style or genre or whatever. I've started with a sentence and followed it to find a whole book; I've created 20K-word chapter-by-chapter outlines and written from that; and I've done everything in between. I firmly believe there's no right or wrong way. For me, it's figuring out what feels right at this particular moment for this particular story.
Marie Lu	Pantser.
Melissa de la Cruz	Plotter.

Daniel José Older	Pantser for LIFE.
Elizabeth Eulberg	Plotter.
Julie Murphy	A little bit of both!
Stephanie Perkins	Plotter.
Alex London	A hybrid. I start by the seat of my pants, panic at about 15,000 words, and start making outlines then, which I often stray from again and again and again.
Sarah Rees Brennan	Plotter! Except for a little pants embroidery around the plot.
Jesse Andrews	Both somehow. More of a pantser, I guess.
Alan Gratz	Plotter!
Soman Chainani	Pantser.
Holly Black	I want to be a plotter, but I do a lot of "discovery writing" despite my best intentions.
Kiersten White	Both.
Maggie Stiefvater	I pants plottily or plot pantsily. I can't tell anymore.
Zoraida Córdova	Plotter.
Gordon Korman	Plotter.
Rachel Caine	Hybrid! I make a relatively small outline that I don't necessarily follow to the letter.
Dhonielle Clayton	I am neither one of those. I am a headlights writer. I'm a plotter and a pantser but can see only a few feet in front of me.
Eliot Schrefer	Plotter.
Z Brewer	I was a pantser for years but learned how to be a plotter because it makes less work in the end and frees me up to just ride the wave.

CHAPTER 7
FINDING YOUR PROCESS

What's the best process to use when writing a book?

It's incredibly important that I say this up front and often: *Every writer has a different process.* In fact, every *book* has a different process! There's no one way to do this, so if someone ever tells you "this is the best way to write a book," turn around and run because that person is mistaken.

I know writers who write meticulous outlines that are almost as long as their books.

And I know writers who sit down and go and don't look back.

I know writers who rewrite and tweak and perfect every paragraph before they move on to the next one.

And I know writers who don't even glance back until they've got a whole draft down.

I know writers who write longhand or type single-spaced or do an entire draft with "Track Changes" on, just to trick themselves into thinking they're doing a rewrite and not a first draft.

Writers are always looking for a shortcut, a scheme, a plan, a strategy, so that this time it will be easy. But it's never easy. And we know that. Still, we keep playing mind games with ourselves—anything that helps to get us to The End.

Pretty much every writer I know has tried a bunch of different things. Some of them work. Some of them don't. But we keep trying anyway because, as we say in this business, you never really learn to write a book; you just learn to write the book you're writing right now.

So there is no one way to do this. But in this section, I'll write about how some of my friends and I do this. Maybe that will help you figure out how *you* should do it, too.

DEAR MELISSA DE LA CRUZ,
What's your process? Are you a plotter or a pantser?

I am very much a plotter. But I also like to surprise myself, so I often dismiss the first thing that comes to mind for a twist, knowing that that's the first thing a reader will think as well. You want to surprise your readers, which is very hard to do. You really have to work at it, which means rewriting the ending many, many times until it works.

What is the process you use to write your books?

Well, as I said, there's no one way to do this! But in case anyone is interested, this is the way *I* do it. (Which, for the record, probably won't be the way you will—or should—do it.)

STEP 1. GET AN IDEA. Struggle with the idea for usually several months. Then settle on the idea and dig in.

STEP 2. STORYBOARD THE PLOT (see "Developing Your Plot") and try to figure out as much of the action as possible.

STEP 3. WRITE A SCREENPLAY. Yes. You read that correctly. I'm a huge outlier because the first drafts of my novels are pretty much always screenplays. I've only heard of one other author doing this, so it certainly isn't the norm but it's what works for me.

Why?

Well, you see, I started writing screenplays when I was in college and grad school, so my "dirty water books" are really screenplays. Are any of them any good? Nope. But when my agent suggested one of those screenplays might make a good novel, I started adapting it and realized it was some of the easiest writing I'd ever done. The whole story was laid out for me—with dialogue! I just had to fill in the writing part. So now I do that every time.

Why not just outline? Well, because I'm terrible at outlining. I know. I've tried it! You see, to me, everything sounds good in an outline. I genuinely won't know if something is awesome or weird or weirdly awesome until I get it on the page.

Screenplays are just action and dialogue—no pretty prose, no character descriptions or super-detailed fight scenes—so they're a quick way of getting the key plot points, settings, characters, etc., on the page. That makes them an efficient way of telling the weird from the weirdly awesome, in other words. So that's what I do first. And it can take me a month or so just to get most of the story hammered out.

STEP 4. WRITE A REALLY ROUGH FIRST DRAFT. And I do mean *really* rough. Usually, I'll leave my house every day and go to a local restaurant where they know me (and kind of feel sorry for me toward the end). I take my AlphaSmart (more on that in a bit) and write pretty much every day for long stretches of time, usually three to six hours at a time with very few breaks.

Because I'm working off those screenplay pages and not starting from scratch, I can have incredibly productive days. (On *Not If I Save You First*, I probably averaged well over 3,000 words per day, which is a lot by most standards.) At that rate, I can finish a 60,000-word book in twenty days. Which means, once I start writing, I can often have a first draft in a month or so.

THIS IS NOT AVERAGE.

In fact, when I read that, even I get really, really freaked out and intimidated. Please don't think you have to write this way. And please don't be too terribly impressed.

Why? Because that first draft probably won't make a lot of sense. That first draft will include subplots that will get cut later and characters that aren't fully fleshed out and, usually, a conclusion that doesn't even start to work.

But the first draft will *exist* and that is a first draft's only job (in my process).

STEP 5. SHOW MY FIRST DRAFT TO MY EDITOR to get notes on the plot and the general direction of the novel.

STEP 6. WRITE A SECOND DRAFT. Honestly, this is, for me, where the hard work begins. At this point, stuff is starting to get real. What I write at this point stands a really good chance of ending up in the finished book, and that's both awesome (no more blank page!) but also terrifying (what if people hate it?).

STEP 7. CRY. Seriously. At any point along here, it's totally okay to cry. A lot.

STEP 8. DO MORE DRAFTS. I'll work for several months getting the book where I like it before I send it to my editor again.

STEP 9. REPEAT STEPS 5–8 AS NECESSARY, until my editor and I both think it's pretty good.

STEP 10. DO A LINE EDIT. This is where my editor and I go through the book line by line. It's painstaking. It's tedious. And it's sooooooooo worth it because, in my opinion, this is where a book can go from good to great. This is the point where you look at a sentence that has ten words and ask yourself, "Can this be better said with six?" This is the point where you look at a really pretty sentence and say to yourself, "I said basically the same thing three pages ago, so should I cut this? I should probably cut this."

This is the point where you make sure every single word makes the book better. If it doesn't serve a purpose, cut it. Initially, I always find this hard, but by the end I'm drunk on power and cutting everything I can because I'm weird like that.

STEP 11. SEND THE BOOK TO MY PUBLISHER TO BE COPYEDITED AND TYPESET. This is when you work with a *different* editor than the one you've been working with all along. A "copy editor" is really a specialist who will go through the manuscript with a finetoothed comb and will answer things like "*should that be fine-toothed*?" "*Fine tooth*"? See? I don't know. But eventually I'll have a copy editor coming along behind me, helping me out.

STEP 13. DO PAGE PROOFS. Page proofs are the very last pass you will ever do of your novel. At this point, you won't be working in Microsoft Word anymore. This time you'll get a file where your book looks exactly like a real book. It will have fancy fonts and pretty interior art and all that fun stuff. It will be your job to do one last pass and make sure everything is perfect!

Because you will never, ever edit that book again. And if you and the proofreaders miss a typo . . . well . . . then you'd better get ready to live with it because there's no going back.

STEP 12. TAKE A NAP. The book is finished.

Again, in no way, shape, or form am I saying this is the best process. I can't even guarantee that when I start my next book, this will be *my* process. But this is how I've been doing it for the past few years, and if something in there appeals to you, try it. You won't know what your process is until you write!

STEP 13. START THINKING ABOUT YOUR NEXT NOVEL.

What's the best writing advice you ever got?	
Daniel José Older	After you finish something and submit it, take a break and then start something new.

Do you write bits, then put them all together, or do you start at the beginning and write through to the end?

This is another one of those things that is going to vary a lot, depending on who you talk to. I know writers who might write the last chapter before they write the first. Then they might move on to chapter 17 or 14, or 40. They just write the scenes as they come, and that process works for them. Which is totally valid.

You have one job, and that's to find the process that works for *you*.

But I'm the kind of writer who needs to start at the beginning and write until I hit The End. Always. I can't even revise out of order. Every single draft starts at page one and goes through to the end.

There are a lot of reasons why this works for me. First, because that's what feels natural. And a big part of this business is finding your groove and then sticking with it.

The other thing I like about writing in order is that no matter how much planning and plotting I might do, I'm always surprised when I start writing. Always. And that's a good thing! (After all, if the author is surprised by a plot twist, the reader probably will be, too!)

So I can't jump around if I don't know exactly where I'm going.

It's also important to remember that you're not just writing a plot. You're also writing characters. And characters have emotions and relationships and ups and downs, and those things are fluid, constantly changing—those things have to be consistent from one scene to the next, and writing in order is the best way I know to put myself in the frame of mind my characters were in in the last scene—to have just written it.

Maybe that's not the case for you. Maybe writing out of order is going to be your process. But I do want to offer one word of caution.

When I have the urge to write out of order, it's usually because there are scenes I'm just not very excited to write, so I want to skip them. Because they're boring. But boring scenes don't need to be skipped. Boring scenes need to be cut or fixed.

As I say elsewhere in this book, there's no room in this business for "filler," so if you've got scenes you're not very excited to write, think about why that is and ask yourself if that also means no one will be excited to read them.

But maybe you're skipping around because that's just the way your brain—and your process—works. And honestly, you won't know until you try. So keep trying!

Do you write chronologically?	
Jesse Andrews	Yes.
Marissa Meyer	Not usually.
Kiersten White	Always start-to-finish.
Maggie Stiefvater	I try to write as chronologically as possible, but the more complex the book, the less likely I am to guess right when the emotional beats are supposed to land.
Dhonielle Clayton	Yes!
Z Brewer	Nope. I'm a cheater. I bounce around to the fun parts, then go back and fill in the "boring" parts.

I was wondering, what do you write on? Is it anything special? By that I mean is there a special program that publishers prefer writers to download, or can they just be written on a stack of notebook paper or Microsoft Word?

The very first book I ever finished was one that I wrote longhand in spiral-bound **NOTEBOOKS** I bought at the dollar store. I think it took six of them. So there. Six bucks, plus tax. That's how much money I had invested in my first book.

Today, I might write longhand from time to time if I need to shake things up, but I've upgraded significantly in the past decade.

I do my outline or "zero draft" in **FINAL DRAFT**, a leading screenwriting software, because it allows me to write action and scene descriptors and dialogue and get a really rough framework for the book down quickly.

After that, I do all of my first drafts on a really old, really cheap, really durable word processor called an **ALPHASMART**. In fact, they don't make them anymore (you can occasionally buy used versions online). I'm so dependent on my AlphaSmart that I have two extra ones because I'm so worried that if mine broke I'd never write again! Why? Because it doesn't have Wi-Fi or email or games. It runs on regular batteries that can last, literally, for months. You can type for forever and then plug the AlphaSmart into a laptop and download everything into whatever word-processing software you like.

So that's something that I love and rely on, but it's in no way mandatory and it might not be for you at all.

What is mandatory is access to a computer of some kind and **MICROSOFT WORD**.

Once you start working with an editor, pretty much everything will be done in Word. That's what your editor will use, and you're going to be passing copies of your book back and forth for months. Word has a feature called Track Changes, which allows you to keep track of who made what edits and also leave comments to each other in the margins. It's absolutely essential for life as an author.

Not to mention that pretty much all other business documents are written in Word as well. So you're going to need that to work on marketing plans, cover copy, publicity interviews, etc.

In addition to Word, a lot of writers sing the praises of a software called **SCRIVENER**. It has a ton of features and can do some really neat things, and I use it occasionally myself. Specifically, Scrivener is *great* for reordering material, so if you want to move a scene from chapter 12 to chapter 17 and put chapter 20 where chapter 10 currently is, then Scrivener is super handy. If you think you might be writing your next book out of order, then Scrivener might very well be the perfect thing for you.

These are a few of the things that other authors and I have found helpful, but here's the thing: *There is no software or gadget or machine that will write your book for you.* Spending thousands of dollars on fancy laptops or finding the perfect pen won't get words on the page. The right software or laptop or notebook might make writing easier or more pleasant, but believe this: The actual writing will always be up to you.

Do you write on a computer or longhand (or other)?	
Shannon Hale	Always a computer. I started writing books the year my family got our first computer, and my brain is trained to respond to the clicking of a keyboard. Also it's frustrating for me to write longhand. Too slow! My thoughts are coming in fast!
Marie Lu	Computer.
Melissa de la Cruz	Computer.
Daniel José Older	Computer.
Elizabeth Eulberg	I brainstorm/outline by hand, write on computer.
Julie Murphy	Both!
Stephanie Perkins	Computer.
Kody Keplinger	Computer.
Marissa Meyer	Brainstorm longhand, write on the computer.
Alex London	Computer until I get stuck, then longhand to break out of a rut.
Sarah Rees Brennan	Usually a computer.
Jesse Andrews	Computer.

Alan Gratz	Computer.
Soman Chainani	Computer.
Holly Black	Computer (sometimes an AlphaSmart or the like for fast drafting).
Kiersten White	Computer.
Maggie Stiefvater	Computer. I'm not a monster.
Zoraida Córdova	Both.
Gordon Korman	Computer.
Rachel Caine	Computer all the way.
Dhonielle Clayton	Longhand.
Eliot Schrefer	Computer.
Z Brewer	Always on a computer, unless I'm scribbling notes on the back of a random envelope or Post-it.

DEAR DANIEL JOSÉ OLDER,
What's your writing process like?

I make sure I've eaten breakfast and have a cup of coffee in hand and some good music playing, and then I generally start with a brief entry into a writing log—it's basically like warming up before you really jump all the way in, gets my gears turning and allows me to settle into the flow of getting words on the page without worrying too much about what those words are. I try to hit a thousand words before breaking for lunch, but I'm not too hard on myself if I don't. Then I do some nonwriting things and go back for an afternoon session.

> **What do you love about that process? What do you hate?**
>
> I love the coming-up-with-ideas part and the seeing-them-play-out-on-the-page part, and I love when things surprise me as I'm going. I don't outline, so it's really fun to watch the story unravel in process. I don't love editing. It's just no fun at all, usually, but it's crucial and must be taken seriously.

People often say, "Don't be afraid of messing up the first draft—just write!" But when you are afraid, anxious, or hesitant, how do you push through and keep writing despite the fear in your gut?

"Paper is cheap."

"Microsoft Word files are free."

I put those things in quotes because . . . I actually said them. Every night. For about a year, as I was writing my very first book. I was so afraid, anxious, and hesitant about getting something wrong that it was easy to find myself frozen, terrified of writing another word. *What if it's the wrong word?*

But then one day I realized that paper is cheap and Microsoft Word files are free. The only thing I was risking was my time, and it was time I would have otherwise spent watching TV.

So, really, the question was: "Is this book idea worth skipping this hour of television?" And the answer was yes.

One of the coolest things about this business is that . . . well . . . at least in the beginning, it's nobody's business but yours.

If you don't like what you've written, scrap it. If you don't think your book is good enough, write another one. You don't have to show it to a single person or spend a single dime until you like what you've got.

All you're risking is your time.

Now, that's not to say that time isn't valuable. It very much is. Between jobs and second jobs and schoolwork and sports and taking care of siblings, there are probably a lot of things competing for your time.

But if you're going to spend an hour staring at a blank page, terrified, you might as well spend that same hour getting something down. Even if it's the wrong thing.

Paper is cheap.

Microsoft Word files are free.

Remember what I said in the beginning: Everyone starts with dirty water. Sure, you might be writing the wrong things now. You might still be writing the wrong things six months from now.

But the only way to get to the right things is to let the water run. Are you willing to risk an hour of your time to write something that might not be great? Because at the end of the day, that's all you have to lose. And if you stay frozen, terrified of making a mistake, you might lose a lot more than that.

What's the best writing advice you ever got?	
Z Brewer	Write the first draft just for you. Tell yourself a story without judging how you're doing so. Entertain yourself. You can fix it later.

When writing your books, what do you do to make sure you sit down and write on a daily/consistent basis?

You'll sometimes hear people say, "Writers write every day. If you're not writing every day, you're not a *real* writer!" Well then, I guess I'm not a real writer. Neither are a bunch of people I know.

I like to say that I write by inertia. When I'm in motion, I tend to stay in motion; when I'm at rest, I tend to stay at rest. Which just means that if I'm deep into a project or on deadline or really on a roll, I'll keep writing. For several hours a day—every day. But I might also go weeks without writing a word.

This is something that's going to vary immensely writer to writer. But the one thing we all agree on is this: Writers write. It doesn't matter if you do it a little bit every day or if you have big marathon writing days a few days a month or a few months a year. It doesn't matter when or how you write. It just matters that you do it.

Also, for the record, writing isn't always . . . writing. Some of the hardest days I have are the days when I don't write a single word—when I just sit on the floor staring at a whiteboard all day, trying to figure out why my plot doesn't make sense. Or there are the days when I'm scouring through research books trying to find a great setting for a scene or a fun fact to work a plot twist around.

A day where I write 4,000 words without a bathroom break is hard. The days when I just don't know what to write are harder.

But both types of days matter. After all, sometimes you have to blast through five feet of mountain so that, the next day, you can lay fifty feet of track.

Both types of days are how you eventually reach The End.

How do you find time to write? It's hard for me to find time between school, homework, and my part-time job to do most things. And when I do get a moment to myself, it's just so much easier to catch up on my latest Netflix addiction than to actually write.

There is always going to be something else to do. Always. Maybe it's school. Maybe it's another job. Or maybe it's something good on TV or a movie or a concert you want to go see. Or sleep. Seriously. Never underestimate the power of sleep.

Truthfully, I'm one of the lucky ones, because writing is my job now. This means not just that I don't have another job eating up my time and energy, but also that when I say "I've got to write today," my friends and family respect that—which makes it easier to find the time in a lot of ways.

But here's the thing that I want to make really clear: Every writer starts off writing for free.

And every writer starts out writing on borrowed time.

I started writing seriously when I was in college and in graduate school. I wrote even more seriously when I had a full-time job. I still had that job when I wrote my first four published books. In fact, most writers *never* have the luxury of writing full-time.

I'd come home from work, exhausted, and have to ask myself: *What do you want more, to watch this hour of TV or to have a novel published one day?*

So I gave up TV. (A lot. Not all.)

What you give up will be up to you.

So what if you literally, genuinely, don't have the time? Between school and jobs and family responsibilities, maybe you've already given up TV and Netflix and hanging out with friends. If that's the case, then I might advise you to try the notebook technique.

My first book (which will never be published, but that's okay) was written literally in spiral-bound notebooks during the time I had to wait at the dentist's office and in the moments in my car when I was five minutes early for a meeting. It was written while I waited for the water to boil so I could make spaghetti for supper.

I wrote that book on stolen time, and I know I'm not alone.

There seems to be this idea that writers sit down on snowy days by crackling fires with old-timey typewriters and, in movie-montage fashion, bang out a perfect novel over the course of a few days of uninterrupted time.

That's how people write in movies.

How people write in real life is uglier than that. It's a heck of a lot less glamorous, and it's a lot more sporadic.

I have friends who have written entire novels while waiting for their kids to get out of soccer practice. I have friends who write books on the bus on their way to work. I have friends who get up at four thirty every morning and write for an hour because they know it's the only hour they're going to have to themselves all day.

If you truly don't have the time to write right now, that's okay. You can read (or listen to audiobooks). You can think. You can pay attention to books and movies and stories and start preparing yourself for the day when you do have the time to sit down to write.

But keep in mind that just because there isn't a clear, obvious block of time already carved out during your day, that doesn't mean you can't steal a few minutes here or there.

Maybe you'll only be able to write 100 words a day. But I'll tell you what I eventually told myself: If you'd been writing a little bit every day for the past two years instead of *talking* about writing, you might have a book by now.

DEAR RACHEL CAINE,

You're one of the hardest-working writers I know. I'll never forget watching you, laptop open, writing before book signings or in hotel lobbies. Pretty much any time I see you—you're working. So... how do you do that? How are you so good at finding (or making) the time to write?

It's kind of a cliché, but you don't find the time... you have to make the time! When I was working a regular job, I discovered that if I left for work at 7:00 a.m., I arrived at my office at 8:30 with traffic... but if I left at 5:00 a.m., I'd get to the Starbucks next to my office at 5:30 a.m., when it opened. So I carved out those three hours for myself prior to regular work time, and then I normally would stay late to write for another hour or two to avoid going-home traffic. I had a mandatory four hours on Saturdays, Sundays, and holidays. But my schedule was mine. Other people like late-night writing, or writing on breaks and lunch hours. No right answer.

As a full-timer, it's oddly just as hard, since there are constant interruptions and (of course) temptations. But I try to mandate a solid eight hours at the computer for five days a week, four hours a day on the weekend, with occasional days off.

How do you keep from getting distracted while trying to write?

This probably depends on when you're writing, where you're writing, and what exactly tends to distract you.

Is it people? Maybe your siblings or your parents or your friends won't leave you alone. Maybe procrastination itself is your distraction and you're always finding something else you could do instead. Or maybe it's technology, and every time you sit down to write, you get a million texts and something cool happens online.

But do you want to know a secret? There's always something happening online. That's why almost every writer I know has some way of turning the internet off when they're working. There are apps you can download that will disable the internet for however long you want it. Sometimes I will literally unplug my router if I really need to get serious.

When I'm on deadline, I like to leave my house with all of its distractions (laundry to fold . . . cookies to bake . . .) and go to a café where I can't get on the internet. So that's two distractions taken care of right there. Then I put on some headphones and turn on a white noise app so that I can't hear the conversations of the people around me. (Another distraction down.)

Then I write like the wind. (True story: One time I was so deep in the zone that when I finished my work for the day, I looked up to find that there were two ambulances and a fire truck in the parking lot and the whole restaurant was going crazy because a man was having a heart attack twenty feet away from me. I'd had no idea!)

You may not be able to go out to a restaurant and unplug like I can, but if writing is a priority, you're going to have to figure out what distracts you and then come up with ways to either turn those distractions off or tell the people in your life that you need a certain amount of time by yourself, alone, to write. Then set a timer or some kind of goal and don't get up until it's met.

What's a GREAT word count day for you?	
Shannon Hale	2,500. 1,000 is more typical.
Marie Lu	3,000.
Melissa de la Cruz	I can do 20,000 words in one night if necessary. But I try to keep to about 3,000 to 5,000.
Daniel José Older	2,000.
Elizabeth Eulberg	2,500 (once did 7K!).
Julie Murphy	Sometimes it's 500. Sometimes it's 3,000. I'm usually happy with anything over 1,500.
Stephanie Perkins	500.
Kody Keplinger	2,500. Which, for me, is about a chapter.
Marissa Meyer	8,000.
Alex London	2,500.
Sarah Rees Brennan	10,000 words. Okay, 7,000 words is also pretty great.
Jesse Andrews	1,000.
Alan Gratz	5,000.
Soman Chainani	1,000.
Holly Black	2,000.
Kiersten White	5,000 to 10,000 words.
Maggie Stiefvater	10,000—but that's usually when I'm at the very end of a draft and I have no more questions to answer. Normally I would be over the moon to accomplish 1,200 to 2,000.
Zoraida Córdova	5,000.
Gordon Korman	1,500.

Rachel Caine	5,000.
Dhonielle Clayton	3,000.
Eliot Schrefer	2,500.
Z Brewer	That depends on my mood and has shifted wildly over the years. At one point, 8,000 was GREAT and 5,000 was good. Nowadays? I'd say anything over 2,000 is GREAT.

How do I raise my daily word count? I see people managing to write 2,000 a day when I can only write like 100, if even that.

The first thing you need to understand is that all writers is different. Some writers labor over every single word and place them lovingly and painstakingly on the page.

Some puke up words and then fix them later. (I'm a puker. And that's okay. That's my process.)

Part of being a young or new writer is figuring out what *your* process is going to be. Maybe you're only meant to write 100 words a day. If you write consistently, you will have a finished book someday. I swear!

But if you really want to write more words at a time, here are some tips and tricks that might help with that.

1. GIVE YOURSELF PERMISSION TO WRITE BADLY. Now, some writers can never, ever do this, and that's 100 percent okay. It's not their process. It may not be *your* process. But you're never going to be able to sit down and write thousands of words at a time if every single word has to be perfect. How do you do that? Well . . .

2. DON'T EDIT AS YOU WRITE. Which may very well mean not *reading* or rereading as you write. Because (for me, at least) to reread means

to fiddle, and to fiddle means to obsess, and to obsess means to spend an hour and a half wondering if that comma really goes there or not.

You can fix the commas later. You can fix the grammar later. You can tighten up the prose and spruce up the dialogue. The things that are wrong today will still be wrong when it comes time to write draft two. So my goal is always to get to the end of draft one first.

3. TRY WRITING ON SOMETHING WHERE IT'S HARD TO REWRITE AS YOU GO. I used to have this very same problem, so that's why I started writing in dollar-store notebooks. It's really hard to totally rewrite something that's written on paper (as opposed to something on a computer), so when I wrote my opening paragraph in that notebook, I didn't really have much choice but to write a second paragraph. And then a third. And so on until I had my very first finished book. If I'd kept trying to write on a computer, I would still be reworking that first paragraph!

4. TRY TO HAVE SOME GOALS IN MIND WHEN YOU SIT DOWN EACH DAY. Start with a realistic word count goal. Don't go crazy. It's okay to start small—maybe 250 words or so—and build up once you realize what a good day for you looks like.

I'd also recommend you set some kind of story goal. For some reason, writing just seems so much easier when there is a point in the story I'm trying to reach or a couple of scenes I'm really excited to hammer out.

What if you don't have any scenes you're excited about or don't know what to write next? Then I probably wouldn't sit down to write just yet because sitting there spinning your wheels is just going to make you feel bad about yourself. So get up. Take a walk or clean your room while you try to think what you're going to write.

Then sit down and write it.

How do you get yourself to write on a regular basis? I always tell myself that I'm going to write one day, but later I get "too tired" and put it off.

You've hit on one of the hardest things about this business: No one makes you do it.

Now, eventually, you may reach the point where you have editors and agents and other people counting on you to deliver, but even then—even now—no one is coming to my house every day to make me do this. I have to decide when I'm going to write and how much I've got to get done.

If it weren't for my deadlines, I might never get anything written. So what are you supposed to do? Well, I'd recommend you give yourself some deadlines.

You might want to look around online, and see if there are any contests you'd like to enter from organizations like the Society of Children's Book Writers and Illustrators (SCBWI) and the various genre organizations like the Romance Writers of America or Mystery Writers of

America. Those contests have deadlines, and having a goal you're trying to hit can be super motivating.

Or maybe you should make a deal with a teacher or a family member. Maybe if you tell a friend that you have to finish your first draft before your birthday or New Year's Eve, then that will be the kick you need. After all, deadlines and goals are a lot easier to keep if you've got someone out there waiting to see the finished product.

When you are writing, do you usually let other people read the draft before it's done? If so, is it friends and family or other people you are less close to?

This is an incredibly personal thing, and it will vary a lot, author to author. Personally, I don't show anyone my first drafts until they're finished. Then I will usually read them through and make sure they make sense before sending them off to my editor.

Now, a lot of authors wouldn't be caught dead letting their editors see their first drafts! But my books have become so plot-heavy through the years that I need my editor to weigh in as soon as possible to help me decide what should stay and what should go.

Think of it like building a house. In the first draft, I'm pouring the foundation and putting up the frame. I want someone to come and have a look at things before I start putting in plumbing and laying down floors. I don't want to spend a week hanging wallpaper in a room that's going to get torn down or moved to the other side of the house! I need to know where everything is going to go—what's going to matter and who the players are going to be—before I get too far along. I've found that, in the long run, it's more efficient to let my editor weigh in early on. In general, my editor is cool with that, so it works for us.

Many authors won't show their editors anything until they're confident the book is close to perfect. So maybe they'll work on their own. Or maybe they'll show their work to a close friend.

Some authors might even have critique partners or groups—usually other writers they know and like and whose work they respect. They might read early drafts and offer feedback, and maybe you'll do the same for them.

Personally, I don't have a formal critique partner, but I love having friends I can brainstorm with and talk to about my (many!) plot problems. Amazingly, just the act of laying out my whole plot for someone usually allows me to see the problem for myself—a lot of times, that's the most helpful part of the process!

But I want to offer one word of warning. When you're starting out, it's hard to know if what you're doing is any good or not. I get it. In fact, I still feel that way a lot of the time. When you show your work to a friend or teacher or critique partner, listen to what they have to say, but also listen to your gut. Nobody knows your book better than you. Nobody knows your characters better than you. So take any and all advice and criticism that rings true in your gut and makes sense, but it's okay to leave the rest. Nobody can write your book better than you can. It's just up to you to do it.

So if you haven't already noticed, the answer to pretty much every question in this book is "Well, it depends." Nowhere is that more true than with process.

That's why I wanted to poll some of the most respected writers out there to show you how many processes there are. There really, truly is no one way to write a book.

I think the hardest part about process isn't just that it varies so much writer to writer but that it can also vary book to book.

I don't know what your process is right now or what your process will be after reading this book, but I can pretty much guarantee you it's going to vary over the course of your life and your career.

Maybe you'll start a book that just cannot (or will not) be written chronologically. Maybe you'll get a new job or have triplets and go from being someone who writes 5,000 words a day to someone who writes 500 (and all of them at two in the morning).

You may not know what your process is. You definitely don't know what your process is going to be. But the most important thing to remember is that *it's not the process that matters*. The book that comes out of the process is the only thing that counts.

145

CHAPTER 8
STARTING YOUR FIRST DRAFT

How does one decide what the perfect opening sentence of a book should be?

People talk a lot about opening lines, but in my opinion, a first sentence has one job and one job only: to make someone want to read the second sentence.

When I was twelve, I broke my leg jumping off the wall between Canada and Germany.

That's the first line of my novel *All Fall Down*, and it's my favorite of my first lines for a number of reasons.

Go ahead and reread the sentence above and think about it. What kind of twelve-year-old willingly jumps off walls? And since when are Canada and Germany next to each other? And why is there a wall between them?

That sentence tells the reader that our main character is something of a daredevil and this book is set in a world that's not quite like our own. That sentence also tells the reader that if they want the answer to those questions, they're going to have to read the second sentence!

It's easy to get hung up on first sentences, I know. I do it, too, and I always have trouble starting a draft until I have a good one. Sometimes they change a little (or a lot), but I can't start writing until the first sentence pops into my head (usually while I'm cooking or swimming or folding laundry or doing something that totally isn't writing-related).

But if you're having trouble with your first sentence, don't worry. Definitely don't let it keep you from writing. Just put something down and come back to it. You can rewrite it a million times if you need to.

DEAR ZORAIDA CÓRDOVA,
What's the hardest part about writing a book?

The number one thing is the doubt that creeps in while you're drafting. This feeling didn't exist when I wrote my debut novel, because I was writing that book for myself. There were no expectations, no deadlines, just me and the page. After the first book is out in the world and you're ready to try again, things are different. Some of those things are good—all of a sudden you have a community of other authors going through the same thing. But the doubt is there, waiting like a creepy little monster looking over your shoulder. It manifests itself in different forms. It tells you you're not good enough to write the next book, or the one after that. Luckily, the community part is stronger, and you know that you aren't alone in this wild business of writing books.

How do you write the beginning of the story? How do you balance making it interesting and introducing the story and characters?

In many ways, the first few chapters of your book are the most important. After all, if readers are bored in chapter 1, they may not read chapter 2. If they're not pulled in by chapter 2, they probably won't even try chapter 3, etc., etc.

I think the biggest mistake that most new writers make at the beginning of a story is to think they have to spell everything out right then, right there. *Look at all the cool stuff I've thought up!*

Instead of hinting at a character's mysterious backstory, a new writer might go into detail about it as soon as the character steps on the page. Instead of layering in details of the world little by little, they might have long paragraphs or pages talking about every single aspect right up front. (This, of course, is called "info-dumping.")

As a rule, I like to live by the "get in as soon as it gets interesting, get out before it gets boring" school of storytelling. Make sure those early scenes introduce your characters and your world, but don't worry about introducing every little thing right then.

It's okay for your reader to have a few questions. You just don't want them to be confused.

Now, I'm going to let you in on something that I've noticed, not as a writer but as a reader. I start a lot of books. I quit a lot of books. One of the things that I have noticed is that a lot of the books I put down have long sections of information and no *scenes*.

As a reader, I want to be grounded in the story. I want to know *who* the characters are and also *where* they are. Are they standing on the deck of a ship? Are they in gym class? Are they lying in a hospital bed? Too often I don't know. Or maybe the character isn't anywhere at all, and it's the author/narrator who is "telling" us backstory and character details and I'm afloat again.

In other words, the author proceeds to *tell* me what's important.

In the books I keep reading, the authors always *show* me what's important.

I'm not reading paragraph after paragraph about how important Prim is to Katniss and how the Hunger Games work. No. I'm watching Katniss smooth Prim's hair and tell her everything's going to be okay even though it's the day of "the reaping." What's the reaping? Well, you better believe I'm going to keep reading and find out!

So a good practical tip for new writers is this: When in doubt, make your opening chapters as scene-based as possible. Put your character in a place doing a thing. When you ground your characters you also ground your reader, pulling them into the story.

Are there phenomenal books that have opened with a more omniscient overview? Absolutely! *The Disreputable History of Frankie Landau-Banks* by E. Lockhart is my personal favorite. The voice of that novel is spectacular, and it grabs you by the collar on page one and won't let you go. It's like a siren song. I just have to keep listening. Which, again, is what you want in an opening chapter.

Whichever approach you choose, just know that it's going to get a lot better—and easier—with practice.

I'm eighteen and trying to write a book at the moment. The biggest problem I have is that my chapters are quite short! How do you pad out your chapters without rambling about inconsequential things?

First, good for you for starting your book! That's the first step!

Second, there is no right or wrong length for a chapter. Some authors write very long chapters. Some authors (or books) have incredibly short chapters. And short chapters can be great, especially for reluctant readers who feel good every time they finish a chapter.

So, short chapters aren't really a problem! That's good news.

Finally, don't ever feel like you need to "pad" anything. Ever. In my opinion, padding is very, very bad. And boring. And . . . skippable. So make sure your scenes have enough conflict, that your characters have a goal that they're working toward and plenty of stuff standing in the way.

When you've completed a scene or reach something that feels like a natural break, it's probably time to start a new chapter. Another good time to break would be if you're changing points of view. Or locations. Or skipping over a period of time. (Like if chapter 12 happens on Tuesday and your next scenes take place on Saturday, then that might be a good breaking point.)

My favorite time to insert chapter breaks is when there's been a big change in the action. The villain shows up! The getaway car explodes! The trajectory that our characters were on changes suddenly and putting a break between those two chapters will accomplish two things: First, it's a mini cliffhanger, and your reader is totally going to want to keep reading. Second, it signals to the reader that the tide has shifted somehow and you're entering a new phase of the story.

Ultimately, there really is no right or wrong way, and you will need to do what feels natural to you.

Is it okay to use bad grammar in your book? Like if you're writing it in a kid's point of view, is it okay?

Sure. Grammar, vocabulary level, sentence length and structure— all of these things (and more) add up to the "voice" of your novel. And voice is very important!

Just make sure that you don't overdo it. You should make your character's voice feel authentic and unique, but you don't want it to be hard to read and you definitely don't want it to take away from the story.

So a good rule might be to add enough funky spellings and wacky punctuation and bad grammar to make your character's voice shine through, but stop just shy of making your reader confused or distracted.

(And FYI, we'll be talking a lot more about voice a little later!)

Do you think humor is something that comes naturally? What advice can you offer about developing a humorous narrative?

Here's the thing about writing humor:

1. It's really, really hard.
2. Funny people usually don't know why they're funny. They just are.
3. There's nothing less funny than someone trying super hard to be funny.

So, in answer to your question: Yes, I think humor is something that comes far more naturally to some people than to others. If you want to write funny books, my best advice would be to read (or reread) books that you think are funny and then annotate them carefully. Write down or highlight the funny parts and ask yourself why that line made you chuckle or that scene worked for you.

And remember, comedy—far more than romance or drama or action—is subjective. Just keep writing and eventually you'll find your voice.

If you're gonna write a story, do you want to use a really advanced vocabulary (college level of writing), or should you keep it at normal range (high school level)? Should I use words that my readers might have to look up in the dictionary?

This is a question that so many people asked when we announced this book! Seriously, *a lot* of you have this question, which I think is really interesting. And it actually touches on a pet peeve of mine.

Years ago, I was on a hiring committee for my day job. We got a lot of applications, but one in particular stood out. This guy had a perfectly fine résumé, but his cover letter was . . . interesting.

It was as if he'd written a regular letter, then got a thesaurus and changed every word to something he thought sounded more impressive. Or fancier. Or smarter. But in the end, he just sounded kind of like an idiot who didn't know that *I'd love to talk to you about this job* is just as good as *I would endeavor to dialogue with your institution regarding this employment opportunity.*

So I am not a fan of using big words *just* to make yourself sound smarter. In my experience, that almost always backfires.

But it's important to say that this is yet another question that doesn't have a right or wrong answer because the words an author uses are *personal*. They are a huge part of that author's voice, and voice is maybe the most abstract thing we'll talk about in this book.

Just know this: Good writing isn't determined by the level of words you use. It's determined by the way they make the reader feel. Sometimes the perfect word is something that might be unfamiliar to some readers. Sometimes that fits with the character and the voice and the tone of the book overall. That's why this is something that's going to vary every single time.

Now, if you wanted to write a book for really little kids? Yeah. Then this might matter. But other than that, if you sit down to write and the book comes out in big words, fine. If it comes out in more basic words, also fine.

The key is choosing the *right* words. Always.

How do you write the stuff in between major (or minor) plot points?

How did you find "fillers" for stories when you weren't sure what to write, or how do you keep the story interesting between climaxes?

What do you do when you have most of your book done but you still need a few fillers to go in between?

How do you avoid skipping the boring parts, and not just write the fun bits?

These are just four of the (many, many) questions we got on this topic, and I wanted to include them all here because I think this is a hugely important point.

Are you ready?

It's going to change your life . . .

Okay.

Here's the thing, folks: *You should only be writing the good parts.*

I remember when I was writing what would become my very first published novel. I still had my day job, and I was trying to cram as much writing as possible into the weekends, and I kept thinking, *I wish I didn't have to write all these boring scenes . . . I wish I could just skip to the interesting scenes!*

And then one day it hit me: Any scene too boring to write is probably a scene too boring to read.

It was a huge light bulb moment for me and one that changed pretty much my entire outlook. Never again would I let (or make) myself write "filler," and you shouldn't either.

But how do you leave the boring parts out? Is that even possible?

Well, for starters, you have to give your readers some credit.

I think a lot of new writers think that if you have a scene with your heroine getting ready for school, then next you have to show her getting in the car, then riding to school, then walking into school, then saying hi to her friends . . . and so on and so on.

But if you show your heroine getting ready for school and, in the next scene, she's already at school, are your readers going to be super confused by how she got there? Or are they going to figure it out?

Next, I think it's incredibly important that each scene accomplishes multiple things. For example, you could have a scene where we meet your heroine. Then maybe there's a scene where we realize what her personality is like. Then another where we learn she has two sisters. Then another where we learn her sisters have magical powers. Then yet another scene where we learn that there's an ancient prophecy that one of the three sisters will turn into a goat on her sixteenth birthday . . . and on and on and on.

Or we could have one or two killer scenes where the reader learns all of those facts in a really interesting way.

I hear aspiring writers talk about this a lot, how they can't cut this scene because it accomplishes this one thing. But the truth is, every single scene—especially early in your story—should accomplish multiple things. For example, you don't need a scene to establish your character's personality. Every single scene should already be doing that all the way through the book.

When a lot of people talk about "filler" scenes, I think they're particularly worried about the middle. And I get it. Middles can be really hard for me as well.

I really struggled when I was writing *I'd Tell You I Love You, But Then I'd Have to Kill You*. Initially, the book was supposed to take place over the heroine's sophomore year of spy school. In the first draft, I had a bunch of interesting stuff happening at the beginning of the book, and a bunch of cool stuff happening at the end of the book, but a whole lot of "filler" was happening in between because, well, there was a lot of school year in there. Then my genius editor said, "Why not make it take place over the fall semester instead of the whole year?"—and like magic, my problem was solved.

That was also when I read Meg Cabot's amazing Princess Diaries series and learned that not everything in a book has to look like a book. Which meant I could have things like a list of "Pros and Cons of What Happened That September" that literally allowed me to skip from August to October and not have a whole month where I had my characters doing stuff that didn't really matter.

I could also do excerpts from my heroine's "Covert Operations Report" written in spy lingo, giving a play-by-play of her missions in a fun, different voice that allowed me to "tell" (and not show) and offered a rundown of a lot of information very quickly. (They were also the source of a lot of humor.)

Finally, I want to point out that this doesn't mean you should write only the fight scenes or the make-out scenes or scenes that are nonstop action. No. Not at all.

I heard once that a great story is like a great song. It shouldn't be the same volume all the way through. It's not going to be the same tempo. It's going to have highs and lows. It's going to build and crest and fall. Make sure there is a rhythm to your story. Give your characters ups and downs—quiet moments and loud—and as long as something is at stake for them in each and every scene, then you're going to be okay.

Plus, if there are boring scenes? You can cut them in revision.

How do you make a story truly meaningful? How do you make your work important, rather than just a silly story?

Silly stories are okay. Silly stories serve a purpose.

On the whole, society tends to believe that dramatic or serious books/shows/movies are way more important than stories that make people laugh and feel good. But laughing and feeling good is important, too. Sometimes, laughing at a book is the only laugh a person has all day. Sometimes, when the world is making you feel bad, a book can make you feel good, and I happen to think that there's a very real value in that.

I've heard from a lot of readers who wanted to thank me for writing something they could enjoy while doing their chemo treatments. I've gotten more than one email from a kid who clung to my books while their parents got divorced.

I don't write the types of books that are going to win awards. I'll never be a critical darling. But sometimes my silly books are read by people who already have enough dark and serious and tragic in their lives. Sometimes I can make sad people smile.

So if you're working on a story that does that, yay! I think that's awesome. See the meaning in your work as it is, and don't spend too much time worrying how it stacks up against all of the great work being written today. Maybe the most important thing about your work is that it makes someone happy for a while.

But what's more important than that?

Do you ever find it hard to balance between writing what you want to write and writing what you think an audience will want to read?

In Stephen King's amazing book *On Writing*, he says that we should "write with the door closed; rewrite with the door open." I think about this advice all the time.

(Here's an assignment for you: Read Stephen King's *On Writing*.)

I think a lot about what my readers might want when I'm trying to decide which of my ideas I should commit to next, but I try to keep the door closed once I start that first draft.

And boy am I glad I've done it that way most of the time.

When I was working on the fifth Gallagher Girls novel, *Out of Sight, Out of Time*, I reached a point near the end of the story where I found my heroine doing something I never dreamed she would do. It was so much darker than anything I'd intended to write, and once I had it down, I absolutely loved it, but I kept telling myself my editor would make me cut it. I never dreamed it would be in the finished book.

But . . . my editor loved it! And it ended up being most of my readers' favorite scene in the entire series.

If I'd been writing with the door open, that scene—everyone's favorite scene—wouldn't exist.

So, in answer to your question, I do let myself think about why people read my books, but the only way to get that first draft finished is to close the door and write!

In your books, you're really good at withholding information and unveiling it at the right moment to surprise the readers. Do you have any tips on how to do that?

Thank you! I think that's something that comes from reading a lot of books, watching a lot of movies and TV shows, and writing a lot of drafts.

Generally, my biggest advice on when to reveal information is pretty simple: Your readers should get information when they need it—never before! And your readers should never know more than your hero or heroine knows (at least not for very long).

Why? Because if we know something the hero knows for a long time, eventually—whether we even realize it or not—we're going to start thinking that the hero is a moron for not figuring it out. After all, we've known that it was coming for forty pages!

(FYI, this is also why I never reveal anything in the descriptions of my books that happens more than fifty pages into the book. Not to save the "twist" but to save the main character from looking like a fool.)

Even more important than *when* a character gets a piece of information is probably *how* the character gets that information.

I remember when I was writing my second Gallagher Girls book, *Cross My Heart and Hope to Spy*, I had a scene where the girls went trotting down to a teacher's office and the teacher explained exactly what was going on in the plot. My editor almost broke her red pen correcting that one. What's the use of writing a book about teenage spies if you can't have them using their skills to get that information for themselves? Where's the fun in that?

Hinting at things is good. Teasing is great. But information is always 100 percent better when the hero or heroine has to *earn* it. Making them earn it is a big part of making sure you have enough story (and conflict) to go the distance.

In my whole writing journey, my writing style has changed many, many times, mostly according to the last book I just read-it'll usually take on the style of that writer. So how do you develop your own writing style?

A lot of people had questions about "writing style," which makes total sense. What you call "writing style" some call "voice." But no matter what you call it, it's really important, really personal, and really, really hard to teach and/or describe.

First, it's important to understand that in a lot of ways there are actually two different types of voice.

AUTHORIAL VOICE is probably what a lot of people think of as an author's "style." It can be everything from word choice to sentence structure to humor to tone to subject matter. It's a lot like an author's literary fingerprint, and even when they don't intend to, something about the way a person writes often carries through, book to book.

For example, last summer, I got kind of obsessed with a particular romance author, and I read a ton of her books, one right after the other. I was super excited when I found out my library had an ebook bundle by her—three whole books I could read (for free)!

I sat down one night and zoomed through the first one and loved it. Then I started the second book and something felt off, but I couldn't put my finger on what.

It was the same kind of plot. It featured the same kind of characters. All the elements that her books usually have were there, but this one just didn't affect me in the same way her other books had. I read the whole thing, and when I was finished, I commented to someone that it wasn't bad but it was my least favorite of her books.

Then I looked back to see what the title was and noticed that instead of a three-book bundle by my favorite author, it was a bundle of books by three *different* authors.

Why had that second book felt like it was written by a different person? Because it *was*.

To me, that's the best possible example of style—or authorial voice. That even if you don't look at the cover page, you can tell who did (or didn't) write it just from the book itself.

The second type of voice is **NARRATIVE VOICE**, and this one is just as important. Simply put, authorial voice is the voice of the author, but narrative voice is the voice of the *character*.

And that's a really important distinction.

After all, Cammie in Gallagher Girls sounds incredibly different from Grace in Embassy Row. Even though they're both first person narrators written by me—and parts of me absolutely crept in! But Cammie is a far more innocent character than Grace, so Grace's voice just has a different tone and feel and style.

Those books sound like me. But they sound like Grace or Cammie more.

I think your problem of having your voice take on the quality of whatever book you just finished is incredibly common. Even now I have to watch what I'm reading while I'm writing. For example, I was writing something in first person *past* tense a few weeks ago. Then I took a break one day and read something written in first person *present* tense while I was eating lunch.

Two hours later, I was back at my desk and realized I'd switched to present tense without even knowing it and had to rewrite a whole chapter.

So voices creep into our heads. Great voices creep into our bloodstreams.

But they don't stay there. The voices that stay there are the voices that come from within.

From within *you* for your authorial voice.

And from within *your character* for your narrative voice.

The best way I know to make sure those voices are true and unique is to read so broadly and so frequently that *all* of the voices influence you. And to write so much that you purge whatever voice might be lingering on the edge of your subconscious.

Remember the water hose theory?

The best way to get to the words and the themes and the styles that are truly your own is to let the water run.

How do you find your authorial voice? How do you then also have a unique voice for each of your narrators/characters?

Maybe it sounds silly, but I write the way I talk, so it's literally my voice on paper. (Okay, so I say "dude" and "awesome" way less on the page.) As for my characters, when I write from their perspective, it's almost like they whisper into my ear what they would say, what they would do, how they feel. I merely transcribe it. I guess you could say that I just do what the voices tell me to.

What's the best writing advice you ever got?

David Levithan	In college, someone told me, "You could never expect Mark Twain to write like Jane Austen." The point being, they're both great, but in their own way. So you can find your own way to be great.

How do you write transitions? For example, I have two major scenes happening and I can't find the middle ground to ease my way into it without just randomly jumping from one extreme to the next.

Wanna know a secret? Transitions are probably my least favorite thing to write. I hate them! I have no idea why it's so much harder to write the sentence that starts a scene than it is to write the entire scene sometimes. But it is.

So how do you do it? Well, I think a lot depends on the two scenes you're trying to transition between. And I think the key might lie in *why* the two scenes were split in the first place.

Is it because a great deal of time has passed between the two scenes? Then the passing of that time—showing the reader how much it is and what all has changed—is a good approach. For example, if you're going from Tuesday night to Wednesday morning, it can be as simple as "The next morning, XYZ character was . . ." Seriously. They don't always have to be fancy or poignant. Sometimes they just need to get the job done.

Are you splitting up two scenes because you're going from one POV character to another? Then your transition should probably show that, both to signal to the reader that we're now in someone else's head, and also because, presumably, that jump was important. For some reason, you needed to know what that other character was thinking or feeling, so get right to those thoughts and feelings when possible.

Maybe you're going from one scene/chapter to the next because something super big just happened, marking the end of one moment and the beginning of a very different kind of moment (taking place just seconds apart). For example, if you've got a scene with your hero and heroine making cupcakes and then a dragon busts through the wall— well, I'd say the dragon is probably a great place to start the next scene. (You'll notice this is all closely tied to the earlier question about when to include a chapter break.)

Transitions need to show a lot of things: whose POV we're in (when writing in third person or multiple first person), where we are, how much time has passed. They can also be really funny sometimes. For example, when you end a scene with *We'll be fine as long as it doesn't rain!* and then you open the next scene with *It only rained nine inches.*

Sometimes a transition is a great opportunity to sprinkle in some backstory.

Imagine the scene that ends with a dragon bursting through the wall. Maybe you start the next scene with something like *When Chloe was six, she wanted a lizard for a pet. When she was seven, she asked for a reptile cage. And for her tenth birthday, she'd begged and pleaded with her mother, arguing that she was now mature enough to handle a much larger animal. But as the dragon turned her mother's favorite dishes into ash, Chloe had to admit that she might have been mistaken.*

In the end, this is one of those things that won't make or break your novel, especially in the first draft. Just write what feels natural and get a draft down on paper. That's your first—and most important—job.

How do you balance/combine what you need to move your plot along and some more "flowery" phrasing that isn't as important for the plot?

My mom is a really, really amazing cook. When I went away to college and moved into my first apartment, I'd get homesick sometimes and start craving some of the things that Mom used to make. So I'd call her up and say, "Mom, how do you make chili?" And she'd say, "Oh, you know . . . you brown some ground beef in a skillet and then you just kind of make it."

Or I'd ask, "Mom, what's your gravy recipe?" to which she'd laugh and say, "There's no recipe for gravy! You make some sausage, then add some flour and milk, and you just make it. You'll be fine. You know what gravy's supposed to taste like."

You can probably imagine how frustrating that answer was to a hungry college student. (No, Mom, if I knew how to make it, I wouldn't be asking you how to make it!)

But eventually I did learn how to make chili. And gravy. And a lot of other things—and now when someone asks me for the recipe, I shrug and say, "I don't know. I just kind of make it."

In a lot of ways, writing is just like this. There isn't a recipe you can follow, a firmly established game plan. It's a matter of taste and feel, experience and gut instinct.

But most of all, it's about *knowing what it's supposed to taste like.*

Look at the books you've loved from your favorite authors. Maybe get a cheap copy of one and mark it up with different colored highlighters. Put the romantic parts in one color, the action parts in another. Maybe bracket the flowery parts and flag those pages with a Post-it. Maybe you can underline the parts that made you laugh.

Go through several books that way, and when you're finished, how many Post-its do you have? Where do they come in, with the blue or yellow or pink highlights? This process isn't just about reading a book; it's about doing an X-ray of a book. This is you taking a look at all the little pieces that you know are in there but you've never really studied before.

So how do I balance prose and action? (Or romance? Or comedy? Or . . . anything else?) I'm not really sure. I just keep editing and working and tweaking things until it tastes right.

DEAR ELIZABETH EULBERG,
What's the hardest part about writing a book?

Overall, it's the faith that I can do it at all. I write at my desk with a set of my finished books staring at me. I often look at them and say to myself, "You've done it before, you can do it again." So much of being a writer is in your mind. You can look for outside validation, but at the end of the day, you have to be happy with the book you've written. It's your name on it. You're the one that will have to talk about it for many years (if you're lucky!). I think everybody struggles with imposter syndrome and I'm no exception.

Craftwise, it's writing description. I want to get to the action, the character banter, the development of relationships, the drama! I usually have to be told by my editor that I didn't describe something. But I also like leaving the main character's physical description rather vague, as I want the reader to be able to put themselves in their shoes. Plus, I figure, would you rather me describe a house or get to the kissing? Yeah, that's what I thought.

How do you balance writing with detail, but not so much that you become redundant?

This is one of those things that is pretty much going to boil down to voice. Some authors can write detailed and elaborate descriptions that paint such an amazing picture that we feel like we're there, looking at that sunset or smile or . . . doorknob. Some authors can go into the same level of detail and it's just a doorknob. And boring. So, so boring.

So how much detail is the right amount of detail? Well, however much you need. How do you know how much you need? I suppose it depends on how many of those details are relevant to the character or the plot. For example, if one of your characters is left-handed and you later find out that the murderer wielded the knife with her left hand, then that's a detail that will need to make an appearance at some point. Otherwise, maybe her left-handedness isn't that important and shouldn't be belabored.

Your job as the writer isn't to tell us everything you know. It's not to supply a list of all the contents of a room or exactly what every character is wearing at every moment. Your job is to describe things in a way that makes the reader see and (most importantly) *feel* a particular way.

For some writers (and some voices), that might mean a lot of detail. For others, it might mean very sparse descriptions. What matters is finding the voice and style that works for you. And you find that by writing.

DEAR CARRIE RYAN,

You have a rich, lyrical voice that really paints a picture. How do you find the balance between narrative/description and action/pacing?

What a great compliment—thank you! I've learned that if I'm bored writing it, I assume the reader will be bored reading it. So when I get bored, I make something happen. I throw a wrench into my character's plans, or give them an unexpected twist. (One time I even blew something up.) Anything to force the characters to react, which will almost necessarily carry the story forward.

Sometimes it can be easy for me to get carried away in descriptions, and I've decided that's okay! I allow myself to dig in as much as I want during a first draft because a lot of the time, that's how I'm discovering and understanding the world. It's in revisions that I worry more about pacing—trimming description where it bogs down the story rather than enhancing it. This is one area where it's really useful to have beta readers. It can be scary to show your unedited work to someone else, but often it's the best way to gauge whether you're getting across what you want to.

What do you do if you feel like you're telling too much and not showing enough?

Ooh. Show, Don't Tell—maybe my favorite piece of classic writing advice. And one of the things that is maybe the most difficult (and the most important) for new writers to understand.

As I've said elsewhere in this book, the very first things that I ever wrote were screenplays. They were really bad and pretty boring, but I learned so much from writing them, not the least of which is "Show, Don't Tell."

I think one of the reasons that a lot of new writers are confused by Show, Don't Tell is because they don't really understand what it means. It may be easier to understand if we look at your story like a screenplay.

Imagine a script that says this:

> *MAGGIE comes into the room and nearly stumbles over a body. She looks down at the floor and gasps as she realizes the dead man is her soon-to-be ex-husband, who has been stabbed with the letter opener he gave her when she stopped modeling and decided to go back to law school. Maggie screams, then runs away.*

Okay. So maybe that's how some authors might introduce a new character in their book. That's fine. But it's also a bad case of Telling. I know because if that were a screenplay and that screenplay were made into a movie, the camera would actually see this:

A beautiful woman comes into the room and nearly stumbles over a dead man with something sticking out of his chest. She gasps, then runs away.

Do you see the difference?

Show, Don't Tell means that you can tell the reader all about Maggie and her husband and that she used to be a model and is a lawyer now. But maybe it would be more interesting to show those things instead?

Personally, I think it would be way more fun to see one of the homicide detectives recognize Maggie and ask if she used to be a model. I'd like to hear them question her about her divorce and why a pretty lady like her would want to read all those thick books.

I want characters. I want dialogue. I want action.

In short, I don't want all the interesting stuff dumped in my lap.

Show, Don't Tell also applies to what our characters are feeling. There's nothing that annoys me more than reading something like:

Julia was so furious she slammed the door.

Really? Julia was furious? I never would have guessed since happy people slam doors so frequently. (That's me being sarcastic, by the way.)

I didn't need to be told Julia was furious—the door slamming was enough for me.

There may very well be times in your book where telling is a quick and efficient way of letting your reader know exactly what's going on, but try to keep this in mind. And when in doubt, think of it like a movie. If a camera were watching this scene, would it see the character's emotions? Would it catch the important pieces of backstory? Would it be able to follow the action? Or is all of that information taking place entirely within the character's (or the author's) head?

Your goal is always to make sure it also ends up on the page.

If we realize, 30,000 words in, that we're telling the story from the wrong character's perspective or using the wrong POV, how should we proceed?

Well, first you cry. Then you will probably need ice cream. And maybe pizza. And you'll definitely want the option of breaking something. Then you'll want to talk to a good friend or family member and sleep for at least ten hours.

After that, maybe step away from the project for a few days just to make sure that you really are using the wrong POV. (It may just be a case of the mid-book crazies—we all get them.) Then come back and reread what you have with fresh eyes. If you still think you're in the wrong POV, you have two options.

You can try to edit your current document, changing the POV along the way. Or you can start with a blank page, using what you have so far as a blueprint, taking the dialogue and story beats that you like but basically starting from scratch. I know both options sound like a lot of work, but believe me, POV is important enough that it's worth it. I promise!

How do you write action scenes?

A better way of phrasing this question might be "How do you *rewrite* action scenes?" because I never, ever get them right on the first try.

Some authors do some very elaborate planning for action scenes. They'll map out the path of the car chase. They'll have friends stage a fight so that they can keep track of who has a knife and in what hand and where the grenade rolled off to.

Sometimes we'll consult real experts in weapons or hand-to-hand combat, which is incredibly helpful in terms of making sure the scene you write is logical and . . . well . . . possible.

All this research is a good thing to do if you find that helpful.

For me, the most helpful thing is often thinking about the setting for the scene itself. When I think about action scenes that I've seen in movies, they can all start to run together, right? I mean, I don't really remember one fight from another. All the car chases start to look the same. But a car chase that happens underground in a subway tunnel (*The Italian Job*), that I remember. A fight that happens on top of a moving train with a helicopter inches away (*Mission: Impossible*)—yeah, that stuck with me, too.

So research. Plan. Visualize. Think about things you've never seen. But most important, don't forget that none of this will matter if we don't care about the characters in the fight and if there isn't anything at stake.

DEAR SARAH REES BRENNAN,
How do you write action scenes?

I actually really love writing action scenes! I didn't always, since I'd think about it in terms of "blocking" for a movie: Where is everybody? Where are they standing? What are they doing? What moves are they making? I signed up for fencing class so I could work out that kind of thing, and got my butt kicked by a sword-wielding eight-year-old. That's all an important part of writing action scenes, but how I learned to love action scenes was the trick of writing them for me—thinking about how action scenes are a fun, dynamic way to showcase a character. Who are they protecting? What kind of weapon are they using? (Expertly wielding a broadsword? Wildly throwing a toaster?) How do they fight—ferociously, or without conviction? What do they say—are they witty, or do they just occasionally holler, "Duck"? If they were hurt, who would run to them? You can show someone's true character by showing who they are when they're in trouble.

DEAR ALEX LONDON,
How do you write action scenes?

I play them out like a movie in my head, then try to describe what I see as clearly as possible, picking the exciting details just like a director would choose which shots to use. Sometimes that's a close-up; sometimes it's an epic aerial shot. I also tend to listen to video game soundtracks when I write, which helps in the actiony parts, too.

How do you build tension in your story?

I think a lot of people think of tension as being tied to plot. And it is—don't get me wrong. But I'd argue that it's just as much (and maybe more) about characters. And POV.

Think about it this way:

Action is having a bomb go off.

Tension happens when your reader knows the bomb is there and cares about whether or not the bomb might hurt a character we love—maybe stop them from achieving a goal that we're invested in.

And don't forget, tension also isn't just about big, external, physical risks. (*Will the bridge collapse? Can she get out of the burning house? Who is the killer?*) There's a billion-dollar industry built on romantic tension: Will he ever say "I love you"? Will she leave her awful fiancé and run away with the man who loves her for who she really is?

Tension is conflict. And conflict is gold.

It's a sense of being unsure or anxious or worried. It's a feeling of wanting a thing—anything—and having serious doubts about whether or not it will happen. It's being concerned about whether or not the characters you care about will be okay.

So you want to have great tension in your story? Start with a great character and then give us a whole lot of reasons to worry about whether or not they'll actually get their happy ending.

Why do you choose not to have chapter titles? Do you ever think that these are a good idea?

I think it can be a great idea if it fits with your voice and the type of book you're writing. It's never really fit with something that I've done, but that doesn't mean I won't do it in the future.

The most difficult thing for me is ending a story. How I should finish? How do I choose the end when

there are so many wonderful (and not so wonderful) possibilities?

In a way, conclusions are my favorite thing to write. After all, the end is in sight (which is a *great* feeling!). You've been writing for a long time, slowly narrowing down all the ways that your story can go, eliminating possibilities until you reach the point where there are only a few ways the story can turn out.

And then I inevitably proceed to pick the *wrong* way. Always. Every time. As a result, endings are almost always the part of the story that I have to work on the hardest during draft number two.

For example, the sixth (and final) Gallagher Girls book, *United We Spy*, had a totally different ending right up until the very last draft. I'd figured out an ending in the storyboarding stage, and I just kept writing it and writing it and writing it, but no amount of rewriting ever made it . . . right.

I knew it. My editor knew it (but didn't know how to say it). Eventually we got on the phone, and I (kind of flippantly) said, "I wish I could just do [X]!" There was a long pause on the phone, and then she said, "Uh . . . why can't you?"

At the end of a book, there are a lot of possibilities. Even if we know, generally, how things are going to turn out, there are still a lot of ways to accomplish it. I had picked a way, and I kept trying to make it fit even though the book had gone in a different direction. (See? I told you I wasn't any good at outlining.)

Do I regret writing that wrong ending? Nope. Not in the least. Because that was how I found the right ending.

Just remember that a right ending will do three very different but very important jobs.

First, an ending must wrap up all the central questions that the book has asked (unless the book is part of a series, in which case some bigger, overarching questions might remain). You've got to tie up all the loose ends, see your character either gain—or lose—their goal, and give us a hint of what that character's life is going to be like from now on.

Second, your ending needs to pay off—which means it has to meet whatever expectations our readers might not even know they have.

Basically, can you imagine the final Harry Potter book if Voldemort had gotten pneumonia and died before the Battle of Hogwarts? What if he'd been hit by another wizard during the fighting and died before Harry even showed up? No. That series was always going to end with Harry and Voldemort duking it out. Always. It had to. Because any other ending would feel like a rip-off. Whether we realized it or not, we'd been promised a Harry vs. Voldemort showdown, and we got it.

Twist endings are great. Surprises are good. But not if the "twist" doesn't include whatever it is the story has been building toward from the beginning.

It's Katniss vs. President Snow. It's Black Panther vs. Killmonger. It's Mia Thermopolis deciding that, yes, she's going to be a princess.

In a way, the good ending is the ending that's inevitable. (Which is why good twists are so great and so hard—it *was* inevitable! We just didn't know it at the time.)

That's what was wrong with the original ending of *United We Spy*. There was a big dramatic showdown at the climax, but it wasn't a showdown between my heroine and the longtime villain of the series. Drafting Me thought that would be a cool twist. But Drafting Me was wrong, and what I ended up with was an ending that didn't pay off.

Once I reminded myself who the ultimate villain was and changed things so that the climax centered on a conflict with her, then everything worked brilliantly.

An ending's third job is probably its most important. People don't just remember how books end; ultimately, they remember how a book's ending made them *feel*.

Sometimes that means giving the reader what they want. Sometimes it means giving them something they didn't even know they wanted. Sometimes it means breaking their heart.

Whatever the case, when a person finishes a book and wants more, it's not because they want to read that book again. It's because they want to feel that way again. That is the ultimate goal.

How do you come up with a title for your books?

Ooh, titles . . .

When I started writing a book about a girl who went to an elite boarding school for spies, the phrase *I'd Tell You I Love You, But Then I'd Have to Kill You* popped into my head, and I knew I'd found my title. Just like that. Just that quickly. And for one brief moment I thought titles were so easy.

I was wrong.

I was very, very wrong.

Now here we are, about a dozen titles later, and all of them were the result of hours upon hours of work and research and worry.

What kind of work? Well, that depends what you're going for, I guess.

For example, it became evident early on that the titles for each

Gallagher Girls book would be a play on a common phrase or idiom. Which means that I spent approximately nine billion hours online, looking up idioms and sayings and phrases and trying to think of ways to twist them into something clever. For every title, there are probably fifty (or 150) on a list of possible titles that didn't make the cut.

(Personally, I'm a little bitter that *Not if I Save You First* won out over such gems as *Wild Moose Chase* and *All's Bear in Love and War*.)

But not every title will (or should) be a twist on an idiom. Sometimes a great title is a line from the book itself. Sometimes it's a description of the character or the name of a place. Maybe it's a single word that summarizes the essence of the story. Or maybe it's a short word or phrase that is so tied to the story in your mind that that is how you automatically refer to it.

If you're hoping to write a series someday, then it's important to think about not just what the title of the first book will be but also about what the titles are going to look like for all future books. They should sound like they go together, so think about what cadence, style, and voice the titles themselves have.

For example, when I was writing my Embassy Row series, as soon as we settled on the title *All Fall Down* for book one (because it was a line in the book itself), it became clear that we were going for phrases people know from nursery rhymes. It was immediately obvious to me that the next two titles in the series should be *See How They Run* and *Take the Key and Lock Her Up*.

The key thing to remember is this: Titles are important. And titles are also hard. If you haven't come up with a great title off the top of your head, then it's okay to just call your book *Untitled Radioactive Hamster Book* for now and come back to it later. The key right now is to get your book written.

In my life, I've met dozens of people who've told me that they're going to write a book someday—that they've got the perfect idea. That they'll do it just as soon as they have the time. I don't know for a fact, but I wouldn't be surprised if every last one of them is still *talking* about writing.

Folks, talk is cheap. Talk is easy. Talk is something you can do without ever running the risk that you might mess it up.

The number of people who talk about writing compared to the number of people who have actually written a first draft is staggering. But there's no way to have a career in this business if you don't move to that second group.

I know it's scary. But you can do it.

Remember that your opening sentence matters, but it can be rewritten.

Filler scenes are scenes you shouldn't even mess with, and voice is something you'll figure out over time. When you're worried about showing versus telling, you just have to imagine your book is a movie and write down only what the camera sees.

Just make sure something is always at stake—that there's something your characters want or need and have to earn themselves, and you should have plenty of conflict (gas in the tank) to get you to The End.

And most of all, remember you can't rewrite a blank page. Ever. So get to writing.

	How long does it take you to finish a first draft?	How many drafts do you usually do?	How long does it take for you to finish a book?
Shannon Hale	Depends on the type of book, since I write early chapter books as well as novels. One week to four months.	A dozen. First chapters might get thirty to fifty drafts.	Two months to seven years.
Marie Lu	Fastest: Two months. Slowest: One year.	Five.	Fastest: One year. Slowest: Two years.
Melissa de la Cruz	I think the average is three months, but I can do it in six weeks if needed. I once wrote a book in two weeks. I don't recommend it!	I usually do three. One full manuscript turned in, one after notes from editor, and one copyedit. But my first drafts come in really clean.	Six months on average, I would say.
Daniel José Older	Between three months and two years.	One and a half.	Six months.
Elizabeth Eulberg	Middle grade: One month. YA: Two months (but VERY sloppy first drafts).	Three or four before my editor sees it.	From idea to accepted manuscript: twelve to eighteen months.
Julie Murphy	It varies. I've taken a month, and I've taken nearly a year. About four to five months is good for me.	Five.	From drafting to edits, about six months on average, but I've taken much longer and much less, just depending.

Stephanie Perkins	Two years for a full draft. Tons of unfinished drafts precede this, though. My first full draft is always close to being publishable, because I've been working on it for so long.	Between fifteen and twenty.	Two to three years.
Kody Keplinger	Anywhere from one month to one year. Depends on the book.	Between three and five.	From starting the first draft to finishing all revisions, it takes me between one and two years.
Marissa Meyer	Between four to eight weeks, usually.	Four to five.	Six months to a year.
Alex London	A few months.	Around five or six.	It depends on the book! Six months to a year?
Sarah Rees Brennan	A month or three years, given my fastest and longest times.	Three or four. Once, eleven, but please, God, let that never happen again.	Usually eight months. Once, four years, but please, God, let that never happen again.
Jesse Andrews	Six months to a year.	Five or so.	One to two years.
Alan Gratz	Three months.	Six.	A year and three months.
Soman Chainani	My first draft is my final draft because I edit as I go along—fourteen months.	Thirty to thirty-five, along the way.	A little over a year.

Holly Black	Six months.	I rewrite as I go, a lot.	Six to eight months.
Kiersten White	Anywhere from six days to eighteen months.	Seven.	One year.
Maggie Stiefvater	The quickest I've ever written a first draft is ninety days–that was *The Scorpio Races*, and I'm sure it was so fast because it was both a book of my absolute heart and also because it had a fairly straightforward sports plot at its core. The longest I've ever taken on just a first draft was *All the Crooked Saints*, which was nearly a year of solid drafting.	Three? Four? Seven? I don't usually make it all the way through the draft before I need to go back and adjust, so it's hard for me to think of them in terms of drafts.	Somehow, I usually have one come out once a year or so, so I guess it must be less than that.
Zoraida Córdova	One to three months.	Four.	A year.
Gordon Korman	Four to six months.	Two.	Eighteen to twenty-four months, planning to pub date.
Rachel Caine	Three months at most.	Two to three.	Five to six months at most.

Dhonielle Clayton	Six to eight months.	Five.	A year.
Eliot Schrefer	Three to four months.	Ten.	A year.
Z Brewer	About four to five months.	Usually three or four.	About nine months.

CHAPTER 9
EDITING YOUR BOOK

If/when I've written the first draft of a novel and want to get it published, what should I do? Do I look around for publishers or write a second draft? Please help.

A lot of answers in this book will basically boil down to "it depends." Not this one. No matter who you ask, the answer to this question will always be: "Do a second draft."

Heck, to be honest, you'll probably want to do a third draft, too. And a fourth. And maybe a fifth. And then you'll probably want to set that entire project aside and work on something totally different for a while. Because I don't know anyone—not a soul—who published the first thing they ever wrote. And I definitely don't know anyone who's broken into this business with a first draft.

Writing is rewriting. Period. And I know that's not what most people want to hear. When I do school visits, aspiring writers are often looking for a magic number—like I can guarantee that their book will work after draft three or seven. Or twenty.

And then it occurred to me . . .

New writers look at their books and ask, "How many drafts do I *have* to do?"

Experienced writers look at their books and ask, "How many drafts do I *get* to do?"

There. That right there is the difference.

A second draft isn't a chore; it's an opportunity. A third draft isn't a punishment; it's a luxury.

Since I've been doing this professionally, I've heard a lot more published, successful authors complain about not having time to do another draft than I've heard complain about needing to do one.

So take all the time—and the drafts—you need to get your book right. Set aside the worry and the pressure of trying to get it right the first time.

When you're first starting out, you get as many shots as you need to sink that ball from half-court. If it takes twenty-five shots, that's fine.

Take as many as you need. Take as much time as you need. The most important thing is that you just keep shooting.

When we finish the rough draft, staring at the daunting pile of words, what is the first thing we should do to begin editing?

Honestly, everyone who finishes a first draft should do one thing first: Celebrate! Give yourself a big pat on the back because that's extremely rare and incredibly awesome. You've officially moved from the huge group of *talkers* to the much more exclusive group of *writers*. Go, you!

Of course, every author is different, but for me, the first step is usually to take a little break from the book, just to clear my head and rest.

I'm very serious about this. I've had the privilege of working with some of the best editors in the business, but I firmly believe that *time* is the greatest editor of all.

Think about it like this: Have you ever had something cooking in your house? A roast in the Crock-Pot? Maybe some fresh bread in the oven? Well, if you're around it all day, you kind of get immune to the smell. But then maybe you go out for a little while, and when you get back, the aroma just hits you! You couldn't smell it before because you were so close to it—you had to take a step away.

Writing is like that. You're right there, in the thick of it, and you can lose all perspective. So that's why I say that, when possible, the first step in any editorial process should be setting the project aside for at least a week. (A month is better. Six months would be better still.) Then come back to it with fresh eyes, and you'll be amazed how different it looks.

Then you may want to block off as much time as you can and try to read the whole manuscript straight through. Don't worry about making big edits now. You're just trying to see what's on the page and—more importantly—what's *not* on the page.

Your next step is probably going to depend on what your process is.

Did you hammer out a first draft really quickly? Then you might be looking at a manuscript full of typos and incomplete sentences, characters whose names change halfway through, a plot that might go all over the place, and a villain that doesn't really work.

If this is your process (and I can speak from experience, since that's my process), then I think your first step will be to pick your battles. What are the big things that you know don't work? And what are the little (but persistent) things that have been nagging at you all along?

What does your gut tell you isn't quite working? There may be parts of your book that aren't technically wrong but are just . . . off somehow. Like having sand in your shoe. It doesn't hurt. But it's annoying and doesn't feel right.

Those gut-level things will probably be what you want to focus on in draft number two.

Now, a lot of people will look at a manuscript full of typos and think: There! Those are the things I have to fix! And those things do need fixing, but *there's a difference between proofreading and editing*.

A big one.

When they're starting out, I think a lot of writers think that their job in draft two will be to catch all the typos and correct all the spelling errors. That stuff is important—don't get me wrong. But that stuff isn't the hard stuff. And you're not going to make it big in this business by just doing the easy parts.

Make no mistake about it: Revising is a very hard part.

But how do you do it? Like . . . where do you even begin?

Well, some authors will go to the first page of their novels and start rewriting with word one. Some writers will jump from scene to scene, rewriting things in an order that feels right to them. Some writers will print out their manuscripts and pull out their highlighters and their Post-it notes, and start marking scenes where there isn't enough conflict or highlighting places where the hero and heroine need to have more tension. Some writers will start with a blank page and just start typing.

In the end, it doesn't matter exactly how you do it.

It just matters that you do it.

Personally, I'll set the book aside for as long as I can in order to get a little perspective. Then, when it's time for me to start rewriting, I'll have a big checklist in my office. A kind of to-do list of the things that my gut (and my editor) have told me need work. These will be things like *Make the friendship more believable; add more villain backstory; tighten up the beginning; flesh out the ending* . . . and on and on.

So very big-picture things. Broad things. Things that probably can't be accomplished by tweaking just a line or two of dialogue.

That's how I get started. With the big stuff.

What is your editing process?

Once I get rolling on my rewrite and have a to-do list of all the big-picture items that need work, I'll go to page one and get started.

Always page one.

Some people might decide to fix the villain backstory first, and they'll leapfrog through the book, going to the places where those changes need to take place. They'll do that for everything on their list, marking them off one by one. But I can't do that, for some reason. I have to go to the beginning and address everything kind of all at once.

As I make my way through the book, I'll keep all of those things in mind, adding or deleting or changing as I go. As soon as I've achieved one, I'll mark it off the list, and I'll keep going straight through, chronologically, start to finish.

Some things can be marked off after a few scenes. Some things may still be on the board when I start draft three. Or four.

Eventually, I'll start focusing on smaller and smaller things. By draft three, I'm starting to get more worried about individual scenes or lines. By draft four, I'm worried about words. By the end, I'm worried about commas.

So that's my editing process—kind of like a funnel. Big at the top but getting smaller and smaller until I'm paying attention to even the tiniest details.

DEAR CHRISTINA DIAZ GONZALEZ,
How do you revise/rewrite?

Every day, before I begin writing, I read a few pages of what I wrote beforehand. I will spend some time revising/ rewriting those pages to get me back into the mind frame I had the day before. Once I am done writing the whole book, I go back and tackle revisions as if I was a reader . . . figuring out where the writer went wrong and how the story could have been better.

When do you decide to rewrite? After each chapter? Once you realize what you're doing isn't working? Or after the entire first draft is done?

This is going to depend entirely on your process.

Some authors rewrite as they go. They'll sit down every day and read/rewrite what they wrote the day before. Maybe they'll start reading from the beginning and only have time to work on a paragraph or two. Maybe they'll rewrite every paragraph as they write it.

That's their process.

My process is to get everything down and then get to the end. After that I'll take a break, go for a swim, see a movie. And then I'll go back to chapter 1 and start over again.

That's my process for a number of reasons. First, I tend to hyper-focus sometimes, and especially early in my career, I'd get fixated on a paragraph or a line and never move forward. There's not a doubt in my mind that I would have never finished a book if I was still trying to rewrite as I go.

Another reason is that, as my career has evolved, my books have become a lot more intricately plotted, so I really need to know what plot elements and twists and characters I'm going to need to pull that thing off. I need to know where I'm going, and the only way to know is to get there.

But again, that's just my process.

The key question is, what is *your* process going to be? You don't have to decide right now. Much like the wand chooses the wizard, the process chooses the writer.

DEAR HOLLY BLACK,
How do you revise/rewrite?

For years, I've been revising as I went along. I would write a chapter and then rewrite it and sometimes even rewrite it again before proceeding on. This was due to feeling as though my plotting was dependent on extrapolating on what came before and that until one chapter was exactly right, I couldn't figure out what came next. Right now, I seem to have finally got some traction with fast drafting, basically by deciding that if I need to write something wrong before I can write it correctly, then I ought to at least write it quickly.

However, even when I was revising many times during the

writing process, I still revised again once the book was done. Then I print out my novel and go at it with sticky notes, high-lighters, and colored pens. I then set a goal of chapters per day (or days per chapter, depending on the book) and go at it. I also read the book out loud, often to my long-suffering spouse.

When rewriting, should I open a new doc and start from scratch, or would it be better to copy and paste, then perform surgery on the project? Are there advantages or disadvantages to one over the other?

I'm so glad you asked this question! I can see where this would be confusing when you're starting out. Unfortunately the answer is, once again, "it depends." But I'll share my system with you. Maybe it will help you to figure out what your system should be.

I always have a folder on my computer where I store all the drafts of each book. Obviously, I'll start out with a first draft. And I'll give that file a name that includes three important pieces of information:

—What book it is (usually a short nickname like *Alaska* or *Embassy 3* or something to help me quickly identify the book itself).

—What draft it is. *Draft 1.*

—What date I started that file.

So the file for this book is named *Dear Ally Draft 1 May 1, 2017.*

That may seem like overkill, but after a few years (and many, many drafts), I've learned that it helps to have as much information right up front as possible.

Then, when it comes time to do my second draft, I'll just save the first draft file with a new name. So draft two will become *Dear Ally Draft 2 August 1, 2017.*

With this system, draft one is still there if I need it—still safely saved on my computer as *Dear Ally Draft 1 May 1, 2017.* But the revision is also there as *Dear Ally Draft 2 August 1, 2017.*

Now, there may be some authors and some occasions where it's easiest to start each draft with a totally new, blank file. If you're going to have to do a massive rewrite, that may be best. It might be especially good if you're going to have to cut a lot of material. After all, cutting something you labored over is never fun. With a blank file, you don't have to actually cut anything—there could just be a lot of stuff you don't bring over.

Whatever you choose, just know there is no right or wrong answer and, eventually, you'll figure out your own system.

Oh, and I'll add that for every book I also maintain a "scraps" file, so I never truly delete anything. If there's a chunk of the book that has to go I'll simply cut it and paste it into the scraps file. That way, again, it's there if I need it. And psychologically, that's so much easier than deleting something forever.

DEAR JULIE MURPHY,
What's the best piece of editorial advice you've ever received?

I think in working with my editor I've learned how to let go of fear and just jump into edits feetfirst, but I've also learned that sometimes editing smart doesn't always mean editing big. Sometimes the edits that carry the most impact are small things that ripple out. Sometimes editing means going in and scrapping entire chapters and story lines, but sometimes it means carefully plucking away at a scene with tweezers until every sentence is working as hard as possible.

My word count is too long. How would you advise I cut it down?

Ooh. Cutting. Yes, I'm weird and kind of evil because cutting is my favorite part of the writing process.

The first thing you need to know is that there are two kinds of cuts:

—the kind you do with a chainsaw.

—the kind you do with a scalpel.

I usually like to do the chainsaw cuts first. This means that you're going to go through your manuscript and think about the *big* things that aren't working (or just aren't necessary).

Do you need the subplot with the best friend trying to get a part-time job? Do you need the part of the heroine's quest where she climbs a mountain for three chapters only to get there and not really learn anything and have nothing really change one way or another? Do you need the character of the snotty next-door neighbor?

You get the picture.

If you don't need it—if it doesn't show something about the character *OR* if it doesn't affect the character's overall goal—then maybe it should go.

After you've taken a chainsaw and cut out all the big things, then it's time to pick up your scalpel. In a way, this is more tedious work, but honestly, I kind of love it, because scalpel cuts can help you turn a good book into a great book. It's where you change all the things that the average person will never, ever see and yet they can tell, when you're finished, that the book is better.

It's when you try to say with six words what you were saying with ten.

It's when you look at a sentence and remember that you said something very similar ten pages ago, so this one is unnecessary.

It's when you notice that a scene has about three lines of dialogue too many, causing it to go on a little bit longer than it needs to.

You'd be so surprised how many extra lines and unnecessary words there are sometimes, and by trimming things up, you can really make a difference.

But . . . be careful. Some authors have very flowy or lavish voices, and all those "extra" words might be what makes their work pop.

Just know this: When I was working on *I'd Tell You I Love You, But Then I'd Have to Kill You*, I was tasked with rewriting the book so that a particular scene took place about thirty pages sooner. I didn't cut a single scene. I didn't cut a single character. I didn't cut anything that actually mattered, it turns out. And yet I managed to cut thirty pages out of the first hundred pages simply by looking at each and every sentence and making sure that not a single word was wasted.

Whether or not your book is technically "too long," keep a scalpel and a chainsaw handy. They're two really useful tools in making your book as good as it can possibly be.

How do you decide if scenes are necessary or unnecessary?

Once upon a time, there used to be a thing where car dealerships would run contests to give away a new car. To compete, people would have to go down to the dealership and put one hand on the car. That's it. Just put a hand on the car. And keep it there. The last person with a hand on the car won it. Simple as that.

Well, as time went on and people got hungry or tired or needed to go to the bathroom, they'd wander off and give up, but the person who stuck it out—the person who kept one hand on the car at all times—was the winner.

Your book should be like that.

Every book has one central story/conflict/plot. There may be subplots. There will no doubt be supporting characters. But every single thing in your book should somehow "touch" that central story/conflict/plot. If there's a scene that doesn't have a hand on the car in some way, then that's a scene that's got to go!

How do you pace your book properly without going too fast or too slow?

Pacing is something that's really important! But, like voice, it's one of those things that's also really hard to pinpoint. It's more of a you-know-it-when-you-see-it kind of thing.

But I can guarantee you this: It's almost impossible to get pacing right on the first try. Or even the second. In fact, pacing is something that's going to slowly evolve with each draft of your novel because, as you make changes, those changes are going speed your book up in some places and probably slow it down in others.

My favorite way to judge the pacing of my books is to step away from them for a few days and then sit down and read the book in one go—start to finish. If there are places where you start to get a little bored or start wanting to skim, then the pacing is slow there, and you need to either cut the scenes (a chainsaw edit) or tighten up the writing (a scalpel edit).

Another great test is to read your entire book out loud. Yep. Have a glass of water handy and make sure you have some time, but know that this is a technique a ton of authors swear by. (See David's answer below.)

The key here is to keep working and give yourself a break if you don't get it right the first time—very few of us do!

DEAR DAVID LEVITHAN,
How do you know what to cut?

I am a big advocate of reading your book in as many different ways as possible before finalizing it. Since I write on a computer, I'm used to reading and rereading drafts on a screen. So the first crucial test is to print it out and edit the printout, pen in hand—I always find things that way that I missed on the screen. Then I read the whole thing aloud. This is, I think, the best way to find boring and unnecessary parts—when you're reading three hundred pages out loud, you can definitely tell when it slows down or when you have two sentences in a row that say the same thing, because reading out loud forces you to come into contact with every single

One of my favorite parts of writing is dialogue. The only problem is that I feel at times my dialogue seems forced or unrealistic. Any tips on how to improve?

There's a knack to dialogue, I'm not going to lie. Some people will tell you to record and transcribe—or just think really, really hard—about how real people talk. And that's not bad advice. After all, what most new writers want is to write dialogue that sounds "realistic." But real people . . .

. . . start sentences without finishing them. . . . misstart and have to backtrack. . . . get off track and meander around, looking for a point.

If you truly wrote dialogue the way people actually talk, then readers would probably get confused and really frustrated!

So the key to writing fictional dialogue, in my opinion, is to write dialogue that sounds realistic (but isn't too realistic).

Some of the best lessons that I learned about writing dialogue came from the world of screenwriting. I mean, think about it: Dialogue really is a screenwriter's best friend. It's pretty much the only time an audience will hear or see the writer's actual words. So screenwriters don't mess around when it comes to dialogue.

One of my favorite screenwriting dialogue tips is to cover up or remove all the character names or attributions. If the line doesn't say

Charlie said, can you still tell that Charlie said it? Does Charlie sound different from the other people in the scene? Does it sound like Charlie? Feel like Charlie? If so, then you're doing at least one thing right.

Another tip is to use some of those false starts and meandering sentences. It's a great idea to include some of the "bad" aspects of realistic dialogue—just don't do it too much. It's like salt. You want enough to add flavor but not so much that you make it inedible.

Finally, my advice would be to read as many screenplays as you can get your hands on. Sometimes libraries will have them (especially at universities or colleges that teach screenwriting courses). Every year about Oscar time, some of the studios will put their "best screenplay" contenders up on their websites for people to read. Sometimes you can even buy screenplays from online bookstores.

And of course, you should be reading lots of books with great dialogue. But remember, your job here isn't to read as a reader; it's to read as a *writer*. Highlight good lines and great scenes. Make notes about all the little clues that might be contained in a line of dialogue. And pay careful attention to the things that *aren't* said.

All the early chapters of *Not If I Save You First* open with a letter from Maddie to Logan, her best friend. But when we see Maddie six years after moving away, her father asks her, "Do you have any letters for me to take on my next run?"

"Did you *bring* me any letters?" Maddie asks him.

Her dad just shakes his head.

"Then that's your answer."

In that exchange, we learn that Maddie must have written Logan letters for a long time. We learn that Maddie isn't writing to him anymore. We can see—just from this short exchange—that Maddie's attitude toward Logan (and the letters) is deeply and fundamentally changed. As the author, I didn't have to spell that out. Instead, I have to trust that my reader is savvy enough to pick up on the clues.

If you can do that, then you don't need two characters to have a long conversation about how they're half siblings. You can just have one of them ask, "My dad or your dad?" Trust in your reader to be smart enough to read between the lines.

Finally, the most important thing to remember for dialogue is this: Your characters aren't speaking to us. Nope. They should be speaking to *each other*. Which means they should never say, "Hello, Cindy, it's so good to see you again, since we are cousins who only ever get together on the Fourth of July because our mothers had a huge argument five years ago and our families became estranged."

No. Just no.

Cindy already knows all that. The other characters know that, too. Which makes that dialogue lazy (and kind of stupid).

Instead, you might try something like this:

"Hey, Cindy."

"Hey, cuz."

"Long time."

"Funny. Fourth of July is the same day as last year."

"So is your mom . . ."

"Still mad at your mom? What do you think?"

"Yeah. Mine, too."

If you struggle with dialogue, don't worry. This is definitely something that takes a lot of time and practice and patience.

Do I need a professional editor, or is it okay if my mom's friend edits my book?

Your book needs to be as good as you can possibly make it. Which means, hopefully, seeing the things about your book that aren't quite working and then fixing them.

So how do you see those things? Well, maybe by talking to your mom's friend or maybe by joining a critique group at your local community college or asking a (very honest) teacher or family member or friend for their opinions.

When I was starting out, I lived in a small town that had a great library with a small book club that met once a month. I asked the librarian if the group would mind reading my book one month and letting me come hear them discuss it. I made six copies of the manuscript and brought six red pens and instructed everyone not to be afraid to use them. That experience was incredibly valuable.

Not because I took everything they said and did exactly that, but because (a) rejection and criticism are constant in this business and you need to get used to it, and (b) I got to hear what was working about the story and some opinions about what wasn't working.

That's something I want to make sure you all know: that the world is full of people who are going to try to tell you how to write your book. Listen to them. Thank them. Consider them and the feedback they give, but at the end of the day, follow your gut and write your book.

Very few people start off working with professional editors or published authors as critique partners. Most of us start off getting feedback from friends and family. And, ultimately, it doesn't matter who is giving you notes on your book. What counts is knowing which notes to use and which notes to ignore and then figuring out a way for your book to be as good as it can possibly be.

How do you know when to just step back and NOT try to rewrite that same sentence for the eighth time because the phrasing doesn't feel EXACTLY right?

This is a really hard thing to do sometimes. But you're right; sometimes this is exactly what's needed! Sometimes the best work we can do is . . . to not work at all. Or to work on something else.

I know it sounds counterintuitive, but I've found that to be really true.

Also, sometimes when there's a line I'm never really happy with, that's a sign that the line shouldn't be in there at all. So I don't fix it. I cut it.

One of the hardest things in this business is perspective. When is something truly terrible? And when do you just have a bad case of The Crazies? Honestly, in that situation, only time will tell.

So take a walk. Take a nap. Go to the movies or see if one of your friends wants to hang out. When you get out of your own head, you're able to get out of your own way. So step back from things for a few hours or even a few days.

When you finally come back to it, I bet you'll have a much better idea what you need to do.

My best friend and I both like to write and I was wondering if you have any advice on how you should go about co-writing a novel?

Since I haven't written a book with another writer, I'm going to pass this question along to three of my friends—Holly Black and Cassandra

Clare, who write the Magisterium series together, and David Levithan, who edits Magisterium and has collaborated with a number of people on YA novels, including Rachel Cohn, John Green, Nina LaCour, and Andrea Cremer.

DEAR HOLLY BLACK AND CASSANDRA CLARE,
Do you have any advice for friends who might be interested in writing a book together?

HOLLY ANSWERS:

I think the best thing about collaboration is that you come up with things together that you never would have come up with alone. People are worried about disagreements, but it's from the disagreements that the really good stuff comes. That's where the other person is going to push you out of your comfort zone and into the challenging but fun part of making up something really new.

That said, to me it's really important to have solo work going on at the same time so that you have a space where you can make all the decisions and more easily conceptualize your shared work as *shared*.

CASSIE ANSWERS:

Set some ground rules when you start about how you are going to resolve any disagreements. If you really want a plot to go one way and your collaborator wants it to go another way, you should sit down and try to figure out a third way because if you're not fighting for your idea, it's easier to come up with something that you both really like.

There's something challenging about giving up complete ownership of something in the service of creating something different and special. Make sure to talk about scenes or pieces of plot you're especially excited about so that, if possible, the person most excited about a particular scene gets to write it. You'll also wind up talking through different life experiences that inform character. Blending them creates characters probably neither of you would have come up with on your own, which means you're getting to write something, and write about people, you wouldn't normally get to do.

If you're like me, you'll travel to faraway lands so your co-writer will be forced to chase you around the globe. Fun vacation time!

DEAR DAVID LEVITHAN,
Do you have any advice for friends who might be interested in writing a book together?

I am always amazed at how Holly and Cassie write Magisterium—they will plot it out together, write in the same room together, even finish each other's sentences. That's one kind of collaboration.

For my collaborations, we always alternate chapters and

never plot things out ahead of time. The fun of the writing is discovering what happens by seeing what your co-author does next. So for *Nick & Norah's Infinite Playlist*, Rachel came up with the premise—two kids from New Jersey, named Nick and Norah, in New York City for a night. That's all we knew about the story going into it. Then I wrote the first chapter and emailed it to her. We hadn't even talked about the fact that we weren't going to talk about it—but lo and behold, a day or two later, chapter 2 was waiting in my inbox. So I wrote chapter 3 and sent it to her. And so on. We've done it this way for five books now, and it's always an adventure. We get to control our own chapters, even if we're not controlling the overall story—I like that balance a lot.

How do you know when a book is finished? Is there a way to tell the right time to stop a book?

Leonardo da Vinci once said, "Art is never finished, only abandoned."

Most writers get this. I mean *really* get this. Because to be honest, I don't think I've ever really finished a book. It's more like my editor ripped it out of my hands because it was either that or cancel the contract, and a girl's got to eat. There's not a single book with my name on the cover that I wouldn't LOVE to go back and edit right now if they'd let me.

I think that's just kind of how a lot of writers are wired. I'm genetically prone to only seeing the mistakes.

Which can be a good thing. Writers need to be critical of their work. We need to always be striving to be better.

But it can also be a bad thing because, frankly, sometimes we try to fix things that aren't broken and we end up making a great big mess.

Now, of course, I have writer friends who I know and trust. I have an editor who wouldn't let me make a fool of myself. But I didn't always have those people in my life! So what did I have when I was working on those screenplays that never went anywhere and the first book I ever queried agents for?

Well, I still had friends. They weren't professional writers, but they were readers. And they were people who I knew well enough to know when they really liked something and when they just said they liked it.

I had resources like my local librarian and the book club members who generously agreed to read my book when it was just a pile of pages.

I also had contests that I found online and entered. In fact, I'm where I am today because one time I won a contest and there was one line on the critique sheet: *Why hasn't this been published?*

That's when I started querying agents.

That's when I knew it was time to take the next step.

Finally, I had my gut—and you have yours, too! If you're writing a lot. If you're reading a lot. If you're watching a lot of TV and movies, and thinking about all of these things—not as a fan, but as a *writer*—then your gut might be the best resource there is.

Every path to success is different—there is no yellow brick road. Maybe you have friends you can ask to read your manuscript. Maybe you have a teacher or librarian who might be able to give you feedback. Maybe you can find a contest or two to enter and see what some judges have to say. And if all else fails, you have your gut. And you have time.

Put that manuscript in a drawer for six months. If you read it with fresh eyes and your gut says it's pretty darn good, then it probably is.

DEAR MELISSA DE LA CRUZ,

You astound me, lady. I don't know anyone who publishes faster than you, so on behalf of every one of our mutual friends, I have to ask, how have you written so many books in such little time?

I think the key to my success and my process is I am a very fast but also very clean writer. I can procrastinate until the cows come home, but I know I can write 40,000 words in two weeks if I have to. This means that mostly it takes me three to six months to write the first 20-40,000 words, but when I'm two weeks to deadline, I know I can pull it out and crank it out. The more pressed I am to deadline, the smarter I am, the faster I write, and the book takes shape during those last two weeks. It's like I'm a different writer at the end. It's like running a marathon and having the endurance and speed at the end. I also revise and polish as I write, so my work is very clean. I don't really do a messy first draft. My first drafts are like third drafts.

Of course, every writer is going to be different, but for me, the editing process is where my books are really made. Sometimes that means chainsaw edits where I have to get rid of whole subplots or change entire endings. Sometimes it means looking at a fifteen-page chapter and using my scalpel to get it down to twelve. Sometimes it means writing extremely carefully and rereading every day so that when you reach The End, parts of your book have already been rewritten dozens of times.

But no matter what your editorial process might be, know this: It matters. It will show in the finished book, and it's what you're signing up for if you really want a career in this business.

I say it all the time: I'm an okay writer, but I'm a phenomenal rewriter. It might be hard at first to see what needs to change, so put that book in a drawer and write something else. When you look at it again in a few months, the things that aren't quite working will be far easier to spot.

I promise.

CHAPTER 10
BEATING YOUR WRITER'S BLOCK

How do you deal with writer's block?

The weirdest part about writer's block is that I never hear writers use that phrase.

Sure, strangers on airplanes talk about it. People at family reunions want to know if I've got it. "But don't you ever get writer's block?" is a question I've answered about a million times. "What do you do when you get writer's block" is one I've answered about a million more.

I've even heard some really amazing authors say that there is no such thing as writer's block—that it's a made-up concept some people use to try to glamorize not wanting to work some days. And I don't think that's entirely wrong.

After all, a lot of people don't understand that words don't magically appear in their heads. Frankly, I think most people have watched too many movies where someone writes the Great American Novel in a three-minute montage that consists of them typing furiously and throwing pieces of paper at a trash can, all while wearing an assortment of cozy sweaters.

Trust me, real writing isn't like that.

So I never really believed that writer's block was real. I thought it was a kind of urban legend until . . .

Cross My Heart and Hope to Spy happened.

So, as I say in the Writing Your Series section, sequels are hard. *Cross My Heart and Hope to Spy* was especially brutal for many reasons. I still had my day job. I had a lot of pressure on me because book one in that series, *I'd Tell You I Love You, But Then I'd Have to Kill You*, had come out and was doing exceptionally well.

But the biggest problem, it turned out, was that I started *Cross My Heart and Hope to Spy* with a premise and not a plot. So while I knew what the book would, generally, be about (boys coming to the girls' school), I didn't know what would actually . . . happen.

Okay. Boys show up at the girls' school! And then what?

My character didn't have a goal.

Which meant my story didn't have enough conflict.

Which meant I didn't have enough gas in the tank.

I'm not exaggerating when I say that writing that book almost killed me, but I did learn a lot during that process. Not the least of which was that the writer's block nonwriters talk about isn't really true, but writer's block itself *is* very much real.

But as Cassandra Clare likes to say, "Writer's block is never the problem. Writer's block is the *symptom*."

My experience taught me that sometimes I can't write because there's something wrong with the story. And sometimes I can't write because there's something wrong with me.

Which is why I believe there are three overall types of "writer's block."

TYPE ONE WRITER'S BLOCK is where you just don't want to write. Which happens. To everyone. All. The. Time.

You think you should write . . . but your heart isn't in it. Maybe you're just tired. Maybe your favorite show just came to Netflix and you want to binge a whole season. Maybe all your friends are posting pictures of whatever awesome thing they're doing without you.

In other words, there are other things your writing mind wants to be doing. You're not even trying.

The good news is that there are two ways to tackle this kind of writer's block. Either you stick yourself in a chair and force yourself to do it—shut down the distractions for an hour, and see what happens.

Or you take the day off. Or the weekend. You scratch whatever itch you've got, and then you get back to work.

TYPE TWO WRITER'S BLOCK is similar to Type One but far more serious. It's where you want to write, but you just can't put yourself in the chair, or if you do, that act alone uses up all your reserves.

In this case, your writer's block might be a symptom of depression or anxiety. Maybe you're really sick. Maybe you're mentally or physically exhausted. But for whatever reason, your well is just dry and you need to take a little while to refill it.

Maybe that means curling up on the couch and reading a billion books. Maybe it means spending some time with friends. It absolutely means getting some professional help if the problem persists.

Because, of course, this is more than writer's block. It's more like "life block," and no one expects you to handle it alone.

In these cases, I think the number one thing you can do is to just be kind to yourself. This might be the time to get on Twitter and mute that person who writes 6,000 words a day. Maybe you just manage to muster 100 words some days and that's a struggle, so feel free to stop the comparison game. Don't fall prey to the you-just-have-to-suck-it-up trap. Get some help and try to think about writing as the thing you do for fun. Because at the end of the day, if writing isn't something that's making our lives better, then why are we even doing it?

TYPE THREE WRITER'S BLOCK is the one that I, personally, struggle with the most.

With Type Three Writer's Block, you're showing up. You're putting your rear in a chair and your fingers on the keys. You're picking up the pen. And nothing's happening.

Or things are happening, but they feel like the wrong things.

With Types One and Two, there's something wrong with you. With Type Three, there's something wrong with your *book*.

And you can't figure out what it is, so you stare at a blank page for hours. You write and delete the same chapters a dozen times.

You cry.

Whereas Type One Writer's Block means you need to suck it up and go to work, with Type Three, you *are* working, but something about your book just feels off.

I think this is a lot like playing a sport. Have you ever worked out and it was really hard? Have your muscles ever ached? Have you ever been out of breath?

Now, have you ever gotten injured? Have you pulled a muscle or twisted an ankle or done something that your body really wasn't supposed to do?

Both things hurt, right? But one kind of pain (the you're-working-out-and-it's-tough pain) is what you're supposed to feel and you have to push through it. The other kind of pain is the kind that tells you something is seriously wrong and you need to stop what you're doing right now.

All athletes learn the difference between those two types of pain. And writers have to learn the difference between these two types of blocks.

Type Three Writer's Block is that second type of pain. It's the kind of hurt that tells you something in your story is broken.

So, yeah. I now believe in writer's block. But I also believe that it's just part of being a writer. It's never, ever glamorous. And it should never be an excuse. And in the end, you always have to keep writing.

DEAR ALEX LONDON,
What's the hardest part about writing a book?

For me, it is finding the courage to keep writing when the voice of doubt creeps in and starts whispering in my ear that I'm no good, that my ideas are trite, that my talent is lacking, and that no one cares. I have to learn to ignore that voice and keep writing through it, to trust the work and my vision and know that I can fix and revise what I write, but first I have to write it. It's hard, but the only way to write a good book is to slog through writing a bad one first. I have to remember with each book that the worst writing I ever do is better than the best writing I never do and then I just keep going.

How do you find the motivation to write when you're not feeling in the mood for it?

This is pretty textbook Type One Writer's Block. And some of that is to be expected. After all, a book can't be written in a day. Or even a week. If you work on something—anything—for a long period of time, you're going to get a little tired of it eventually. And some of that is okay.

So on the days you just aren't in the mood for it, I guess you have to ask yourself why. Are you sick? Are you exhausted? Is this your body's way of telling you that you need to take a break and take care of yourself?

Or are you just . . . tired of writing?

It's okay to take some breaks—go see some movies, read some books, hang out with your friends. Maybe set your book aside for a long weekend and play around with something new? (Just don't forget to come back to your original project come Monday!)

I find that I write so much better if I take an "official" day off and then tell myself that tomorrow I have to go back to work. But the key there is simple:

Tomorrow you have to go back to work.

If you rest and relax and refuel and you still don't want to write, then I think you might need some deadlines—they're essential for me! You may not have an agent or an editor waiting for your book, but I bet you can make a deal with one of your friends or teachers. Make a bet with yourself.

At some point, every writer faces a blank page and the knowledge that this is optional. It's not for a grade. It's not for a paycheck (yet). It's something that we do, first and foremost, for ourselves. And we all have to ask ourselves, what is more important, having a finished book someday or spending the next three hours on the internet? Which would I rather be, someone who has finished my first book or someone who binge-watched an entire season of television this weekend?

And if it doesn't happen right now? If you don't have a finished novel (or ten) before you graduate from high school . . . well, that's okay. Writing should be fun. It should be something that enriches your life—not something that defines your life—and if it takes you a few years to find that balance, then there is no shame in that.

Just keep writing.

You'll find your stride eventually.

DEAR DANIEL JOSÉ OLDER,
What do you do when the writing isn't going well?

Step away! The age-old writing advice is always BUTT IN CHAIR, but the truth is, most writing gets done when you're anywhere but in the chair! Why? Because staring at an empty screen with the blinking thing blinking at you is stressful! And stress is bad for creativity. But being out and about in the world—walking around or working out or sitting somewhere quietly—can often open up all kinds of imaginative doors that stress closes. That doesn't mean you never write, because of course, writing does take many, many hours of actually sitting in front of the computer or open notebook, clacking or scribbling away. But it's important to take breaks and it's important to allow yourself time to dream and let your mind wander as well. For me—I'll go to the gym or take a long meandering walk if I'm stuck, and listen to some really good music, and that does the trick!

What do you do when you get writer's block? I've heard some people plan out the entire story beforehand to avoid such issues, but I prefer to just start writing. I often know that I want to get to point B but I don't know how to traverse the space between A and B.

To me, this is a textbook case of Type Three Writer's Block. When you want to write—when you know you *need* to write—and you're trying. You really are. But you don't know quite *what* to write. Or everything you write just seems a little bit off.

I know this feeling.

I am the queen of this feeling.

Sometimes this happens because you genuinely don't know what to write next. Maybe you've written your character into a corner and you don't know how to get her out. (Which is actually a good thing! A book where the characters never get into trouble is a very boring book.)

Sometimes this happens because you have too many ideas for what happens next. Maybe you have a list of ten possible ways that your hero can find out his mentor is the one who is trying to kill him, and you can't quite decide which one works the best.

Whatever the case, in many ways, the solution for Type Three Writer's Block is the exact opposite of what you should do for Type One.

For Type One, the solution is, ultimately, to duct-tape yourself to a chair and not get up until you've met your goal.

For Type Three, you need to get out of that chair! You need to take a walk or go for a swim. You need to take a nap or a shower. (Seriously. I know so many authors who figure out their books in the shower.)

A lot of people think that, when the writing isn't going well, they just need to work harder. In fact, a lot of times, that just means you need to work differently. Or, honestly, to take a break.

Researchers have learned that there's actually a scientific reason why we tend to think of things after we stop trying to remember them. Or why we can go to sleep worried about how to get a character out of a jam and then wake up with the perfect solution right there in front of us. Turns out our brains have two different networks in them. One focuses on creative thinking (the awesome ideas). One focuses on "effortful thinking" (getting stuff done). And we can only really use one network at a time. So while we're in the trenches, focusing on our daily goals, the idea pathway is closed off.

That's why the good ideas usually come when you step away from the computer and put down the notebook—you're turning off the let's-go-to-work part of your brain and turning on the let's-come-up-with-an-idea part of your brain.

And this type of writer's block needs the idea part.

So give it some room to work.

> ### DEAR DAVID LEVITHAN,
> What's the best advice you've heard about getting over writer's block?
>
> Here are a variety of strategies I've heard. Any of them could work for you.
>
> 1. Take a break and come back to it. Taking a walk or taking a shower seem to be the two leading suggestions for letting your mind take some time off.

2. Talk it over with someone. It doesn't have to be another writer. Talking about something uses a different part of the brain than writing it, and sometimes explaining out loud what needs to happen next unlocks the solution of what has to happen.

3. If you don't know what happens next, list all the possible next steps.

4. Ask your character what you should do next. It's strange how often they'll have an answer.

5. Work on something else. If you're not excited by the thing you're working on, find the thing that will make you excited about writing again and dive into it. That may pull you out of the writing slump.

6. Back up a little, then restart. If you're stuck midway through chapter 7, open a new document with just chapter 7. Then delete everything but the opening line and start writing it again. See if it leads you somewhere else.

7. Make the wrong choice. If the idea you have for what comes next sucks, write it anyway. It may never be used, but in seeing why it's wrong, you might discover the right course.

8. Do what it takes to get to your ending. I was co-writing a book and didn't feel my character was really falling in love with my co-author's character the way he should have been. I complained to my co-author about it, and she said, "Well, then write the thing that will make him fall for her." And that was exactly the direction I needed, to get back on course by steering the story in that direction in whatever way worked.

I always get super involved at the beginning of a writing project, but as time goes on, the story gets flat and I find myself disinterested. How do you suggest keeping your story engaging?

The only thing harder than beginnings (and endings) are middles.

Think about it this way: Writing a book is kind of like going on a really long airplane ride. When you first get on the plane, you might be super happy about going to Australia or Japan or wherever. You're going on an adventure! And you just can't wait; you're so excited.

Well, that excitement might last for a few hours, but about the time your back starts to hurt and you can't sleep and the person next to you is snoring and you're all out of snacks, then it's not nearly as much fun.

After a few hours more, you might start thinking that this was the worst idea ever.

But here's the difference: You can't get out of a plane mid-flight, but you can stop working on your novel mid-draft. And a lot of people do—which is a mistake, because in a few hours, you might look out the window to see the Alps! Or some gorgeous island or the Great Wall of China! In a few hours more, you can actually see the reason you got on the plane to begin with, and then all your discomfort will be very much worth it.

Middles are like that. It's easy to get bogged down with all the stuff that's not going well. It's easy to get bored or tired. It's easy to start thinking that you're doing all this hard work for nothing and you might as well give up. But that would be a mistake. Don't think that because the middle of your book is harder to write than the beginning that you're doing something wrong. It's like that for everyone.

Just remember that your story should be constantly changing. Never think of the middle as the place where you have to tread water. The middle should advance the plot. Your character should be on their quest, working toward their goal. They should be having ups and downs, and most of all, they should be facing obstacles.

Conflict is gas in the tank.

And if you're disinterested, ask yourself why. Think about what could happen in the story that would make it more interesting to you. Odds are good that will make it more interesting to readers as well.

Keep the tank full of conflict, and I have no doubt that you can make it to The End.

And when you finish your big, long flight, I have no doubt that you'll be really glad you made the journey.

I've been a writer for as long as I can remember, but when I look at my writing compared to others' around me, I just feel so insecure. I just don't think I have the creativity or discipline to become an author, but it's always been a dream of mine. Any advice on how to handle that?

I've been really, really lucky in my career, because I've gotten to know some amazing writers. We're all really different, coming from different backgrounds with lots of different styles and voices, interests, and hobbies. But one thing we all have in common is that we all pretty much live in constant fear that someone is going to find out we're imposters.

"That *New York Times* bestseller I wrote? Oh, that was a fluke."

"That big, fancy award I won? Oh, yeah. I totally didn't deserve that."

Every writer I know has had moments of feeling like we just can't do it. We don't know how we did it before. We're pretty sure we can never do it again.

So take it from me—confidence doesn't write novels. Arrogance doesn't write novels. Egos don't write novels. Novels only get written when people spend hours and hours and hours . . . writing.

The next time you get the urge to compare your manuscript to a book you're reading, don't. If you're paralyzed from looking at the work of your friends or other aspiring authors online, stop.

In fact, I don't read as many YA novels as I used to because YA is just so good and, inevitably, I always end up in the fetal position on the floor, rocking back and forth, mumbling about how my book will never be as good as the book I just finished.

So now when I'm working on a book in one genre, I'll read books in a totally different genre. Now when I look back at my last book and compare it to my work in progress, I'll remind myself of what my mother told me in our kitchen all those years ago: You should never compare your first draft to someone else's finished draft. (Even if the book you want to compare your book against is your own.)

There's something my writing friends all say: Eyes on your own paper. There's no shortage of comparisons in this business and no shortage of ways for us to feel intimidated. Someone will always be selling better, winning more awards, writing faster. So the next time you start doubting yourself, remember the bestsellers and award winners and writers that you love are—right this moment—doubting themselves, too.

But in the *next* moment, they'll be writing.

DEAR JAY COLES,

When you're working on a novel, do you ever feel like giving up and starting something new? How do you know when to stick with it and what makes you keep going?

Oh, all the time. I'm always starting manuscripts and giving up halfway through or a couple of chapters in. There's just that feeling in my gut that something isn't working or it isn't that particular manuscript's time yet, so I know I'm meant to be working on something else. I have over forty started and half-written manuscripts that I may never again revisit. When I'm writing, I think I know to stick with a particular project/novel when the story clicks—I have a good sense of the characters and their agency and world, I have a good sense of where the story starts and maybe even the ending. Things fall into place. And something that's an especially helpful indicator is when you come back the next day to write and you're still thinking about the characters from the last writing day and you're excited. When that happens, I keep coming back because my heart, mind, and soul are now so invested.

How do you overcome the fear of letting other people read your work? Not just for feedback but friends and family, because what I choose to write about can be so personal?

The good news is that you don't have to show your work to anyone—ever—if you don't want to.

There are many advantages to having writing as a hobby/dream/career. It's relatively inexpensive. You can do it anywhere. You can do it anytime. But you can also do it in absolutely secrecy if that's what works for you. It's what worked for me! I wrote for years without telling a soul what I was doing, and that's what allowed me the freedom (and the confidence) to keep writing.

And your job is to do whatever it takes for you to keep writing, too. If you need to keep your work to yourself for a while, that's fine. If you decide to keep it private for forever, that's fine, too. What matters is that you keep writing and you keep writing for yourself, first and foremost.

It's hard thinking someone might laugh at you, or judge you, or mock you for something you've written. I still worry about it all the time! These feelings might get a little better as you get older, so keep in mind that you don't have to try to publish today or tomorrow or ever. You just have to write, and if and when you feel like sharing your work with the world, then that will be very exciting.

What's the best writing advice you ever got?	
Eliot Schrefer	Some friends will tell you that everything you write is great. Still send your manuscripts to them. Softball cheerleading is very useful!

How do you find inspiration to keep writing a book? I'll get a great idea for a new book and abandon the other one to work on the new one, but none of them have maxed 20,000 words. I'll try going back to the other ones but I just give up. What should I do?

It sounds to me like you have a bad case of the New Shinies!

Now, this isn't a technical term, but it's what I call that feeling of being in the middle of a project you (used to) love, and then out of the blue you get a shiny new idea that looks so much funnier.

And more romantic.

And thrilling.

And mysterious.

And just . . . *better*.

Clearly, this new, shiny idea is bound to be better than that old idea you've been working on for months, right? Well . . . maybe. But maybe not.

All books get hard eventually, and if you give up and start a new project every time that happens, you will never have a finished book. And in my opinion, it's a lot more important that you get your book finished than you get your book perfect. Perfect you can't control. Perfect you can't always hit.

But finished? Finished is totally up to you, and you can do it. So start a file for this shiny idea. Jot down your thoughts. Make some notes. Capture what you know and why you're excited. But don't let it distract you for too long.

In the meantime, maybe try setting yourself some goals for your existing project. (When you hit 10,000 words, you can see that movie you've been waiting for!) Maybe experiment with your process and see if writing out of order might help? Maybe show what you have so far to your most supportive friend and get some cheerleading.

But whatever you do, just keep writing.

Always keep writing.

Alex London	Finish what you start. There is magic in getting to the end of a project. Sometimes that's the only vantage point to see the whole landscape of what you've created. And then the real work of revision can begin.

I can't guarantee much about this business, but I can promise you this: There will come a time when your book stops being fun and starts feeling like work. Then it will stop feeling like work and start feeling like Mount Everest and you can't help but wonder why you ever thought it was a good idea to climb it.

That's going to happen. How do I know? Because it has happened to every single author I have ever known. And it will happen to you.

So when that happens, don't get down. Just stop and think and remember that writer's block isn't a problem, it's a symptom.

ARE YOU TIRED AND JUST NEED TO RECHARGE YOUR BATTERIES?

Then do that. That's okay. Nobody works all the time. It's not healthy. I always write way more efficiently after taking a day off than I would have written slogging through a day I just didn't have it in me. And furthermore, I'm a big believer that writers write better when they have experiences to draw from. So don't forget to experience. Don't forget to live!

ARE YOU STRUGGLING WITH OTHER LIFE THINGS AND HAVING TROUBLE FOCUSING IN GENERAL?

Then be kind to yourself and remember that writing isn't the most important thing in the world. It's not even in the top ten. And if writing becomes the thing that makes you feel worse, then taking a little hiatus isn't a bad thing. Just focus on getting better.

ARE YOU EAGER TO WORK, BUT THE WORK ITSELF JUST FEELS . . . WRONG?

Then stop working. I know that sounds counterintuitive, but your creative brain needs a break. Not a long break. Not forever. But you do need to go for a walk or a swim. You need to see a movie or take a nap. You're not going to write through whatever's wrong. You've got to find a way to write around it, and you'll do that by stepping away for a few hours.

ARE YOU STANDING AT A CROSSROADS OF YOUR STORY, LOOKING AT A DOZEN PATHS IT COULD TAKE AND FROZEN WITH INDECISION?

This one happens to me. A lot. Like . . . every few days. That's why I have notebooks and whiteboards and Post-it notes coming out my ears. Basically, I'll map out all the different possibilities. There will be flow-chart-looking things all over my house. And even then I pick the wrong route sometimes. And then I back up and try another path. I just have to accept the fact that mistakes are part of the journey and every one I make eventually leads me to The End.

DID YOU READ A SUPER-GREAT BOOK LAST NIGHT AND SO, TODAY, YOU CAN'T HELP LOOKING AT EVERY WORD YOU WRITE AND THINKING THAT THEY'LL NEVER BE GOOD ENOUGH?

Stop. You have no idea what that book looked like before it got published. And you really don't know how good (or horrendous) the author's early work was. Trust me. We all start out with dirty water.

DOES IT LOOK LIKE EVERYONE IS FINISHING BOOKS AND WINNING CONTESTS AND GETTING AGENTS BUT YOU?

Then eyes on your own paper! Several years ago a good friend of mine went on a big international book tour. She was posting the most glamorous photos, and I was so jealous. Then, when I saw her, I said something about how amazing her tour must have been. She turned to me—dead serious—and said, "Ally, Twitter lies." Turns out, she'd had food poisoning and jet lag and had been deathly ill and miserable the whole time.

So while it might look like everyone is having huge breakthroughs but you . . . well . . . Twitter lies.

DO YOU HAVE A SHINY NEW IDEA THAT'S BURNING A HOLE IN YOUR POCKET?

Then give yourself a day to write it down and put as much as you can on paper before you forget it. Just don't forget to go back to your "real" project. Otherwise, when this new, shiny project gets hard (and it will) you might quit it, too. And so on, and so on.

CHAPTER 11
WRITING YOUR SERIES

Do you recommend starting a writing career with a single book or starting with a BANG by writing a series?

Series are tricky things. Not just writing them, but also the many, many business considerations that go with them.

For a long time, series have been really popular and somewhat common in books for teens and young adults. It started, of course, with Harry Potter. Then Twilight and the Hunger Games and all the big series that came along with them.

But for every series that made it mega big, there are dozens that had disappointing sales for books one and two. Which meant that no one was excited about book three and, in many cases, they weren't even published, and all those authors never got to finish the series they had been so excited to write.

So should *you* start with a series?

Honestly, most publishers would love nothing more than to find a great new writer with a great new book. If it turns out that book is a hit, they would probably *love* to hear you've got an idea for a book two. Or three. Or seven. But most publishers would also probably prefer to have that first book stand alone, just in case the sales aren't strong enough to warrant publishing any more.

A phrase you hear a lot is "a stand-alone novel with spin-off potential." If you're really itching to write a series, that might be a safe place to start.

I wish this question had a character/craft/story/conflict answer. But it doesn't, I'm afraid. This is where the business part of this business comes into play. And when speaking about series, in particular, the business elements are always going to have to be considered.

DEAR MARISSA MEYER,

Any words of wisdom for someone who's trying to write a series?

If your series involves any sort of villainous opposition to the protagonist, I like to think about each book as a progressive level in a video game. You know how you could never beat the ultimate dungeon boss after just the first level, but you're *just* strong enough and have gathered *just* enough weapons or abilities to defeat one of the boss's minions? It's the same sort of thing. Every book should show your character(s) getting a little stronger and a little more capable, and testing those skills against increasingly difficult opposition, until they finally have to face off against the series's greatest foe in the climax of the final book.

Do you start off knowing you are going to write a series? Or is that something a writer figures out along the way?

I'm of the opinion that there are three types of series.

THE HARRY POTTER MODEL: This is the one that most teens and young adults think about when they think series. After all, it's how J. K. Rowling did it! And plenty of the big series that have happened since.

The Harry Potter Model means that the series is really one big story told over several volumes. There's an overarching plot (can Harry defeat Voldemort?), but each book has its own stand-alone story. (Can Harry save the Sorcerer's Stone? Will Harry survive the Triwizard Tournament? Etc.)

In answer to your question, I think most writers who end up utilizing the Harry Potter Model know that they're writing a series (or hoping to write a series) from the get-go. For example, when I sold *I'd Tell You I Love You, But Then I'd Have to Kill You*, I didn't know that I'd get to write six books, but I knew that I was hoping to write a lot, so I gave my heroine a missing father and a lot of unanswered questions—I gave myself a whole lot of conflict that I could potentially play with down the line.

When I sold my Embassy Row series, I had some more experience and a more established track record, so I was able to sell all three of those books at once, and in doing so, I was able to have a general story arc all planned out from the beginning.

Neither way is better or worse. Those are just two different ways of thinking about the Harry Potter Model.

Of course, there's also . . .

THE NANCY DREW MODEL: Most mysteries (both on TV and in books) follow the Nancy Drew Model, but a Nancy Drew Model series doesn't necessarily have to be a mystery. They just have to be the types of books that lend themselves to more "episodic" stories (meaning that each individual story is self-contained, even though some characters recur from book to book). And in my opinion, these series are incredibly rare in teen fiction (which is a shame). In fact, my Heist Society series is one of the few examples I can think of.

For the Nancy Drew Model to work, you really need a character, story, and situation where a new—totally separate—problem can show up at the beginning of each book. Every time, you'll need a new case or a mystery or a job or a game or . . . something. You need a setup that lends itself to stories that have clear beginnings, middles, and endings. And you need them to be the kind of stories you can *duplicate* in another book (without writing the exact same book again).

There is kind of a spectrum of books in the Nancy Drew Model. For some, like Nancy Drew or shows like *Law & Order*, it doesn't matter if you start with volume one or volume twenty. You don't have to read/watch them in order to understand exactly what's going on because each story truly stands alone.

Other stories in the Nancy Drew Model will have plots that stand alone, but there might be character arcs that cover multiple books. So even though you could, technically, read them out of order, you get a better experience if you can follow the characters from book one.

My Heist Society series is like that. In each book, Kat and her crew of teenage thieves take on a new "job," but their relationships with each other are constantly evolving, so people probably do enjoy them more when they're read in order.

THE ROMANCE NOVEL MODEL: Romance is a billion-dollar industry. (Yes, that's *billion* with a *B*!) And for good reason. A lot of really amazing, smart writers are working in that genre, and they figured out a long time ago what readers want: *Books that are exactly the same but totally different.*

Really, that's the key to any series, no matter the model. Sometimes a person picks up the second book in a series because they need to know what happens next, but I think they're more likely to pick up another book because they want to feel the way the first book made them feel.

Romance novelists have perfected this. Which is why the vast majority of romance novels truly and totally stand alone. They tell the story of two people falling in love. But a lot of times those people will have a friend or a brother or a neighbor who happens to be single . . . and in the next book, that person falls in love . . . usually with someone who has a friend or a sibling or a neighbor who—you guessed it—falls in love in the next book.

Most people call these *companion novels*, and honestly, for writers just starting out, this might be a great place to start.

Tell one story. Tell it really, really well. But introduce us to a character or a place or something that the reader might want to read more about next time.

DEAR DAVID LEVITHAN,
Which series model is the best?

I honestly think all the models you've mentioned work well. When I started as an editor at Scholastic in the 1990s, we had three big series, and there's one for each of your categories. Animorphs followed the Harry Potter Model—it was one long saga over many, many books. The Baby-sitters Club was the Nancy Drew Model, driven by the characters and with each book standing alone, even as some character arcs played out over multiple books. Goosebumps was the Romance Novel Model—the stories were largely unrelated, but every time you pick up a Goosebumps book, you know you're going to get fun, funny horror thrills. Each of these series sold tens of millions of copies . . . and still have fandoms over twenty years later.

So, in answer to your question, I suppose it depends. The key to writing a series—especially early in your career—is to not get lost in the fact that your favorite books have been series or that the authors you admire most have written series or that writing a series is your BIG DREAM.

Series are nothing more than a collection of several books. So focus on the books first. Preferably, focus on a *book*. And make it as amazing as possible—make it as *complete* as possible, with a beginning, middle *and* end. If it's meant to be a series, then that will happen in due time.

DEAR JULIE MURPHY,

Your amazing novel *Dumplin'* now has a companion novel, *Puddin'*—not a sequel. Why did you decide to go that route and what did you learn from it?

I actually decided to write a companion novel to *Dumplin'* because the moment I was done writing that book, I felt a little bit homesick. I think that's pretty normal any time someone finishes a book, but this was a nagging feeling that wouldn't go away. So I thought long and hard about what loose threads I'd left behind and who (of the characters in *Dumplin'*) I felt like deserved their own moment in the sun. I think there's a careful balance you have to strike with a companion novel. You want the book to feel reminiscent of the first, but it still has to exist as a stand-alone.

How difficult is the first book related to, say, the third or fourth?

If you do find yourself writing a series, don't be surprised if some books are harder than others. After all, all books are different! Books within a series are no exception. Gallagher Girls 2 almost killed me. Gallagher Girls 3 was the easiest book I've ever written.

Why? I'm not sure. But I have noticed that—*for me*—book two is almost always the hardest.

I'm not sure why that is. I think it has something to do with the fact that I've already described all the characters my favorite way . . . in the first book. And I've already said all my favorite things about the world . . . in the first book. And I usually used a lot of my favorite plot devices . . . in the first book.

And then I have to write a whole new book not using any of my favorite things! In short, I have to write a whole new book that is exactly the same but totally different from the first book. And let me tell you, that is easier said than done.

I think that's why there's one rule that almost every series follows to some extent: *With every book, the world gets bigger.*

This is really, really important. Every book should be bringing new characters and new places. Every book should bring new conflicts and new challenges.

I mean, can you imagine Harry Potter if every single book took place at Privet Drive and Diagon Alley and Hogwarts? If there wasn't a new Defense Against the Dark Arts teacher every year? I don't think it's a coincidence that book one saw Harry getting on the Hogwarts Express and book two had him arriving at school via a flying car. I like to imagine J. K. Rowling was sitting down with a cup of tea, thinking, *I've already described this bloody train!* So she (in a stroke of genius) got him to school in a totally different—and very exciting—way that both allowed her to write something totally new and different and served to introduce one of the big questions or mysteries of that novel (why couldn't Harry and Ron get onto the platform?).

You can't expect to keep going back to the same places and involving the exact same people time after time, book after book, and not run out of gas in the tank—and not run out of conflict.

So as you think about where you want your characters to go in your series, try thinking about that *literally*. What new places do you want your characters to see? Who do you want them to meet? What kinds of new experiences and fresh characters can you add to the mix along the way?

Keep expanding your world and you'll keep expanding your options as a writer.

I want to know, in a book series, how do you end the first book? People say it should be a cliffhanger, but how do you build the suspense that makes people want to read more?

The only way I would recommend ending a book in a cliffhanger is if you already have a very well established career and fan base and, frankly, if you already have that next book under contract.

There have been so many successful series in YA fiction that, I think, most readers assume all series are really successful. I'm afraid to say that just isn't true. I know so many authors who had big, awesome plans for big, awesome stories they were going to tell over a whole bunch of books, but many of them never got the chance.

And the people who ended their first or second books with cliffhangers . . . some of those authors have readers who are still hanging because the publisher decided not to publish book three. Or four. Or whatever. It's really sad.

My heart goes out to any author or reader in that situation, but those are the harsh realities about this business: Books have to make money. And if they don't make enough money, publishers won't be publishing any more of them.

So, if you can't have a cliffhanger, how do you end a first book in a way that makes people want to read more?

Well, really, this starts with writing a good book. Give them characters they're invested in. Give them a rich, vibrant world that they love. Give them heart-stopping suspense and heartbreaking story lines, and they'll want to return to your world over and over again.

You will often hear authors of beloved stand-alone novels talk about how fans are constantly asking for sequels. But *The Outsiders*, for example, is meant to stand alone. And I'd argue that fans don't really *want* a sequel. What fans want is to read *The Outsiders* for the first time again. What they *need* is to feel the way *The Outsiders* made them feel.

So start by writing a book that makes readers feel so strongly that they crave that feeling again and again. Then, think about how you can

1. give the reader a satisfying ending to your story.
2. give the reader a taste of what the conflict in your next story might be.

Which leads me, I guess, to a pet topic of mine: cliffhangers vs. game changers.

Honestly, *cliffhanger* might be the most misunderstood and misused term in all of fiction.

After all, there are people who still complain that I ended the Gallagher Girls series on such a "cliffhanger" because we don't know if Zach and Cammie got married, had kids, what those kids' names were, and where the kids went to school.

So to a lot of people, *cliffhanger* means "there is something—*anything*—that I don't know."

But that's not what a cliffhanger is.

If those are your standards, then I'm sorry, probably every book you'll ever read for the rest of your life will be a cliffhanger.

A "cliffhanger" actually means that a character is in imminent peril (hanging off a cliff). I can even go with those who say a cliffhanger means that a book/movie/TV episode ends at a point of maximum suspense with the central questions of that book/film/TV episode being unanswered.

Where I think a lot of people get confused by the term is when the core plotline of that book is wrapped up and then the author—or storyteller—chooses to introduce something that will alter the plotlines of *future* stories.

I like to call these *game changers*.

For example,

Harry Potter has just competed in the Triwizard Tournament. We know how his name got into the Goblet of Fire. We know how he survives. We know who dies. But . . . at the end of the book we also know that the world in which Harry lives is going to be very different from now on.

Does *Harry Potter and the Goblet of Fire* end in a cliffhanger? No. Does it end in a way that makes you eager and anxious for the next book? Yes!

But that, my friend, is not a cliffhanger. It's a game changer. And I love them so, so very much.

I've been doing this for a while now, and this is what I've learned: To keep a series fresh, every now and then you have to change the game.

DEAR MELISSA DE LA CRUZ,
What are some mistakes to avoid when writing a series?

Not planning the series from the beginning. I think you really have to know the background story before you plunge into a long series; otherwise, you will write contradictory elements that you will regret in the later books. So

Do you map out your plot for a whole series, go book by book, or just go with the flow?

Again, this is going to depend on what series model you're using. But let's assume you're going with the Harry Potter Model (since that's what most teens are into).

There is no right or wrong way of doing this. In fact, I've done it both ways.

For Gallagher Girls, I didn't have a whole lot of time when I was writing book one. And honestly, I was so new to writing that I probably wouldn't have known how to sit down and plan out a whole series if my life had depended on it. But luckily, I did know enough about stories to know that if I was ever going to get to write a whole bunch of books, I was going to need a whole bunch of conflict.

So I didn't plan the whole series out, but I did give my heroine some really big problems that it would, logically, take several years to solve. What happened to her father? Is he alive or dead? What was he working on when he disappeared? What is her mom not telling her? What is her dad's best friend hiding?

Those questions had nothing to do with the plot of book one, but they were there, simmering under the surface, and most readers were able to figure out that those were the questions my heroine was going to have to answer eventually.

When it came time to sell my third series, Embassy Row, I wanted to try it the other way. That time, I knew I wanted to do three books and I had a much better idea of what would happen in each one. Now, does that mean I sat down and outlined all three books at once? No. (But you could certainly do that if it suited your process.) For me, that just meant that I had a really good idea what the big, overarching plot was going to be—that I was writing a story about a girl who had seen her mother murdered and that this would be a series about figuring out exactly who had done it and why.

When I started out, I didn't know every single beat of all three books, but I did know how each book would start and how each book would end so that I had some goalposts to shoot for. I knew, in general, what direction the series was going to take, and that worked out well for that series. (Though I wouldn't necessarily do it that way every time.)

At the end of the day, much like each writer is different and each book is different, every series is going to be different, too. And you just have to follow your gut, be open to new things, and work really, really hard.

DEAR SOMAN CHAINANI,
What do you think is the most important thing to keep in mind when writing a series?

A series is tricky because you have to stay ahead of your readers. Young readers are exceptionally intuitive; they can sense your patterns, and in the time between books, they often can leap ahead of you in the story, simply by putting puzzle pieces together. As the author, each book has to step up the game so that it continues to challenge young readers—especially since they're growing in age. At the same time, a series usually has a built-in readership, so it also lets you take risks you wouldn't on a first book in a series. While writing *The School for Good & Evil*, I made sure each book has a different genre at its heart—book 1 is a fantasy, book 2 is really an Almodovar-style farce, book 3 is a Western, book 4 a court romance . . . If I challenge myself as an author, it'll challenge the readers as well.

How far ahead do you plan certain plot points in your series? In Gallagher Girls, the first book is where Cammie mentions the circus, but that one little comment sets up the resolution as seen in the fifth novel. Did you look back and try to incorporate things from old books or was that planned from the beginning?

I didn't really have the time (or, frankly, the know-how) to plan out the entire Gallagher Girls series when I started it. Which is kind of amazing because I truly love how the story turned out. And if I'd sat down with a game plan that I'd written years before, I might have been stuck with that plan in my mind, and I might not have been open to the really cool twists and turns and changes that appeared along the way.

But in a way, it's also dangerous. And terrifying. Because this system basically means walking up to a cliff and jumping, trusting yourself to learn to fly on the way down. But I tend to work/write/think better when under pressure, and this was the best pressure possible!

I always thought it was sheer, dumb luck that I could go back and tie those little throwaway lines (like the one about the circus) into the ultimate story, but now I'm not so sure. I've spent a lot of time thinking about that George R. R. Martin quote about how some writers are architects, planning elaborate cities, and some are gardeners, planting seeds to see which ones will later grow.

When I wrote that line about the circus—really, when I wrote anything about Cammie and her father—I was planting seeds. I had no idea which ones would grow to be useful later on, but somewhere deep inside me, my gut knew that some of those would matter someday. I just didn't know which ones—or how—at the time.

So if you're working on a series and you don't know exactly what's going to happen six books from now, that's okay. Just be sure you plant some seeds as you go along. You never know when you might need them.

Series can be like a siren's song to an aspiring writer. Big stories! Sweeping worlds! Epic love! (Not to mention fame and fortune.) But it isn't always possible for every series to play out like the author intended, so if you choose to go that route, consider all the business and creative factors that will come into play.

What kind of series are you writing, and how will you give your readers a satisfying conclusion if you only get to write two books (instead of ten)?

How are you going to expand your characters' world in every book? What new places will we see and what new people will we meet?

And most importantly, where is your conflict coming from? Because if you think conflict is important to a book, let me tell you, it's absolutely essential for a series.

You can do it! Just think about it carefully and plan for both the best—and the worst—case scenarios.

CHAPTER 12
PUBLISHING YOUR BOOK

Do you have to be a certain age to get a book published? How can we get publishers to take our work seriously even though we are teenagers?

This might be the publishing question that YA writers get asked the most. Which makes a lot of sense. We're writing for teens, after all, and a lot of them have just figured out that writing is a job. It's a job they want. It's a job they want *right now*!

So believe me when I say that the short answer to this question is no: There isn't a certain age you have to be to get a book published. Gordon Korman, for example, published his first book when he was fourteen years old! S. E. Hinton started *The Outsiders* when she was fifteen. Christopher Paolini was nineteen when a publisher bought *Eragon*.

But I wouldn't be doing my job if I didn't also say that those cases are pretty rare.

I also wouldn't be doing my job if I didn't say that I think you might be asking the wrong question. Instead of asking, "Do you have to be a certain age to get a book published?" I think you'd be better off asking, "How do I write a book that's publishable?"

Because honestly, publishers don't care if you're thirteen. Or thirty. Or sixty. From a publicity standpoint, they'd probably love to discover a thirteen-year-old literature prodigy. They could book you on all the talk shows and get you covered in all the newspapers and magazines. The media loves a hook, and "thirteen-year-old pens novel of the year" is a good one.

So it's not that publishers are opposed to publishing teen authors. It's that . . . well . . . first, you have to write the novel of the year.

There is one guaranteed way of getting publishers to take you seriously even though you're a teenager: *Write a great book.*

That's it. That's the "trick."

Always.

Without exception.

Every time.

I mean it.

You have to write a great book if you want to get taken seriously. So that is where your focus should really be.

But there is a second part to your question (that nobody ever talks about).

Authors get asked all the time if teenagers *can* publish books. No one ever asks us if a teenager *should* publish a book. Which is a really different—and maybe even more important—question.

Personally, I hate to see teens obsess about publishing. I'd much rather see them super excited about *writing*.

Why do I feel this way? Because *writing* and *publishing* are two extremely different things.

Writing is creative. It can be fun, frustrating, exhilarating, perplexing, challenging, stimulating, and very, very satisfying.

Writing is you in a room with all of your imaginary friends, playing massive games of "what if" . . .

"What if Lisa and Bob get stuck in an elevator?"

"What if Mona and Mindy find out they bought the same dress?"

"What if the world's worst magician moved in next door to me?"

Like that.

Writing is what writers do. Period. If you write, you're a writer. It doesn't matter if you're twelve or twenty or eighty. If you put pen to paper or fingers to keys or whatever your method of choice is, you're a writer.

Publishing, however, is the business of creating, distributing, and selling books. And the most important word in that sentence is *business*.

Publishing means taking the work of very few writers and crafting that work very, very carefully and then positioning it in the marketplace in a way that will hopefully appeal to as many book buyers as possible. Publishing means deadlines and nasty reviews and getting edit letters that make you throw up. And then cry. And then throw up again. (Which I've done.)

Publishing means missing Thanksgiving dinner because your book is late. (Which totally happened.)

Publishing means not seeing your friends because you have thirty-six hours to turn around your copyedits. (Which is inevitable.)

Publishing means having people you don't know say nasty things about you and what you've created. (Which happens every single day.)

In some cases, publishing might even mean death threats because people don't like that this character and that character didn't end up together. (Ooh . . . I could tell you stories.)

So writing and publishing aren't the same thing. Not at all.

It's like an ACT question: *All sunflowers are yellow, but not all yellow things are sunflowers* . . .

So all writers write, but not all writers publish.

And that's okay.

Just remember . . .

Writing is a fun, great, and rewarding hobby.

Publishing is a competitive, stressful, and complex business.

So when teens ask me whether or not they can get published at a young age, they need to understand that they're not talking to me about *writing*; they're asking about *publishing* . . .

They're talking about *going pro*. And that's a very different conversation.

My next-door neighbors have an adorable daughter who is ten. Every day after school, she spends about thirty minutes in their driveway playing basketball—dribbling, shooting, practicing bounce passes off the garage door.

Do I think this is a good, healthy, positive thing for her to have an interest in? Absolutely.

Do I think she should try out for the NBA next year? Definitely not.

And that's exactly what we're talking about here.

Publishing isn't writing. Publishing is writing at a professional level with professional stakes, pressures, and consequences. *And people get hurt.*

So the moral of the story is this, gang: No matter how old you are, write if you're a writer. Nothing can take that away from you.

But don't say that you're only going to shoot hoops in your driveway if you think you're going to get drafted into the NBA. Shoot hoops because you love shooting hoops.

And if you do it long enough and well enough, then you may have a chance to go pro when you're ready. If you want to.

DEAR GORDON KORMAN,
What was your experience like publishing as a teen? Do you have any advice for teens who are looking to do the same?

I was incredibly lucky to publish my first book so young, and on some level, I totally understood that. Sad to say, though, when I think back to those days, the feeling I remember most is an overpowering sense of impatience. I wrote *This Can't Be Happening at Macdonald Hall* at twelve, signed a contract at thirteen, and didn't have a book in my hand until I was fourteen. All that waiting was killing my preteen/teen self. Thinking about my career today, things aren't much quicker, but I've got a lot more balls in the air to keep myself busy. And of course, as a wily veteran, I know what to expect.

My advice to teens is to make writing a part of their daily lives. I know so many kids who want to write—but they never actually do. It's as if they're waiting for some magical alignment of the stars or something. Ninety-five percent of what I know about writing comes from doing it—writing, rewriting, trying, struggling, crashing, burning, and occasionally succeeding.

Is it hard to get a book published?

Yes. And no. The truth of the matter is that it's probably easier to get a book published than it is to write a publishable book.

So many people who set out to become writers want to skip right over the get-really-good-at-writing part and go straight to the beautiful-people-star-in-the-movie part, but I'm afraid it doesn't work that way. (Which you know! Because you're reading *this* book!)

Honestly, very few authors are able to sell their first book. Or their second. Or their twentieth. And most of us will tell you that, in hindsight, we're glad it worked out that way because those first books weren't good enough.

Once you are writing at a professional level, you could very well get something published eventually. Maybe not your first "good" book. (Sadly, sometimes a book is ahead of its time. Or slightly behind the times. Or there might be other reasons that will make it harder to publish.)

But I can guarantee you that agents want to sign and work with amazing new writers. Every editor I know would love to find the Next Big Thing.

Sadly, I have no doubt that, through the years, there have been a lot of really amazing books that never got their chance. For example, for years the big traditional romance publishers maintained imprints dedicated to writers and characters of color. Oftentimes, those books weren't shelved with the rest of the genre. They weren't carried by many stores, and even when they were, they were hard to find. The reason? Publishers maintained that there wasn't a big market for diverse romance. Well, then self-publishing came along, and as soon as authors were able to sell their books directly to readers— when they were able to cut out the traditional publishers—sales of diverse romance novels went through the roof, proving that the demand had been there all along. Publishers just hadn't been willing or able to see it.

For decades, a lack of diversity behind the scenes in publishing has translated to a lack of diversity on bookstore shelves. I know for a fact that a lot of really amazing books by amazing writers never got their shot. But I think that might be changing. Organizations like We Need Diverse Books (check them out at diversebooks.org) are doing tremendous work. More doors are opening every day.

In the meantime, all you can do is keep writing. Keep challenging yourself. And know that the first step in becoming a traditionally published writer is always—for everyone—writing.

What matters now is that you keep writing!

DEAR MAGGIE STIEFVATER,
How many rejections did you receive before you found an agent?

Dozens. Hundreds. Billions. I began submitting query letters when I was sixteen, and began receiving rejection letters by the bushel (this was because my novels were terrible). I have rejections from my current agent and my current publisher (they were right). I never found the piles of rejections particularly discouraging, though; they were concrete proof that I was trying. Moreover, they started getting encouraging once I started getting better. Agents would write little handwritten bits of encouragement on them: "Not for me, but probably for someone!" So I could kind of track my lumpy progress.

How many rejections did you receive before you found an agent?	
Shannon Hale	About 100?
Marie Lu	600+
Melissa de la Cruz	Probably 6.
Daniel José Older	40
Stephanie Perkins	3
Kody Keplinger	Too many to count.
Marissa Meyer	8 or 9
Alex London	None! I stumbled into my agent.
Sarah Rees Brennan	1

Jesse Andrews	Dozens
Soman Chainani	16
Holly Black	I sold my first book without an agent.
Kiersten White	50
Zoraida Córdova	0
Dhonielle Clayton	25
Eliot Schrefer	0
Z Brewer	Combined rejections from three books = 248. (Yeah . . . I know. I sent them to EVERYONE, which isn't a wise approach.)

How do you know your work is good enough to be published?

This might be the hardest thing about this business. Even now, ten years and fifteen books into my career, I ask myself this question almost every day, so I'm not sure it's something you ever really get over.

When I was first starting out, it was especially hard to know. That's why, before I started querying agents, I made a deal with myself. I decided to enter my book in a contest run by my state's writers' association (something most states have and pretty much anyone can join). I told myself that if I won the contest I'd take that as a sign that I was ready to take the next step.

Well, imagine my surprise . . . and my joy . . . and my fear . . . when I actually won the contest. Even then, I was about to talk myself out of submitting to agents (it's a scary thing!), when I got the judge's notes back, and saw that he'd asked only one question: *Why hasn't this been published?*

That was it—the sign I'd been waiting for! So I took the next big step.

Now I'm of the opinion that you need three things before going pro.

1. OBVIOUSLY, YOU NEED A FINISHED BOOK. Not an idea. Not a draft. Not even a second draft. Nope. You need a book you've rewritten a whole bunch of times and polished to perfection—a book you can put in a drawer for six months while you work on something else and still like when you read it again with fresh eyes.

2. YOU NEED REALLY POSITIVE FEEDBACK FROM PEOPLE WHO WILL BE HONEST WITH YOU. Maybe that's your parents or your friends or your teachers. But personally, I think it's also worth your time and effort to enter some contests. Just watch out for scams, because there is no shortage of people looking to take advantage of writers and their dreams. For that reason, you might want to start with the contests associated with writing conferences and organizations. If you are a student in grades seven to twelve, you might want to consider the Scholastic Art & Writing Awards (artandwriting.org). It might be good to "compete" (for lack of a better word) against a whole bunch of people who, theoretically, have been working just as hard as you have— maybe harder! It's important to know how you stack up.

3. YOU NEED TO BE READY (EMOTIONALLY, PHYSICALLY, SPIRI- TUALLY) TO GO PRO. That's what you're trying to do. You're not trying to "get a book published." You're trying to begin

a publishing *career*, and you need to be ready for what that means. Rejection. Deadlines. Pressure. More rejection. Paralyzing self-doubt. Rejection. Disappointment. Joy. Rejection again.

And crying.

So, in short, try to get some independent feedback from people who know a good book when they see one. And then try and ask yourself if you're ready—not your book, *you*—for all that this business entails.

There's no shame in setting a book aside and writing another one. And another. And another. Until you feel like you're ready to "go pro." It's not a decision to be taken lightly.

DEAR JENNIFER LYNN BARNES,
You wrote your first (published) book when you were very young. What do you know now that you wish you'd known then?

I wrote my first published book when I was nineteen; it came out a couple of years later. Looking back, I'm not sure that my experience was much different from any other published author, except that I wrote my first four published books while I was still in college. Every author has to learn how to manage their time. For me, this meant not only balancing class work and writing but also balancing writing with having a life! I didn't want to look back on college and feel like I'd lost out on having a real college experience because of writing, so I made a rule for myself that I would only write when my friends were sleeping. Even when I really wanted to, I didn't turn down social invitations or extracurricular opportunities to stay home and write. Writing late at night meant that the only thing I was missing out on was sleep (and I compensated for that by avoiding morning classes when I could and sleeping in).

Basically, I think young writers should try to do three things: read a lot, write a lot, and do things that aren't reading and writing. Sometimes, people get the idea in their head that being a writer means not loving to do anything but write, but I'm a big believer in cultivating multiple passions. Every experience you have will give you more to write about, so one of the most important things as a young writer is to make sure that you're giving yourself the opportunity to pursue interests, passions, and opportunities outside of writing, even once you start publishing.

The other big piece of advice I have for young writers is to avoid saying or thinking, "I want to be published by the time I'm [X] years old." In the long run, it doesn't matter how old you are when you publish your first book. The most special thing about the books you write will never be your age. Ultimately, readers won't care how old you were when you wrote the book; they'll care about the way the book makes them feel. And if you want to be a career author and not just someone who writes one book, then how old you were when you wrote your first book matters even less as time goes on. Most people in the publishing industry don't even realize I was a teenager when I wrote my first book. My readers certainly don't!

Long story short, I recommend that young writers don't define themselves as being *young*, but as being *writers*. You won't always be a teenager, but you will always be a writer, so long as you write.

How does the publishing process work?

Really, books come about in seven steps.

STEP 1: WRITE AND REWRITE YOUR BOOK. This is no doubt the most important step. And it's the step that most people never, ever do because it's hard and a lot of work and there is absolutely no guarantee of success.

Most people aren't willing to give up all their free time for months—or years—in the hopes that someday, maybe, they might get rewarded for it. So if you've already completed step one, go, you! That's a big accomplishment.

STEP 2: FIND A LITERARY AGENT. This is the next step that a lot of people never make it past. Maybe because their book isn't ready yet and they need to work on their craft a little more. Maybe because they've written a great book that's just going to be too hard to sell to a publisher. Maybe because they didn't do their homework and they're querying the wrong agents. Maybe because they just gave up too soon. We'll talk more about finding an agent in a little bit.

Unless you want to self-publish (which we'll also talk about later), step two will be necessary before you can move on to step three.

STEP 3: SELL YOUR BOOK TO AN EDITOR AT A PUBLISHING HOUSE. Editors do a lot of things. They edit (obviously), but they also acquire books for their employers (the publishers), so this might be a little confusing because you might sometimes hear the terms *editor* and *publisher* used interchangeably. For the purposes of selling a new book, at least, that is kind of true.

For example, this book, *Dear Ally, How Do You Write a Book?*, was acquired by David Levithan at Scholastic. (David is both an editor and an author.) So some people might say I sold it to David. Some people might say I sold it to Scholastic. They'd both be right.

The key to remember here is that most publishers/editors will only look at books sent to them by reputable literary agents, so you can't skip step two!

STEP 4: WORK WITH YOUR NEW EDITOR TO MAKE YOUR BOOK AMAZING. Theoretically, your book is already really good—otherwise no editor would have bought it! But it's a really tough world out there, and no editor is going to publish a book they haven't tried to make as great as possible, so all editors will have edits.

These might come as a letter with broad, overarching suggestions. *I don't feel like the villain's motivation is really clear. We need a little more insight into her backstory.*

Or they might come as a very detailed line edit. *On page 73, let's tighten up paragraph four or cut it altogether.*

Or both.

Whatever the case, this is a really important step, and it should not be taken for granted. Listen to your editor. Learn from them, and remember, this person is your most valuable asset within the publishing house. They're the coach of your team, and it's important to work together.

STEP 5: YOUR BOOK IS COPYEDITED. At this point, the heavy lifting is pretty much done. Now your editor will send your book to a copy editor (who is different from your overall editor).

Copy editors are the comma gurus and the grammar goddesses. They go through your manuscript with a fine-tooth comb and make sure it is as close to perfect as possible. Then they'll send it back to your editor, who will then send it to you to accept/reject their changes or fix any big mistakes they might find.

STEP 6: YOUR BOOK GOES INTO TYPESETTING. After all the commas are fixed and the typos are found, your editor will send your book "into typesetting," which means it disappears for a while, and the next time you see it, it will look almost like a real book.

It will have fancy fonts and cool chapter headings, and it will be so surreal you'll want to cry. At this point, you'll want to print it out and do one last read-through because this is your very last chance to fix any errors that might have slipped through (although there will still be proofreaders checking for errors after your work as the author is completed).

You'll need to type all of those up and send a list to your editor and maybe say a prayer and cross your fingers because . . .

STEP 7: YOUR BOOK IS A REAL BOOK. Congratulations! It's done, and you're finished.

Now it's time to get started on a new book and do it all again!

DEAR ALAN GRATZ,
Was your first novel published on the first try?

I sold my first book through the slush pile. It was the third book I wrote. The first two were never bought and published, and received dozens of rejections. The book I finally got published, my first novel, was rejected fifteen times by publishers before someone said yes.

DEAR DAVID LEVITHAN,
So how was this book acquired, from your side of things as the editor?

Wearing my proverbial editor hat here (and not my author hat) . . . here's how it worked from the publisher point of view (in this case, Scholastic).

I'd worked with Ally on four novels, and one day, she told me she had an idea to do a writing guide for YA writers. I said, "Awesome! Send me a proposal." So Ally worked on a proposal and sent it to Kristin Nelson, her agent. Then Kristin sent it to me. I had a couple of notes on the proposal, so Ally revised it so it would make sense to all the people who were going to be reading it. Once I had the proposal in hand, the next step was for me to take it to our acquisitions meeting. (Note: I usually need a full manuscript to bring to this meeting, but since Ally was someone we'd published before, and since her proposal was so detailed, I didn't need her to write the whole thing.)

The acquisitions meeting is the place where all of the heads of all of the departments for our trade division get together to talk about the books we've been submitted. An editor has to be VERY enthusiastic about a book to take it to the acquisitions meeting. There, the department heads (sales, marketing, publicity, and others) and the key sales reps (from national accounts, indie accounts, and online accounts) will weigh in on whatever materials they've been given to read—in this case, the proposal. We'll also make a projection on how many copies it will sell, and run the numbers—this is called a P&L (for profit and loss statement). While we certainly look at the numbers, I can honestly say that what matters the most is the read. In this case, everyone thought this book was a great idea, and that Ally was the perfect person to write it. So I then got to go back to Kristin and make an offer. After we went back and forth on a few of the terms (this pretty much always happens), Kristin accepted the offer (after talking to Ally, of course), and as a result, we had a deal—and you now have a book in your hand that's published by Scholastic.

DEAR DAVID LEVITHAN,

Anything you'd like to add here about the role of the editor, since you're the editor of this book?

I think a lot of people are confused about what an editor does—at worst, they think it's the same as a teacher correcting a paper. But the editor does much more than that. My allegiance is threefold—to the author, to the story, and to the reader. For the author, I am there to be a sounding board, and to help draw out the best book possible. I am there to make suggestions (sometimes many, many suggestions), but I am never there to make demands. The author has the final say (their name is on the book, not mine), so my job is to be a voice as strong as the ones in their head, advocating for what I think will bring out the best in their writing.

My allegiance to the book is to make sure it goes out into the world in the strongest way possible—not just in the writing, but in the cover art and design, the marketing, the cover copy, and the interior design.

As for my allegiance to the reader—I always say that I am the readers' representative during the editorial process. My role is to read it as they would read it, and to point out things that might be confusing, or might be boring, or might be uneven. Then I go back to my allegiance to the writer, to figure out how to make it better. It's also VERY important for editors to point out everything that IS working, as well as the spots that aren't—I believe writers learn as much from praise as they do from criticism.

DEAR JACKIE HORNBERGER, THE COPY EDITOR OF THIS BOOK,

Would you like to add something about how you see your role?

As the copy editor, I read the manuscript only in its near-final state, so I may find inconsistencies "held over" from previous drafts and edits. I look out for typos and grammar issues, and a whole bunch of other things: I check to make sure the timeline of the story works (within the story, as well as with any real-life events mentioned), details about characters are consistent, and details within the series are consistent. I also confirm the spellings of the names of real-life people and places, and fact-check specific details mentioned. (And I'm the kind of person who thinks that's a lot of fun!) I also look out for any sensitivity issues. I see myself as a "neutral third party" who should ask any questions remaining to be asked.

DEAR DAVID LEVITHAN,

So, from a publisher's point of view, how long does it take to make a book?

If we're talking a novel (and not a picture book or a graphic novel), an editor likes to get a book about a year and a half before publication date. This gives about four months for editing and polishing the first draft. The book is usually due into copyediting roughly fourteen months before the publication date. Copyediting takes a month, then the page proofs and various proofreads will take another two to three months, which is also when the cover comes together. If all goes according to schedule, the author's work will be done about seven months before the book is actually published.

Why does it take so long?!

The reason we have to get everything ready so early is that the sales reps—the people who sell our books to bookstores, who in turn sell them to you—have to present the books to the stores about six months ahead of time (sometimes as much as nine months ahead of time, for big books). We will create advance reader's copies of books for booksellers, for conventions, for librarians, and for the media, to build the buzz and convince people to bring the book into their stores and libraries. Which is why we need the book to be done so far in advance of when we actually print the book. A book is actually printed and bound about two months before its pub date; if we didn't want so many people to read it ahead of time, we could print them much faster!

Do I need an agent? What do they do?

Assuming you would like to traditionally publish your book and have it in bookstores across the country, then, yes, you're going to need an agent. With very few exceptions, most major publishers don't read unsolicited manuscripts (or the "slush pile"). But they will read things sent to them by agents. So you're going to need one for this (and so, so, so, so, so much more)!

In addition to helping your book find a publishing home, agents really are an author's champion. They're the ones who go to bat for you when a cover just isn't working or when you don't think your publication date should be moved. They negotiate your contracts so that you don't unintentionally end up selling the rights to your soul as well as your book. They'll keep track of the money that your publisher(s) owe you, and if a check's late, they'll get on the phone and make that problem disappear.

Simply put, your agent is your advocate. And bad cop.

They work on commission (typically 15% for US publishing rights. Foreign rights and film rights will be slightly different), so if you don't get paid, neither do they.

A lot of people might look at that 15% and ask why you should give some stranger 15% of your hard-earned money. Well, I'd rather have 85% of a big pie than 100% of a small one. But it's more than that: My agent makes my career better. Which, in turn, makes my life better. And easier. And more sustainable in the long haul.

Trust me, when you get an agent, that 15% commission will be the best money you ever spent.

How am I supposed to get an agent when I don't know any?

The first agent I ever spoke to was my agent when she called one day to offer me representation. And I am very much not alone. In fact, most people don't know any agents when starting out in this business. And the good news is that agents know that, and so most of them (the ones who are looking for new clients) have a system in place that lets them hear from aspiring authors every day.

Here's what you do:

1. RESEARCH.

Seriously. The most important part of this might be research. Because you want to query agents who are:

a. looking for new clients.

b. looking for clients like *you*.

This is so incredibly key. You can have the best book in the world, but if you query an agent who hasn't signed a new client in five years and never intends to sign one again . . . well, you're probably going to get rejected. If you've written an amazing mystery but you send it to an agent who represents only romance, you're probably going to get rejected.

So how do you know which agents to query? Here are a few ideas. You may very well need all of them:

—Look at the authors who are writing books like the one you've written. Go to their websites, look at the acknowledgment pages of their books. You can probably find out who their agents are somewhere if you try hard enough. Then go to those agents' websites and find out if they're accepting queries.

—Every year, there are thousands upon thousands of people trying to find an agent. (My agent, Kristin Nelson, gets at least thirty thousand queries every year.) Which is a bad thing because it means you can get lost in the crowd. (Last year, out of those thirty thousand queries, Kristin signed *three* new clients.)

But it's also a good thing because there are a ton of resources available online to help you do your research.

PublishersMarketplace.com has a free weekly newsletter that gives a rundown of the big publishing deals that were announced that week, so you can keep track of which agents are selling what types of books.

QueryTracker.net is a free website you can join that lets you search agents and see where other aspiring authors are submitting (and what kind of luck they're having).

ManuscriptWishList.com has lots of information about what agents wish they had in their inboxes, as well as a searchable agent database.

SCBWI.org is the homepage for the Society of Children's Book Writers and Illustrators, an organization centered around helping authors and illustrators improve their craft and better navigate their industry.

—Look up agents and follow them on social media. Now, I'm not saying query them on social media. I'm saying follow them. You can get a sense of who they're representing and what they're selling, what their personalities are like and if you think you'd get along.

Plus, nobody knows more about pitching to agents than agents themselves. Some agents don't have much of an online presence at all, but some really enjoy the networking and educational aspects of their jobs, so they have a ton of blog posts and articles, newsletters and tweets that help inform potential clients about their likes and dislikes.

2. LOOK OUT FOR SCAMS.

Sadly, any time you have a huge number of people trying to follow their dreams, there will be people who want to take advantage of them. The publishing world is no different.

So the bad news is that there are a lot of "scam" agents.

The good news is that they're pretty easy to spot.

Here's the thing: **NO REPUTABLE AGENT WILL EVER ASK YOU FOR MONEY.**

No. Not ever. Never. Not once.

Agents work on commission, so they only get paid when you get paid. If they're asking for a fee—even if it's a "reading fee" or a "consulting charge" or any type of money at all—that's a huge red flag. Run, don't walk, in the other direction.

You'll also want to go to any possible agent's website and look to make sure they're selling real books to real publishers. If you can't find their clients' books in any bookstore, then that's another red flag.

If you can't find mention of any deals that they've done, then that's a red flag, too.

There are also some websites that track these "scam" agents, and I'd recommend you check out places like <u>WriterBeware.com</u> or the "Beware" section of <u>AbsoluteWrite.com</u>.

Do your due diligence because this is your book. Your life. Your future. It's up to you to make sure you're in business with the best people possible.

3. WRITE AN AMAZING QUERY LETTER.

Most agents are going to require some kind of letter (or email) from you. Which only makes sense. They need to know who you are and what you've written.

They're also going to need to know your book's genre, its word count, and why you chose that agent to query out of the hundreds of agents out there. And most importantly, they're going to need to know a little bit about your book.

"Why do I need to tell them about my book? Why can't they just read it?"

"If I could tell my story in a paragraph, I wouldn't have written a whole book!"

"I can't wait to get an agent so that I never have to summarize my book in three sentences ever again!"

Those are just some of the things that aspiring authors say about this portion of a query letter. I probably said them myself.

But not a day goes by that I don't have to summarize my books in a sentence or two. Trust me, this is a skill you're going to need for the rest of your career, so I'd highly recommend you work on getting good at it.

Query letters are very important. They need to be professional (but not pretentious), clear (but not boring), clever (but not "cute"). They are the first thing of yours that an agent will read, so show them that you're ready and you've done your homework and you're someone they should consider going into business with.

But don't take my word for it. There are about a billion articles on this topic online. The problem won't be finding information. The problem will be finding too much information. Seriously. People have been posting and blogging and talking about this for decades. So do even more research and try to put your best foot forward!

4. QUERY

So you have your list of reputable agents? You know who you'd love to work with? You know that they're taking clients and what their query procedures are?

Good!

You've got a clear, concise, and interesting query letter?

Yay! You're ready!

Now you've got to go through your list of potential agents and follow their query instructions exactly! And I do mean *exactly*.

If they ask you to email them a one-page cover letter about your background and a ten-page synopsis of your book, then that's what you do.

If they ask for a cover letter and the first twenty-five pages of your manuscript, you send them that.

If they say they will accept only electronic or online submissions, then do not FedEx them your entire manuscript printed out on hot-pink paper so it will stand out.

Don't hire a singing telegram person to rap your prologue while standing in the foyer of their office.

Don't send cookies with your manuscript because they're just going to throw those cookies in the trash because you're someone who can't follow directions (and might want to poison them).

Again, my agent gets thirty thousand queries every year.

Last year, she signed three new clients.

The first cut will always be people who can't (or just refused to) follow directions. Don't be in the first cut.

5. REJECT. REVISE. REPEAT.

In a way, querying agents is like going on blind dates. They're not all going to be love at first sight.

So keep at it and don't give up. If you're not getting any nibbles at all, maybe revise your cover letter or your synopsis or your pitch? Maybe look at querying different agents?

But most of all, you should be working on a new book! I've met a lot of aspiring authors who have literally been revising the same novel for twenty years, thinking this will be the year an agent wants it.

That always makes me sad. Don't put all your eggs in one manuscript. Not when the vast majority of writers get better with every thing they write!

DEAR KRISTIN NELSON,
Do you really find authors in the slush pile?

Yes, I do find terrific authors in my slush pile—including you, Ms. Ally! If memory serves (we've been working together for so long), you originally sent me a query letter, and I signed you based on the strength of your writing. That's also how I connected with Scott Reintgen, Stacey Lee, and quite a few other authors on my roster.

What is the biggest tip you'd give teens who might want to query an agent?

Do not mention your age until an agent offers representation. This is a business, and you are a professional writer looking for an agent, so initially your age doesn't matter. But once an agent has expressed interest, you must disclose if you are under eighteen because a parent or legal guardian must be on the phone with you. Also, never use your teen status as an excuse for lack of experience, either in writing or industry savvy. I shouldn't be able to tell by reading your query letter that you are a teen writer! However, when a young writer does mention in their query that they are a teen, if the query is well written and professional and the story hook is interesting and unique, then we treat that query like any other.

What is the biggest mistake people make when they query?

The biggest query mistake is not nailing your story pitch. Your ability to write an excellent query letter (75 to 80 percent of which is your story pitch) is your opportunity to show a literary agent that you are ready to be taken seriously as an author. Good writers write awesome query letters. By the way, good writers often get help, feedback, and critiques for their query letters *before* sending them to an agent. This is all legit. No one says you have to do it all on your own.

I've met many teen writers at writers' conferences, and the savvy ones approach their writing as a profession. They dress in business-casual clothing, they approach agents with professionalism, and they network with other writers. It's so awesome to see. Often a parent or guardian also attends the conference, but they don't participate in agent pitch meetings. These teens fly solo, and they never fail to impress me.

DEAR JAY COLES,
How did you find (and get) your agent? Were there any resources that were particularly useful in the search?

I got my agent the old-fashioned way. Querying. I followed my agent on Twitter for a while and really had an interest in working with her because (a) she was at a really distinguished literary agency and (b) her client list was very impressive. I sent my agent a manuscript and she liked it. Before she had the chance to offer, I had sent her another manuscript that would become my debut (*Tyler Johnson Was Here*). She liked that one even more and saw potential in me, so she offered really quickly. Throughout the whole process, QueryTracker was a resource I kept going back to.

How many agents can you query at one time and how many did you query before you found one?

Good question!

You definitely don't want to query every agent in the world your first time out. I think I started with twenty.

And then I got twenty rejections.

And then I sent number twenty-one to Kristin, who has now been my agent for fifteen years.

Twenty-one queries might sound like a lot, but it isn't. I was really lucky. I know authors who queried hundreds of agents over the course of several years (and with several different books), so keep at it! Keep writing! And never give up!

My research says that when sending queries to literary agents, they would prefer works that have won awards, or writers with a lot of training. I don't have that. Will my manuscript stand a chance?

Do you know how much formal writing training I'd had when I signed with my agent? None. I had literally never taken a writing class.

Do you know how many awards I'd won? One. It was the Best First Pages of a Novel award given by the Kansas Writers Association. It cost about fifteen dollars to enter, and it was open to anyone in the state.

Don't get me wrong, I'm sure a lot of agents would really perk up if they got a query from a writer who has graduated from a fancy master's of fine arts degree program and has won lots of awards.

But those things aren't necessary.

Not even a little bit.

Especially if you're writing genre (as opposed to literary) fiction.

What you have to have is a *great book*, a *polished and professional cover letter*, and a *list of agents who are actively acquiring books like the one you've written*.

Oh, and patience.

You're going to need a lot of patience.

Is it smart to write under a pseudonym?

Pseudonyms (or "pen names") are not all that common. But they're definitely not uncommon either! And there are definitely good reasons why they're used from time to time.

First of all, it's important to understand that, for writers, our name is our brand.

For example, if you pick up a book by Holly Black, you're going to expect a book with some sort of fantasy or magical element. A Jenny Han is going to have romance. And an Ally Carter book will have teenagers involved in some kind of international intrigue and hijinks.

But what if I decided to write an adult horror novel someday? If my fans picked that up, would they be disappointed? Yeah. Probably. Because that's not what they've come to expect from me.

It's like buying a Coke and having it taste like Sprite. It's not that Sprite is bad. It's just that when you buy one brand, you expect that brand, not something else.

So authors will frequently (but not always) use a pseudonym if writing something new or off-brand.

A new name is also a way of having a fresh start in this business. I've had the privilege of meeting some amazing authors who have been doing this for decades, and a lot of them have written under different names at various points in time. As soon as one market or "brand" cooled down, they'd switch to something else and keep going. And then they'd do it again. And again. And through it all, they kept writing!

I also know people who just write too quickly to publish everything under one name. There's a limit to how many times a year a bookstore can promote a new book by Author X. To some extent, there's a limit to how frequently fans will buy a new book. Being a fast writer can have a lot of advantages, but publishers can be leery of putting out too many books too quickly. That's why Nora Roberts, the queen of modern romance, started publishing thrillers as J. D. Robb several years ago. She was just writing so quickly that her publishers were afraid she might flood her own market, so a whole new name—a whole new author brand—was born.

Sometimes people might use a pseudonym if their name is incredibly hard to spell or, maybe, if they have the same name as another author or celebrity. (If your name is Jonathan Greene, then, yeah, a pseudonym might be in order.)

The final reason someone might use a pseudonym is for reasons of privacy, though I have to say it's pretty hard to keep a name secret. It can be done, but you have to be amazingly diligent and careful, and you'll probably need a few layers of paperwork between you and the public. It can happen, but you're going to need to know very early on that that's your goal and then you'll have to plan accordingly.

How do you find publishers that won't ask for too much money? Because some of us teens can't afford to pay too much.

Finally, a question whose answer *isn't* "it depends"! Nope. This time there is one correct, non negotiable answer, and that answer is:

Never, ever, ever give a publisher money.

Ever.

I mean it. Don't do it.

Don't give a publisher a dime! An agent either.

In fact (this may blow your mind), publishers are supposed to pay *you*. And reputable agents always work on commission, meaning that they take a percentage of what you're paid (usually 15%), so you don't pay them either!

(As I said earlier, but I'll say it again because it's important: Paying my agent 15% of my income is something I will never complain about! She earns her commission and then some, so don't think that being in this business without an agent will save you some money. I promise, in the long run, agents more than pay for themselves!)

Writing is a passion for a lot of people. But it's also a dream, and where there are dreams, there will never be a shortage of people looking to take advantage of the dreamers. Which means the world is full of "publishers" who are more than willing to take your money. Some may call it an editorial service. Some might say that the author has to pay for the art. *All of them are scams*, run by people who want to take advantage of people who want nothing more than to see their words in print.

I know it's hard, getting rejection after rejection. I know it's tempting to want to put your manuscript in book form. Maybe once it's out there . . . Maybe once it has a great cover . . . Maybe once it looks like a real book, publishers will want it?

The bad news is that none of that is true.

The good news is that you can save your money.

Should I self-publish my book now to get my name out there?

Ebooks changed the world.

No. Really. They did.

Before ebooks, self-publishing was mainly what I talk about above— paying a "publisher" (a term I use very loosely) to "publish" your books (which basically meant typesetting and printing books with not-great covers) so that people could try to sell those books to their family and friends. But then ebooks came about and a whole new avenue of self-publishing opened up.

All of a sudden, authors could self-publish their books and actually sell them to readers instead of driving around with a box of really badly done books in the trunk of their car.

Self-publishing went from being largely a scam (with a few exceptions) to a legitimate business strategy. Now some of the smartest, savviest, and best writers I know are self—or "indie"—publishing.

So is it something *you* should do?

Well, like many of the answers in this book, that depends.

1. WHAT GENRE ARE YOU WRITING?

There are some genres where ebooks are incredibly popular and common, so indie publishing is a viable option. Are you writing romance? Science fiction? Then indie publishing could work out for you since those are the genres where ebook sales are the strongest.

2. WHAT AGE ARE YOU WRITING FOR?

Kids and teens don't read ebooks. Yeah. I know. A few do. But on the whole, most readers under the age of eighteen vastly prefer physical books to ebooks, and since we live in an age where self-publishing is pretty much dependent on strong ebook sales, that means that indie publishing isn't ideal if your primary audience is going to be teens or young adults.

A lot of indie authors will also have a way for die-hard fans to order physical, hard-copy books, but they aren't really in stores (where teens browse), and they're very rarely in libraries. They're never in Scholastic book fairs. And a huge part of the YA and teen market is dependent on school and library sales, book fair sales, and a whole host of other things that you have to have a physical book to do.

Now, are there self-published YA books available? Absolutely! Have they made money? Yes. Some have no doubt made a lot of money. But it seems like (at this point in time) most of those books are being bought and read by adults who like to read YA fiction—not by teens themselves. Which makes this a very different market.

So if you've written a YA book that you think will appeal to adults more than teens, yeah. This could possibly work for you. But if you've written a YA book that you think will appeal mainly to teens themselves, then this might not be in your long-run best interest.

At least not now. In a few years, this may very well change.

3. HOW GOOD ARE YOU AT MARKETING, DESIGN, AND OTHER BUSINESSY STUFF?

When you decide to self-publish, *you* become your publisher. You and you alone. Which means you've got to hire a cover designer and a copy editor and pay for both up front and out of your own pocket (which is different from paying a "scam" publisher like we discussed earlier). You're going to have to either pay someone—or learn how—to do the technical stuff that goes into turning a Microsoft Word file into an ebook that's up on all the major vendors.

You're going to have to pick your keywords and categories and other metadata.

You're going to have to set a price point.

And if you don't know what any of those terms mean, then you're either going to want to do a whole lot of research on indie publishing or just go the traditional route. Because you can't succeed at indie publishing without knowing those things and a whole lot more!

Then, once the book is up—once it's one of about a million other books that people have uploaded—you're going to have to find a way of marketing and promoting your book and setting it apart from the pack.

But don't most authors have to promote their books even when they're published by a big New York house anyway? Yes. They absolutely do some of it. Sometimes they do a lot of it. But with indie publishing you're doing 100 percent of it, all the time.

Again, I know people who have become very successful indie publishing, and without exception, they're all really smart, really dedicated, really savvy people who went this route because it was a great business decision.

I don't know any über-successful indie authors who are only in indie publishing because they didn't want to mess with getting an agent.

4. HOW QUICKLY DO YOU WRITE?

Without a doubt, one of the things that most successful indie authors have in common is how quickly they're able to turn out new books. There are a lot of reasons why that is (and some are very complicated, involving the algorithms that online booksellers use to determine where a book falls in its ranking), but the key thing to remember is that successful indie authors are turning out multiple books a year. (I have a friend who published *twelve* books a few years ago! Yes, a book a month.)

If that matches your process . . .

If you feel like you can write a whole bunch of books pretty quickly . . .

If you are kind of a publishing geek (like me!) and you think, *Yay! I can do my own metadata!* . . .

If you want to write for adult readers in genres where ebooks are selling really well . . .

Then self—or indie—publishing might very well be for you.

But self-publishing is NOT for you if . . .

—You think it will be less work than working with a traditional publisher.

—You think having a book for sale online will automatically impress agents or editors.

—You think putting *published author* on your application is going to automatically get you into Harvard.

—You think it will be easy to stand out among the massive number of books self-published every year.

There really is no easy road to success in this business, I'm sorry to say. But paths to success do exist, and if you're smart and patient and if you work really, really hard, you could very well find one!

DEAR CARRIE RYAN,
You know more about self-publishing than anyone I know. Is that something you'd recommend to teens who are just getting started writing?

This is always such a difficult question to answer because it depends on what the goal is. If your goal is simply to publish a book, then I say go for it. If it's to sell a lot of copies of that book and build a career . . . That's when I'm a little more hesitant to recommend that route when you're just starting out, because now you're becoming your own publisher, which is a lot of work.

I feel like sometimes young writers turn to indie publishing because they're too impatient with the process. They want to skip to the end. But I don't think that's the best way to build a solid, long-term career. When you're starting out is the time you should be experimenting with writing: taking risks, trying new voices and styles. You're building the foundation for what comes next and that's not something you can shortcut around. I have reams of unpublished fiction in a filing cabinet in my garage, and I'm okay with it staying there. If indie publishing had been an option when I wrote it, I might have tried to go that route, but I doubt I would have found much success. My writing just wasn't that great—I had to move on to new projects, I had to learn and grow and study craft and figure out how to revise.

Also, it's easy to forget that indie publishing is a business. If you want to sell a lot of copies of a book, it's going to take work and it's very different work from writing. Some people love being their own publisher—there are many benefits (like having complete control). But some authors want to focus on the writing and not worry about the rest (like sourcing covers, setting pricing, designing ad campaigns). So right now my advice is that

> if you want to indie publish, make sure you know what you're getting into. It's not a shortcut but its own path with unique challenges and rewards. And of course there's always the option of going hybrid: being both traditionally and indie published.

How do you become a writer without having a publisher nearby?

One of my absolutely favorite things about being a writer is that you can do it from anywhere. I mean literally anywhere! You could write and publish a book from the moon as long as you had the time and a decent internet connection.

In the movies and on TV shows, writers seem to always live in New York (or maybe Los Angeles), but that's not necessary in real life. Publishers don't care where you live. They care about the book you've written. So get to writing that book!

> ### DEAR JULIE MURPHY,
> You live a heck of a long way from NYC. How did you find an agent? Any advice on the subject?
>
> I found my agent the old-fashioned way—querying! Of course there's lots of value in attending conferences and meeting agents in real life, but I think it's also okay to be honest with yourself and know your strengths. For me, that meant I didn't feel confident in my ability to pitch an agent in real life. I feel like those are always the flashiest stories, but I came straight out of the slush pile and so did many of my peers.

What should I do if a publisher rejects my work?

This isn't something that might happen. This is something that *will* happen. I'm sorry to say it, but rejection is like death and taxes—it's something that no writer can avoid forever.

I'm not going to tell you not to take it personally, because it's always going to feel at least a little bit personal. But just know that there are a lot of reasons why publishers (and agents) might reject a book.

Maybe the market for that book just isn't what it used to be, and if you'd sent them that same manuscript eighteen months ago, they would have happily signed you.

Maybe they just bought a very similar book and they don't need two books about faeries or dragons or girls whose braces give them ESP.

Maybe they just don't love the book. This one is hard to hear because it feels like they're saying, "I don't like you. I don't think you have any talent. You're stupid." But really, when an agent or editor says, "I just don't love the book," what they mean is . . . they just don't love the book. It's like trying on a pair of jeans, and even though they're well-made jeans that might look great on someone else, they just don't look great on *you*, so you decide to buy a pair of jeans you love instead.

Editors have a limited amount of room on their desks. They only get to work on so many books a year, so they're only going to work on the books that they love! Which is good, actually. You want an editor who loves your book. You want an editor who is going to passionately support your book in-house and when everyone is sitting around, saying, "Which book should be on the cover of our catalog or featured in the big ad we're taking out in *Entertainment Weekly*?" you want an editor who will scream, "This book! This book right here! I love it!"

And most of all, just because one editor (or agent) passes on a book, it doesn't mean everyone will. There are a ton of stories about books that got rejected all over town and then went on to be huge bestsellers or win fancy awards. So getting rejected by one publisher doesn't mean getting rejected by them all.

But now I'm going to talk about the final (and hardest) reason why a publisher might pass on the book: Sometimes the book just isn't good enough. Yet.

This isn't something anyone wants to hear. Ever. But no one got better at writing by only being told how perfect their writing is, and I want y'all to get good at this! I want you to be ready for what's to come.

The fact of the matter is that this is a business run by professionals, and very few people write at a professional level right out of the gate. It does happen! Absolutely! But even people who published when they were really young didn't publish their first books. No. Usually they have ten or twenty (or more) other books that they'd started and stopped and finished while they perfected their craft and honed their stories.

So what do you do if a publisher (or agent) rejects your book? You write another book. You submit to another publisher or agent.

And another.

And another.

And another.

Until you write the right book at the right time and in the right way. Stick with it! It's worth it. I promise.

DEAR MARIE LU,
How do you deal with rejection?

By drowning myself in sugar. Okay, but honestly, though—I try to remind myself that I am not the same thing as my book. Early on, I signed with my agent with a manuscript about Mozart, but that story never sold. It was a combination of bad writing (my craft wasn't quite there yet), which I could work on, but also because of bad timing (the market wasn't interested in historical fiction), which I had no control over. That's the thing about most rejections—many times, it's not personal. And rejection never stops either, even after publication; there will be critical reviews, or low sales, or readers who didn't like your work. So be kind to yourself. Even though I always put a piece of my heart into everything I write, my self-worth is not my work. You are more than your book. Keep doing your thing and improving your craft, and eventually you will find your way. Also, you never know if a rejected story might someday see the light of day again. Ten years after my Mozart story was soundly rejected, I rewrote it, and it is now being published by Penguin in 2019. You never know.

If I write a book and more than two publishing companies are willing to publish it, do I get to pick? Or is it whoever asked first? Or is it your agent's choice?

If you've got two or more publishers interested in your book, congratulations! That's awesome. In that case, you'll want to talk with each, get a sense for their marketing plans for the book. Maybe ask when they'd like to put the book on shelves, if they have any comparable (comp) titles that they've put out, and where they see your book fitting into the market.

You'll want to chat with both editors and ask what notes they might have for a revision. Where do they see you going with your career? And most of all, you'll want to gauge which editor just feels right. This is a person you're going to have to work closely with for (potentially) a very long time. Finding the right editorial fit might be far more important in the long run than which house is willing to give you what amount of money, though that should absolutely be considered as well.

You'll want to ask all these questions because this is a really big decision, and it is in every way *your* decision! Your agent will absolutely weigh in (which is their job), but the final decision is up to you.

Agents work for you. You don't owe publishers a thing until you've signed a contract. Your book isn't just your book—it's your career! So these decisions matter and they're, ultimately, in your hands, so get as much information as you can. Consider it carefully, then make the call and . . .

Go write another book.

Seriously. You should always be writing the next book.

Good luck!

Has there ever been a moment when you thought that maybe all the effort to get published wasn't worth it?

Every.

Single.

Day.

But you know what? I've wanted to do this since I was twelve years old, and very few people get to do what they've dreamed of doing since they were kids. So I know I'm one of the lucky ones. And I try to remind myself of that as much as possible.

DEAR RACHEL CAINE,
How do you cope with rejection?

I'm fairly secure about it now, but that's at the end of a very long road (more than twenty-five years). Early in my career, I had no rejections, right up to the moment I was dropped by my publisher and unable to sell under my own name. That was tough, and it required thinking hard about what I wanted to write, and why, and what I was genuinely good at doing. I had to find my voice, and I think it took me several years to do it. I get proposals rejected from time to time, and I put them aside and look at them again to see what didn't work about it, based on the feedback. But it doesn't feel nearly as personal anymore.

If you're a first-time author, how do you market your book and spread the word? I realize publishers might do some marketing, but how would someone new to the industry promote their book?

Oh, how I wish I had an answer to this question! I really, truly do.

I'm afraid marketing and promotion is one of those things that are almost mystical. If you get a bunch of authors together and listen to us talking, you might think we're trying to find the Holy Grail. But no, we're just trying to find a way to consistently and successfully market and promote a book.

One thing I've learned in the past ten or so years in this business: No one knows. What will work. What won't work. Why something worked extremely well in one case but didn't even start to move the needle in another.

But there are a few things that I know for certain:

—People do judge books by their covers.

—No one ever put their book on the bestseller list simply by being on social media.

—Absolutely nothing is more important than writing your next book.

Honestly, there are a few things that I know for a fact will sell books. Unfortunately, none of them are things that an author actually controls.

Getting an amazing cover, for example. Your publisher is in charge of that. Also, where your book is shelved in stores. You know those big tables where books are displayed when you walk into the store? How about the fancy tables or displays where there might be a cool grouping of books, kind of like "If you read X, try Y"? Those things definitely move the needle, but they're also out of the author's hands.

And of course, maybe the most important factor in sales: How hot is the genre your book is in? Truthfully, timing is a huge thing in this business. The "big book" is always a moving target, and it's one that's almost impossible to hit intentionally. After all, the book you start today won't be on shelves until a year and a half from now—at the earliest! No one knows what genre is going to be super hot in a year and a half, so you can only write the book you love and hope for the best.

For example, in the wake of the Twilight phenomenon, vampire books and romances with other paranormal beings (werewolves, fairies, etc.) became the hottest thing in publishing. But nobody knew that was going to happen until it was already happening.

Now, all of this is a little bit different if you choose to self-publish. Then you are the publisher, and you do get to design the cover and set the price. You can even get a book out fast enough to take advantage of a hot genre if you write quickly enough.

But the downside of being your own publisher is . . . you have to be your own publisher. And as I say elsewhere, there are pros and cons to that.

I've seen a lot of new authors obsess with marketing and promotion. Personally, I spent thousands of dollars and hundreds of hours and nothing—not a single bit of it—made any difference. My career took off when I wrote the right book at the right time. When I got an amazing cover. When booksellers and librarians around the country discovered my stuff and started supporting me.

I could have spent the past ten years promoting a book that was never going to sell, but instead I wrote another book and I'm grateful every day I made that decision.

So I'd highly recommend you write your next book, too!

I like to post my work online in order to get feedback and to feel like I'm being seen. However, if I ever become successful, there presumably comes a point

where posting my work may be counterproductive. Is there a way to know when I've reached that point? Should I take down the old work?

One of the hardest things about writing is working on something for months (or years!) and having absolutely no idea if you're doing anything right. Or if you're making something worse. If you're wasting your time or on the verge of the next big thing. Sometimes it can feel like you're writing inside a black hole, and you'd show your work to anyone just to get a little feedback.

I know. I've been there. I am there almost every day.

This is a complicated issue, but if you need the reinforcement that comes from getting feedback, if you need "fans" asking for your new pages and keeping you on task, and if posting your work online is part of what makes writing fun for you, then you should keep doing it.

BUT . . . you're right that you can't do that forever. If you get an idea that's incredibly high-concept. If you have a story that you're working on that feels bigger or better or more real than the others. If you're getting to the point when you think it's time to start maybe thinking about querying agents, then it's also probably time to start keeping your writing private—or at least sharing it only with teachers and family members and close friends.

DEAR DAVID LEVITHAN,
As an editor, what do you think about aspiring authors posting things on sites like Wattpad?

I think it's great to try out your work and build a following using online platforms. But if you end up selling your book to a publisher, odds are good that you'll have a conversation first about what's going to stay up and what's going to come down. If what's online is a rough draft of what you're now polishing into a novel—either you're going to want it to come down or you're going to want to make it clear that what's up there is just a first draft. If what you're writing is an extension within the same world of what's been posted (but not the same story), or if it's completely unrelated, then you'll probably want to keep it up, as a way of getting people ready for what you're going to be publishing. The key here is to be up front with your publisher about what's already out there—and to make sure you have enough new material that it's worth your readers buying it rather than getting it for free.

Do you believe that writing fanfiction is valuable for honing one's writing skills and developing the craft?

Fanfiction is a bit of a minefield, to be honest. On one hand, I'm a huge fan of anything that gets people writing. This is something that you learn to do by doing, so the more you do the better.

However, writing fanfiction isn't the same as writing original fiction. A huge part of this business is creating characters and worlds, and it's important that you learn to create your own—that you practice and plan and really live inside your own story as much as you can.

I think writing fanfiction is a lot like learning how to ride a bike with the training wheels on. There's something there to support you and keep you upright and get you started, but eventually, you will have to take those wheels off if you want to write a story of your own.

What will the differences be between my life before and after I publish a book? (For wisdom purposes, say this book is a bestseller, well-known, and very popular.)

The average person's life changes very little when they publish a book. After all, very few people make enough from their books that they're able to quit their day jobs.

Very few people go on a book tour.

Very few people are on bestseller lists.

And VERY few (I mean a teeny tiny percentage) have a movie made.

Usually the call saying you're on the *New York Times* list comes about the same time your cat throws up on your bed and you have to go wash your sheets. Life's just like that.

If anything, getting a book published just means you're getting ready to have to work a whole lot harder because now you're not just writing for fun—you're writing professionally! And that takes the stakes and the pressure and the responsibility to a whole new level.

But having a successful book has also changed my life in some tremendous ways. I get to do what I wanted to do when I was twelve years old. I have made some phenomenal friends who are smart and funny and so incredibly talented I still can't believe they ever hang out with me. And I don't think any feeling compares to hearing from a reader whose life has been made better because of something that I wrote.

In a way, the more successful your books are, the more some problems go away. (You might be able to quit your day job. You could sock some money away for a rainy day. Maybe people who used to turn their noses up at you suddenly think you're cool.)

But in another way, you'll be trading those old problems for some new problems. (Your publisher needs you to do six months' worth of work in the next two weeks and the stress of it puts you in the hospital. People you've never heard of threaten to sue you for stealing their idea. You start getting asked nine million times a day how people can try out for a movie that doesn't exist.)

Comparatively speaking, these are all good problems to have!

But your life won't be problem-free. Sadly, few lives ever are.

I kinda thought that once I was a Published Author, life would be easier, simpler. I'd feel validated. And maybe even . . . special. But being published doesn't change the core of who I am, and neither does winning that award, or hitting the *New York Times* bestseller list. And once I finally found an agent (after all the rejections), the rejections didn't stop. And once I found a publisher (after all the rejections), still the rejections didn't stop. Rejection is part of this business forever, just like it's a part of life. That surprised me. But even more, I was surprised to discover that that was okay. And I would be okay.

Writing can be an incredibly fun hobby and cathartic pastime. But publishing is a brutal and professional business. Even if you love the former, the latter might not be right for you. Or right for you *right now*.

If and when you decide to "go pro," there are a lot of things to consider, remember, and keep in mind.

—Beware of people who will take advantage of you and your dreams. No legitimate agent or publisher will ever ask you for money of any kind.

—The best way to find a legitimate publisher is to query legitimate agents and follow their instructions and requirements exactly.

—You shouldn't query any agents until you have a finished and polished manuscript. Not an idea. Not a draft. It will take a great book to land an agent, so only go out with something if it's as strong as you can make it.

—Never stop writing. If you're looking for an agent for Book A, you need to be writing Book B. Or Book C. Or Book W. No point in this process is a point where you should stop writing.

—Depending on the genre and age range you've written for, self-publishing might be a viable route for you, but don't fool yourself into thinking it's an easier route. Sure, there are zero hurdles that you have to clear to throw something up online and call yourself a "published author," but the route to actual success is hard no matter which path you choose. So choose the hard you're best equipped to handle.

—If and when you publish a novel, your life may or may not change. Most books don't make a lot of money. Most authors have at least one other source of income. Most careers span, at most, a few books—not a few decades.

So do this for the love of writing. Do it because you can't imagine not at least giving it a try. And if it doesn't happen overnight, don't worry. Overnight success stories usually were made over the years before the rest of the world was paying attention.

CHAPTER 13
PLANNING YOUR FUTURE

When did you realize you wanted to take writing seriously? Was your family supportive?

I first got the writing bug when I was in middle school and read *The Outsiders* by S. E. Hinton. When I found out that that novel had been written by a teenage girl . . . and *I was a teenage girl* . . . well, that made me want to write so badly.

That's when I started scribbling in notebooks and trying to come up with my own stories, but I didn't really talk about it until much, much later. I was always a pretty private kid, and I knew actually having a career as a writer was a long shot. What were the odds that I'd ever get a book published? They were slim. The odds that I could someday do this for a living without starving to death were even slimmer.

But my parents were very supportive of my writing. I still remember my mom buying me my first writing book, *Screenplay* by Syd Field— where I learned a lot of the stuff that I shared in this book.

Not everyone is so lucky. But the good news is that writing is something you can actually do in secret if you want to. You never have to tell a soul until you're ready. You don't have to quit your job (in fact, you really, really shouldn't quit your job) or move across the country. You don't have to accumulate thousands of dollars of student loan debt or loads of specialized equipment.

Really, as far as dreams go, writing is one of the cheapest ones there is. You just have to find something to write on and carve out the time to do it. And you can. If you want it badly enough, you eventually will!

How can I make my love for writing a job?

Good question! I know a lot of people think "author" when they think about writing-related jobs, but in fact, the ability to write well is an asset in almost all jobs. When I was an agricultural economist at a university, writing research papers and articles was a really important part of my job. And if an agricultural economist needs to write well, then pretty much everyone does!

If you want writing to be the focus of your job, then maybe you want to write for magazines or newspapers. If you really love fiction, then maybe you want to work behind the scenes as an editor or maybe even in Hollywood, writing for the film and TV industry.

I should warn you, though, these are all industries where there are a lot more people wanting the job than there are jobs, so they only take the best. All the more reason to start writing now! Practice. Practice. Practice. Even if what you write never gets published, you may very well be honing the skills that you're going to be using for the rest of your life.

I have a question about careers. I have cool ideas for novels and I really enjoy coming up with good stories, but I also really enjoy science. I am studying to become a doctor, but I also don't want to give up on my dream of writing a book. Do I have to choose between them? I don't know what to do.

The bad thing about being a writer (even a published one) is that most people have to have a second job.

But . . .

The good thing about being a writer (even a published one) is that most people get to have a second job!

Every writer I know has had a totally different occupation at some point or another (and many have a second job—or source of income—even now). And those occupations are all over the map.

I was an agricultural economist. Some of us were lawyers or teachers, engineers, or artists. If there's a job that exists, chances are there's a writer who has had that job. So you absolutely do not have to choose between them! Most every writer I know wrote their first book at night or on weekends, over vacation or on their lunch break—whenever they could find the time.

So go ahead! Go to medical school. Get amazing at science! The only person who can take this dream away from you is you!

If you've quit your day job, when did you quit and why?	
Shannon Hale	I quit my day job about six months after having my first baby so that I could be with him. I'd only sold three books at that point and I couldn't have lived on my writing, but I was married with a working husband. Our family wasn't able to live on our book income until I'd published about fifteen books, including multiple *New York Times* bestsellers.
Marie Lu	I quit about six months after my first book sold, when it became clear I wouldn't be able to commit to the travel required for promoting my first book. It was kind of a leap of faith.

Melissa de la Cruz	I actually think I was laid off! I never went back. I decided I wanted to become a starving artist and I was really happy. I never looked back.
Daniel José Older	I quit three years ago, because I was ready and I had good support plans in place for when writing didn't hold me over.
Elizabeth Eulberg	After second book was published, third almost done. I'd saved up money for a year and wanted to take a break, but I didn't think I'd last more than a year!
Julie Murphy	I quit my day job just before my second book came out, because I knew my touring schedule would be much more intense and I couldn't do both at once. That said, I loved my former job and would go back to it if I ever needed to.
Stephanie Perkins	I quit when I got an agent, but I don't recommend this. Often, it can still take years to go from having an agent to having a book deal. I was extraordinarily lucky that I got my first book deal within a few months. Also, I have help! My husband's job provides health insurance and money to pay the bills. If it weren't for him, I would still need a second job.
Marissa Meyer	The moment I had my first book deal, because it was enough to pay the bills and I was ready to pursue this dream full-time.
Alex London	I quit being a YA librarian in 2008 to do research for a book I'd sold, and I've been lucky enough to keep selling enough books that I haven't had a day job in a decade!
Sarah Rees Brennan	I quit when I got my first book deal, because I wanted to move back to my homeland of Ireland! But I still supplement my writing career with teaching.
Jesse Andrews	I quit editing textbooks about seven years ago because I was paying the bills with writing.

Alan Gratz	I quit in 2002 before I'd sold my first book to be a stay-at-home dad for my baby daughter. I sold my first book before she turned one year old!
Soman Chainani	I quit tutoring after book #3, because I had the resources to focus on writing.
Holly Black	After my third book came out and I had five books under contract. I thought I had enough money to live on for a while (that was only sort of true, it turned out).
Kiersten White	I'm a stay-at-home mom, so that day job is still going strong!
Maggie Stiefvater	I quit when my third book—*Shiver*—was published. Although I loved being an artist, it was a sixty-hour-a-week job and it was impossible to do that, promote *Shiver*, and write the sequel at the same time, particularly with two toddlers at home.
Zoraida Córdova	2016 because they wouldn't let me travel for writing events.
Gordon Korman	I was fortunate enough to graduate college directly into full-time writing.
Rachel Caine	2011, because I had too many appearances and tours, and the stress was wearing me very thin. My health was being compromised by lack of sleep and stress!
Dhonielle Clayton	I used to be a middle school librarian and had to quit because of all the deadlines and travel.
David Levithan	This is a trick question, right? 😊 I mean, I'm doing my day job right now, as I edit this book. Not only do I love editing as much as I love writing, I also feel I enjoy my writing much more because I am *not* relying on it for my income. I also am lucky because I have a day job that understands what a writing life is like.

Do you have to go to college to become an author? If so, what major/minor is best to study?

I know writers who have PhDs in literature. And I know writers who never went to college. I know people who studied science or law or, like me, economics. So what I'm trying to say is this: No, you don't have to go to college to become an author. And if you do go, it doesn't seem to matter what you major in.

When I was in college, I used to contemplate changing my major sometimes. After all, I knew what I wanted to do—why would I study something else? But then I realized that you don't actually need a degree to sell a book. *All you actually need is a book.*

But you can't practice law without a law degree. You can't become a doctor without a medical degree. You can't teach without a teaching degree.

So I didn't have to have a degree to write, but I would need a degree to do the other jobs I was interested in. If I was going to spend my time and money pursuing a degree, shouldn't it be a degree that was actually necessary? After all, even with a degree in writing, there's no guarantee of getting a publishing deal. And in hindsight, I'm incredibly glad it worked out that way because having professors and classmates critiquing my work might have changed me and the way I write. And the way I write has worked out pretty well.

So that was the philosophy that worked for me.

Other writers have taken other paths, pursing degrees in creative writing or English. I know a lot of people who have even gone on to get master's of fine arts degrees, and they swear by the experience. It makes you read broadly. Think critically. Learn to take criticism and rejection—all things that are absolutely essential in this business. Plus, if you'd like to teach writing for your day job, then that degree will be especially valuable.

So that's the approach that has worked for them.

Whatever path you choose to take, there isn't a wrong option. The only thing that matters in the end is what kind of book you write. Just do whatever you need to do to make sure that book is as good as possible.

DEAR Z BREWER,

What kind of educational path did you take and what path do you recommend to aspiring writers?

I don't believe that you need a degree in order to become a successful writer. Take me, for example. I barely graduated high school, flunked out of two colleges, and dropped out of a third, and I'm a bestseller. So long as you have your writers' tools (which you learn in English class all through middle and high school), you don't need someone to teach you how to write. You just write . . . and teach yourself.

That being said, do get a degree—but get a degree in marketing. Two reasons: (1) You'll need marketing skills in your career as a writer, and (2) you want to have a day job backup plan so you can support yourself while you're fighting to make your dreams come true.

I'm introverted and extroverted. Writing is typically a solitary activity, which is fine, but is there enough interaction with the outside world? I don't want to always be at home.

You're right. Writing can be a really solitary activity. And that suits some writers just fine. Other writers might need some interaction with the outside world from time to time. Some people find that they get enough of that just through the course of their daily lives. But some people like to get a little more interaction, particularly with other authors!

The great thing about writers is that most of them are really, really nice. And there are so many conferences and festivals and social media outlets where writers gather together and hang out that most people eventually make some friends.

If you live near other authors, it can be fun to get together and write at a café or coffee shop a few times a month. Maybe you'll be in a position someday to attend some writers' retreats (either ones you sign up for or ones you plan yourself).

There are some great organizations like the Society of Children's Book Writers and Illustrators and the Romance Writers of America that put on amazing conferences every summer where hundreds of authors come together to learn from each other. I've met some wonderful friends at events like that.

And don't forget, most writers will always have some kind of non-writing job as well, so you may very well be around people all day long and then love coming home to a quiet house to write.

So much like there's no one way to write a book, there's no one way to find your place in the writing community. Just know this: It *is* a community. Writing itself might be a solitary activity, but if you're willing to put in the time and the effort to meet some other writers, it doesn't have to be lonely.

As a writer, there must be times when you feel like giving up. What inspires you to keep going and keep on writing?

I've never known a writer who didn't doubt themselves at least once a week. Heck, once a day! I know I, personally, feel like giving up all the time. And the short answer to your question, I guess, is to say that I can't give up because this is my job and I have bills to pay and if I don't write, I don't eat.

But it's more than that, really. Sure, my editor is counting on me to deliver my book on time, and my readers are looking forward to reading the books I've promised them. But at the end of the day, this isn't something you can do for other people.

Writing isn't something you do because it's your job—otherwise, most of us wouldn't have made it past all those years before it *was* our jobs. No. Writing is something you do because it's who you are.

I couldn't stop asking "what if?" if my life depended on it. I couldn't stop coming up with book ideas or trying to guess what's going to happen on my favorite TV shows if I tried. This is just who I am. And so giving up really isn't an option for me.

I just keep writing.

Because that's what writers do.

ABOUT THE CONTRIBUTORS

JESSE ANDREWS is an author, screenwriter, and former German youth hostel receptionist. He was born and raised in Pittsburgh, Pennsylvania, and is a graduate of Schenley High School and Harvard University. He currently makes his home in Berkeley, California.

JENNIFER LYNN BARNES is the author of more than a dozen young adult novels, including *Little White Lies*, *The Naturals*, *Raised by Wolves*, and *The Fixer*. She has advanced degrees in psychology, psychiatry, and cognitive science, and received her PhD from Yale University in 2012. She is currently a professor of writing and psychology at the University of Oklahoma, where she studies the psychology of fiction and why we like it.

HOLLY BLACK is the author of bestselling contemporary fantasy books for kids and teens. Some of her titles include The Spiderwick Chronicles (with Tony DiTerlizzi), The Modern Faerie Tale series, the Curse Workers series, *Doll Bones*, *The Coldest Girl in Coldtown*, the Magisterium series (with Cassandra Clare), and *The Darkest Part of* *the Forest*. She has been a finalist for an Eisner Award, and the recipient of the Andre Norton Award, the Mythopoeic Award, and a Newbery Honor. She currently lives in New England with her husband and son in a house with a secret door.

SARAH REES BRENNAN was born and raised in Ireland by the sea, and she still uses Ireland as a base for her adventures. She's the author of the critically acclaimed Demon's Lexicon trilogy and the Lynburn Legacy series, a romantic Gothic mystery about a girl who discovers her imaginary friend is a real boy. Sarah's latest book is *In Other Lands*, the story of the crankiest nerd who ever fell into a magical land. She's devoted to reading widely, making bad jokes across the world, and making friends both real and imaginary.

Z BREWER is the *New York Times* bestselling author of the Chronicles of Vladimir Tod series, as well as the Slayer Chronicles series, *Soulbound*, *The Cemetery Boys*, *The Blood Between Us*, *Madness*, and more short stories than they can recall. When not making readers cry because they killed off a character they loved, Z is an anti bullying and mental health advocate. Plus, they have awesome hair.

Z lives in Missouri with a husband person, two children people, and four furry overlords that some people refer to as "cats."

RACHEL CAINE is the *New York Times*, *USA Today*, Amazon Charts, and *Wall Street Journal* bestselling author of more than fifty novels, with breakout series in multiple genres, including young adult and adult thrillers. She's published in more than twenty-five languages around the world. She lives in Fort Worth, Texas, but writes anywhere.

ALLY CARTER is the *New York Times* bestselling author of fifteen novels, including *Not If I Save You First* and the Gallagher Girls, Heist Society, and Embassy Row series. Together, her books have been published in more than twenty-five countries and have sold over three million copies. She lives in Oklahoma and online at allycarter.com.

SOMAN CHAINANI's debut series, the School for Good & Evil, has sold more than 1.5 million copies, been translated into twenty-seven languages across six continents, and will soon be a film from Universal Pictures, with Soman co-writing the screenplay.

A graduate of Harvard University and Columbia University's MFA Film Program, Soman began his career as a screenwriter and director, with his films playing at over 150 film festivals around the world. He has been nominated for the Waterstones Prize for Children's Literature, been named to the Out100, and also received the $100,000 Shasha Grant and the Sun Valley Writers' Fellowship, both for debut writers. Soman lives in New York City.

CASSANDRA CLARE is the author of the Dark Artifices series, the Bane Chronicles series, the Magisterium series, the Infernal Devices series, and the Mortal Instruments series. She was born to American parents in Teheran, Iran, and spent much of her childhood traveling the world with her family, including one trek through the Himalayas as a toddler where she spent a month living in her father's backpack. She lived in France, England, and Switzerland before she was ten years old.

Since her family moved around so much, she found familiarity in books and went everywhere with a book under her arm. After college, Cassie lived in Los Angeles and New York, where she worked at various entertainment magazines and even some rather suspect tabloids, reporting on Brad and Angelina's world travels and Britney Spears's wardrobe malfunctions. She started working on her young adult novel, *City of Bones*, in 2004, inspired by the urban landscape of Manhattan, her favorite city. She turned to writing fantasy fiction full-time in 2006 and hopes never to have to write about Paris Hilton again.

DHONIELLE CLAYTON ("Dhon" like "Don" or "Dawn," not "Danielle") spent most of her childhood under her grandmother's table with a stack of books. She hails from the Washington, DC, suburbs on the Maryland side. A self-proclaimed school nerd, she loved covering her books with brown paper, Lisa Frank folders, having a locker, putting headings on her homework, odd-looking pens and freshly sharpened pencils, and researching mythical creatures. She rediscovered her love of children's fiction by rereading *Harriet the Spy*, which pushed her to earn an MA in Children's Literature from Hollins University and an MFA in Writing for Children at the New School. She taught secondary school for several years—at a pre-professional ballet academy and a private K-8 school. She spent most of her twenties in and out of America—living in London, Paris, a small Japanese town, Bermuda—and wandering the planet. She's been on five out of seven continents, and has grand plans to reach all of them. She is a former librarian and co-founder of CAKE Literary, a creative kitchen whipping up decadent—and decidedly diverse—literary confections for middle grade, young adult, and women's fiction readers. She is also one of the We Need Diverse Books team's librarians, and the co-chair of the inaugural 2016 Walter Award for YA fiction.

JAY COLES is a young adult and middle-grade writer, a composer with ASCAP, and a professional musician residing in Indianapolis, Indiana. He is a graduate of Vincennes University and Ball State University, and holds degrees in English and Liberal Arts. When he's not writing diverse books, he's advocating for them, teaching middle school students, and composing music for various music publishers. Jay's young adult novel *Tyler Johnson Was Here* is about a boy whose life is torn apart by police brutality when his twin brother goes missing, inspired by events from the author's life and the Black Lives Matter movement.

ZORAIDA CÓRDOVA is the award-winning author of the Vicious Deep trilogy and the Brooklyn Brujas series. Her short fiction has appeared in the *New York Times* bestselling anthology, *Star Wars: From a Certain Point of View*, and *Toil & Trouble: 15 Tales of Women and Witchcraft*. She is a New Yorker at heart and is currently working on her next novel.

MELISSA DE LA CRUZ is the #1 *New York Times*, #1 *Publishers Weekly*, #1 Indie Bound author of over fifty books for readers of all ages. Her books include the inspiring anthology *Because I Was a Girl: True Stories for Girls of All Ages*, *Something in Between* (about an undocumented Filipino

American teenager), Disney's Descendants series, the Alex and Eliza series, the Blue Bloods series, and the Witches of East End series, which was turned into an hour-long television show on Lifetime. Her TV movie *Christmas in Angel Falls* was the number two movie of all time on Hallmark's Movies and Mysteries. She is also the co-director of YALLFEST and the co-founder of YALLWEST, two of the biggest teen book festivals in the country. She lives in West Hollywood with her family.

ELIZABETH EULBERG was born and raised in Wisconsin before heading off to college at Syracuse University and making a career in the New York City book biz. Now a full-time writer, she is the author of the young adult novels *The Lonely Hearts Club*, *Prom & Prejudice*, *Take a Bow*, *Revenge of the Girl with the Great Personality*, *Better Off Friends*, *We Can Work It Out*, *Just Another Girl*, and *Past Perfect Life*, as well as the middle grade series the Great Shelby Holmes. She lives outside of Manhattan with her three guitars, two keyboards, and one drumstick.

CHRISTINA DIAZ GONZALEZ is the award-winning author of several books including *The Red Umbrella*, *A Thunderous Whisper*, the Moving Target series, and *Stormspeaker* (part of the Spirit Animals: Fall of the Beasts series). Her books have received numerous honors, among them the American Library Association's Best Fiction for Young Adults, the Florida Book Award, the Nebraska Book Award, and Junior Library Guild selection. Christina currently lives in Miami, Florida, with her husband, sons, and a dog that can open doors. You can read more about her and her books at christinagonzalez.com.

ALAN GRATZ is the bestselling author of a number of novels for young readers, including *Samurai Shortstop*, *The Brooklyn Nine*, *Prisoner B-3087*, *Code of Honor*, *Projekt 1065*, the League of Seven series, and *Ban This Book*. His novel *Refugee* is the story of three different refugee families struggling for freedom and safety in three different eras and different parts of the world. A native of Knoxville, Tennessee, Alan is now a full-time writer living in Asheville, North Carolina, with his wife and daughter. Visit him online at alangratz.com.

SHANNON HALE is the *New York Times* bestselling author of over twenty-five books for kids, teens, and adults, including the Newbery Honor award winner *Princess Academy*, graphic novel *Real Friends*, several books in the popular Ever After High series, and *Austenland*, now a major motion picture.

With her husband, Dean Hale, she pens the Unbeatable Squirrel Girl novels for Marvel Press and the Princess in Black early chapter book series. They live in Utah, where they care for their four children, two cats, and a small plastic pig. Find Shannon at shannonhale.com or on Twitter @haleshannon.

KODY KEPLINGER is the author of several books for teens, including the *New York Times* bestseller *The DUFF*, which was adapted to film in 2015. She is also the author of *Lying Out Loud*, *Run*, and *That's Not What Happened*, as well as the middle grade novel *The Swift Boys & Me*. She lives in New York City and teaches at the Gotham Writers Workshop.

GORDON KORMAN is the author of more than ninety novels for kids and young adults, most recently *Whatshisface*, *Restart*, and *Supergifted*. His writing career began at the age of twelve, when his seventh-grade English assignment became his first published novel.

Now, more than four decades later, he is a full-time writer and speaker, with over thirty million copies of his novels in print in thirty-two languages. Each year he travels extensively, visiting schools and libraries, bringing his trademark humor and adventure styles to readers everywhere. A native of Ontario, Canada, he lives with his family in Long Island, New York.

DAVID LEVITHAN is the author of many bestselling and acclaimed novels, including *Every Day*, *Two Boys Kissing*, *Nick & Norah's Infinite Playlist* (written with Rachel Cohn), and *Will Grayson, Will Grayson* (written with John Green). In 2017, he was awarded the ALA's Margaret A. Edwards Award for his contribution to young adult literature.

David started in the editorial department at Scholastic as an intern when he was nineteen years old . . . and he's been working there ever since.

ALEX LONDON is the author of the middle grade series Tides of War, Dog Tags, and the Wild Ones. His young adult debut, *Proxy*, was an ALA Top Ten Quick Pick for Reluctant Readers and a 2014 Best Fiction for Young Adults selection. His young adult novel *Black Wings Beating* is an epic fantasy set in a world of cutthroat falconry. He lives in Philadelphia, Pennsylvania.

MARIE LU is the #1 *New York Times* bestselling author of the Legend trilogy and The Young Elites trilogy. She graduated from the University of Southern California and jumped into the video game industry, working for Disney Interactive Studios as a Flash artist. Now a full-time writer, she spends her spare time reading, drawing, playing Assassin's Creed, and getting stuck in traffic. She lives in Los Angeles, California (see above: traffic), with one husband, one Chihuahua mix, and two Pembroke Welsh corgis.

MARISSA MEYER is the #1 *New York Times* bestselling author of the Lunar Chronicles, *Heartless*, and *Renegades*, as well as the graphic novels *Wires and Nerve* and *Wires and Nerve, Volume 2: Gone Rogue*. She lives in Tacoma, Washington, with her husband and twin daughters. Find out more at marissameyer.com.

JULIE MURPHY lives in North Texas with her husband (who loves her), her dog (who adores her), and her cat (who tolerates her). After several wonderful years in the library world, Julie now writes full-time. When she's not writing or reliving her reference desk glory days, she can be found watching made-for-TV movies, hunting for the perfect slice of cheese pizza, and planning her next great travel adventure. She is the author of *Side Effects May Vary*, *Ramona Blue*, and *Dumplin'*, which is now a major motion picture. *Puddin'*, the companion to *Dumplin'*, is her latest release. You can visit Julie at juliemurphywrites.com.

KRISTIN NELSON is owner and founding literary agent of Nelson Literary Agency, LLC. She has represented Ally Carter since 2003 and still has on file the infamous email between her and Ally that launched the internationally bestselling Gallagher Girls series. Find out more about Kristin and her agency at nelsonagency.com.

DANIEL JOSÉ OLDER is the award-winning author of both young adult and adult books. His latest books are *Star Wars: Last Shot* and the historical fantasy Dactyl Hill Squad series, his first middle grade books. His *New York Times* bestselling young adult novel *Shadowshaper* was a New York Times Best Book of the Year, and its sequel, *Shadowhouse Fall*, was also highly acclaimed. His other books include the Bone Street Rumba novels, including *Midnight Taxi Tango* and *Half-Resurrection Blues*. Winner of the International Latino Book Award, he has been nominated for the Kirkus Prize, the Locus and World Fantasy Award, and the Andre Norton Award. *Shadowshaper* has been optioned by Tony-winning actress Anika Noni Rose. You can find his thoughts on writing, read dispatches from his decade long career as an NYC paramedic, and hear his music at danieljoseolder.net, on YouTube, and at @djolder on Twitter.

STEPHANIE PERKINS is the *New York Times* and international bestselling author and anthology editor of several books for teens including *Anna and the French Kiss, My True Love Gave to Me,* and *There's Someone Inside Your House.* She lives in the mountains of North Carolina with her husband. Visit her online at stephanieperkins.com.

CARRIE RYAN is the *New York Times* bestselling author of the Forest of Hands and Teeth series, *Daughter of Deep Silence,* and *Infinity Ring: Divide and Conquer,* as well as the editor of *Foretold: 14 Tales of Prophecy and Prediction.* She's written the Map to Everywhere series, a middle grade series co-written with her husband, John Parke Davis, and is working on a new young adult novel. Her books have sold in over twenty-two territories and her first book is in development as a major motion picture. A former litigator, Carrie now lives in Charlotte, North Carolina, with her husband and various pets. You can find her online at CarrieRyan.com or on Twitter at @CarrieRyan.

ELIOT SCHREFER is a *New York Times* bestselling author and has twice been a finalist for the National Book Award. In naming him an Editor's Choice, the *New York Times* has called his work "dazzling and big-hearted." He is also the author of two novels for adults and four other novels for children and young adults. His books have been named to the NPR Best of the Year list, the ALA best fiction list for young adults, and the Chicago Public Library's Best of the Best. His work has also been selected to the Amelia Bloomer List, recognizing the best feminist books for young readers, and he has been a finalist for the Walden Award and won the Green Earth Book Award and Sigurd Olson Nature Writing Award. He lives in New York City, is on the faculty of the Hamline and Fairleigh Dickinson MFAs in Creative Writing, and is the children's book reviewer for *USA Today*.

MAGGIE STIEFVATER is a writer, artist, and musician, and the *New York Times* bestselling author of the Shiver trilogy, *The Scorpio Races*, The Raven Cycle series, and *All the Crooked Saints*. Stiefvater lives in Virginia with her husband and their two children. You can visit her online at maggiestiefvater.com and follow her on Twitter @mstiefvater. For more information, please visit: mediaroom.scholastic.com/maggiestiefvater.

KIERSTEN WHITE is the *New York Times* bestselling author of many books for teens and young readers, including *And I Darken, Now I Rise, Bright We Burn, The Dark Descent of Elizabeth Frankenstein*, and the Paranormalcy trilogy. She lives with her family near the ocean in San Diego, where she perpetually lurks in the shadows. Visit Kiersten online at kierstenwhite.com and follow @kierstenwhite on Twitter.

GLOSSARY OF TERMS

WRITING AND PUBLISHING PHRASES THAT YOU MIGHT NOT KNOW BUT ARE USED WITHIN THIS BOOK

ACT: a section of a story where all the action seems to be moving in a particular direction. Then a **PLOT POINT** will happen—it will hook into the story and spin it around in a *new* direction—and a new act will begin.

ADVANCE READER'S COPY (ARC): ARCs are paperback versions of a book that are printed up before the book is actually published. They are promotional tools given to librarians, booksellers, the media, and other people who can help build buzz about the book before its publication. (It can also be referred to as a bound galley.)

AGENT, aka literary agent (aka your best friend): Generally, agents serve as a go-between for authors and publishers. They help sell books, negotiate contracts, and champion an author's career. Ethical agents always—and only—work on commission. If an "agent" ever charges you money of any kind (processing fees, reading fees, flat fees for shopping a book, etc.), then you need to run in the opposite direction because you're being scammed.

AUTHORIAL VOICE: This might best be described as an author's fingerprint. It's the combination of the words an author uses, the way he or she uses them, and the type of stories they tend to tell. Basically, if you read a book that didn't have a cover and could guess who the author was anyway? Then that author has a strong authorial voice.

BACKSTORY: Any of the events that happen to a character (or world) before a book begins.

CANON: The official version of a story, as written or produced by the author or owner(s) of the source material.

CLICHÉ: A phrase so commonly seen or used that it's considered lazy or unoriginal.

CLIFFHANGER: When a story ends with the characters in immediate danger (as if they are hanging off a cliff).

COMPANION NOVEL: A novel with some overlapping characters and worlds but with a plot that totally stands alone.

CONFLICT: Anything or anyone that might stand between a character and their goal. Author Susan Elizabeth Phillips once described conflict as this: "If your hero is a fire fighter, your heroine had better be an arsonist."

COPY EDITOR: Unlike an "acquiring editor," who might buy a book for a publishing house and work with the author to develop the characters and the story, copy editors work to proofread and perfect manuscripts. The copy editor is one of the last people who will work on a book before it's published.

COPYEDITING: This is where you go through your manuscript, checking for typos, grammatical errors, and inconsistencies. For example, if your heroine has blue eyes on page 163 and brown eyes on page 235, this is where you're probably going to catch it.

CRITIQUE PARTNER OR GROUP: People (often groups of writers) who exchange manuscripts and give suggestions and advice to each other. Sometimes they're friends from school or people who meet online or at conferences, but they always serve as a support system and sounding board for each other. They are also totally and completely, optional.

DAY JOB: A job or profession that a writer does in addition to writing. Pretty much every author has a day job when they're starting out, and the vast majority will have one throughout their entire writing career.

DRAFT: A version of a book that exists during the writing process. A writer will often write many drafts before the book is finished.

EDITING: The process of revising a book, with either large or small changes.

EDITOR: A person employed by a publishing company to acquire new books and work with authors to make those books as great as possible.

An editor is often an author's contact person and main advocate within the publishing house. Also sometimes referred to as an "acquiring editor."

EPILOGUE: Material at the end of some books, after the final chapter of the story, often showing the characters in the future and indicating how their lives turned out.

EPISODIC SERIES: A type of series where each story stands on its own and where the books can be read in pretty much any order—like Goosebumps or Nancy Drew.

FIRST PERSON POV: A point of view where the story is told through the eyes of one character, in that character's own voice. It will use pronouns like *I/we* instead of *he/she/they*.

FREELANCE EDITOR: An independent editor an author can hire to work on their books. Some authors might hire a freelance editor if they want to self-publish their work. Other authors might choose to work with a freelance editor to make their work as strong as possible before publishing with a traditional publisher (though that is rare and certainly not required).

GAME CHANGER: An event, usually at the end of a book, that alters the world or the characters in a way that means future books in the same series will be significantly different from the book(s) that came before.

GENRE: A category of books where all the stories have similar elements and styles. Science fiction, fantasy, thriller, romance, and horror are all examples of genres.

HEAD HOPPING: When an author jumps from one character's point of view into another character's point of view within the same chapter or section.

HIGH CONCEPT: Stories where the conflict or premise is easily described in just a sentence or two. "A Secret Service agent's daughter must save the president's son when he's kidnapped in Alaska" would be an example of a high-concept story (*Not If I Save You First*).

INFO DUMP: When an author piles a whole lot of information on the reader all at once. This is especially common early in books and when introducing characters, and it's something that, as a rule, should be avoided.

NANOWRIMO: National Novel Writing Month, an annual program where people accept the challenge of writing a 50,000-word novel during the month of November.

NARRATIVE VOICE: The style, flow, cadence, tone, word choice, etc., of a particular story. If you can see a paragraph from the middle of a book and guess which book it is, then that's a book that has a strong narrative voice.

NARRATOR: The person—or voice—telling the story.

PACING: The rate at which a story progresses.

PANTSER: A writer who doesn't necessarily know what will happen in their book as they write it, and is said to "write by the seat of their pants."

PAST TENSE: When a story is told as if it has already happened and the narrator is looking back on events.

PLAGIARISM: When you copy someone else's words and use them without giving credit to the original source or author. It's actually a really complex subject, and you can visit plagiarism.org for more information.

PLOT: What happens in a book—the actions the characters take to achieve their goals. A plot is often closely related to the premise, but they're actually two different things.

PLOT POINT: Any part of a story where the story line turns in another direction. It could be something big (like getting accepted to magic school or learning you're a princess). Or it could be a smaller setback or change in your character's journey (like having your car die during a road trip and having to take the bus. Then having the bus break down. Then having a blizzard hit and . . . etc., etc.). Plot points generally mean starting a new **ACT**.

PLOTTER: A writer who figures out the general plot of their book before they begin to write.

POINT OF VIEW (POV): The perspective from which the story is being told.

PREMISE: The general idea, concept, or "setup" of a story. This is often confused with the plot, but actually they're two different (yet semi-related) things. For example, the premise of Harry Potter is "boy goes to magic school," but once you get to magic school a million different things could happen—you could have a million different plots.

PRESENT TENSE: When a story is told as if it is happening right now. It will use present tense verbs. (Like *I run down the street* instead of *I ran down the street*.)

PROCESS: The way an author works, including the number and type of drafts they might do, the tools they might use, how much planning they do before they start, and how long it takes. Processes will vary widely from author to author and book to book, and an individual's process will likely change or evolve over time.

PROLOGUE: A (totally optional) section that an author can insert before chapter 1, often showing backstory that is essential to understanding the world or the characters.

PROSE: Any writing that uses an ordinary rhythm or flow and doesn't have the metrical structure of "verse" (or rhyming or metered poems). In the book world, when people talk about the prose of a novel, they're usually talking about the words themselves and not the characters, plot, world building, or other parts of the novel.

PUBLIC DOMAIN: Material to which a copyright doesn't apply, so anyone can take those characters or world or plot and use them as their own. For example, Sherlock Holmes is now in the public domain, so you can have dozens of Sherlock Holmes movies, TV shows, and books being made at the same time.

QUERY: The act of reaching out to a literary agent or editor in hopes that they might represent or buy your book.

QUERY LETTER: The letter you might send to a literary agent, describing you and your book in the hopes that the agent might want to represent you.

SCENE: A segment of a story usually taking place in a specific place and time that has a beginning and an end.

SECOND PERSON POV: This is the least-used point of view. The entire story is written as if the reader is the main character. So instead of saying *I was late for school today* (as in first person), a story written in second person would say *You were late for school today.*

SENSITIVITY READER: Someone an author can hire to read and critique a manuscript to help the author appropriately represent people of other ethnicities, races, backgrounds, abilities, or sexual orientations. You should never expect a sensitivity reader to work for free.

SERIAL SERIES: A series that tells one story over many books. You can always tell if a series is "serial" if you start with book three and are super confused.

SHOW, DON'T TELL: I could *tell* you what "show, don't tell" means, but I'm going to *show* you instead. See, instead of writing *Joe had never been angrier* (where we have to take your word for it that Joe was angry), write *Joe slammed the door and yelled at the top of his lungs* (where we see Joe acting like an angry person and draw our own conclusions).

SLUSH PILE: The (sometimes literal) pile of unsolicited manuscripts and query letters that accumulate at publishers and literary agencies. (Note: Most publishers do not accept unsolicited manuscripts and never read anything from the slush pile. Some agents, however, do.)

THIRD PERSON LIMITED POV: A point of view where the story is told through the eyes of one character, but without using that character's direct voice. It will use pronouns like *he/they* instead of *I/we*.

THIRD PERSON OMNISCIENT POV: A point of view where the story is told by an unknown/unseen narrator who knows all and sees all. It will use pronouns like *he/they* instead of *I/we*.

TROPE: A story element or type that is incredibly common—especially within a particular genre. Like when fantasy novels are about a "chosen one" or a romance is about "friends to lovers." Avid readers will often have favorite tropes that they read over and over and over.

UNSOLICITED MANUSCRIPT: Any manuscript that is sent to a publisher or editor (even though they didn't ask for it).

VERSE: Novels written in verse are novels that are, essentially, book-length poems. They have carefully chosen words with a specific rhythm or flow, and they will not read or look like novels written in prose.

WORLD BUILDING: The process of creating the social, political, and physical environment in which your characters live. It's generally thought of as something you do for genres like science fiction and fantasy, but most contemporary fiction has world building, too.

ACKNOWLEDGMENTS

This book wouldn't have been possible without the help of so many wonderful people.

First, my agent, Kristin Nelson, who, in addition to contributing her expertise, didn't tell me I was crazy when I told her what I had in mind for this project. Next, I could never have done this without the hard work and amazing guidance of David Levithan, who saw the need for this book and helped me bring it to life, and Maya Marlette, who was our sounding board and co-conspirator every step of the way.

I'm incredibly grateful to everyone at Scholastic for championing my work for years now and taking on the challenge of making and marketing this book.

And, finally, I have to thank the tremendously talented authors and editors who shared their experience and expertise on these pages. This truly would not have been possible without each of them.

ABOUT THE AUTHOR

ALLY CARTER is the author of three *New York Times* bestselling series for young adults: Gallagher Girls, Heist Society, and Embassy Row. Her most recent bestseller is her first stand-alone novel, *Not If I Save You First*. She lives in Oklahoma and online at allycarter.com.